Interpreting the
Ripper Letters

Interpreting the Ripper Letters

Missed Clues and Reflections on Victorian Society

M. J. Trow

PEN & SWORD
TRUE CRIME

First published in Great Britain in 2019 by
Pen & Sword True Crime
An imprint of
Pen & Sword Books Ltd
Yorkshire - Philadelphia

Copyright © M. J. Trow, 2019

ISBN 978 1 52673 929 2

Printed and bound in England
By TJ International Ltd.

Pen & Sword Books Ltd incorporates the Imprints of Pen & Sword Books
Archaeology, Atlas, Aviation, Battleground, Discovery, Family History, History,
Maritime, Military, Naval, Politics, Railways, Select, Transport, True Crime,
Fiction, Frontline Books, Leo Cooper, Praetorian Press, Seaforth Publishing,
Wharncliffe and White Owl.

For a complete list of Pen & Sword titles please contact

PEN & SWORD BOOKS LIMITED
47 Church Street, Barnsley, South Yorkshire, S70 2AS, England
E-mail: enquiries@pen-and-sword.co.uk
Website: www.pen-and-sword.co.uk

or

PEN AND SWORD BOOKS
1950 Lawrence Rd, Havertown, PA 19083, USA
E-mail: uspen-and-sword@casematepublishers.com
Website: www.penandswordbooks.com

Contents

Acknowledgements

My thanks to all who have contributed ideas and suggestions for this book, from the disturbed and peculiar in Victorian society to today's earnest researchers who doggedly search for the world's best-known Unknown Subject.

My thanks also go to Heather Williams and her team at Pen and Sword; a pleasure to work with, as always.

Most especially, a special thank you to my wife, Carol, who not only typed out the manuscript but literally kept me alive to write the book at all.

Ripper Buyer – Beware!

As I put the finishing touches to this book, a Ripper postcard has fetched £22,000 at Grand Auctions Ltd, of Folkestone. It was put up for sale by the widow of an ex-Metropolitan police officer, who was given the postcard when he retired in 1966. This is precisely the problem with Ripper literature and the reason why so many letters are missing. The Met had no right to give away archive material to anybody. Such artefacts should be in the public domain, not private hands.

For the record, the card is addressed 'To the High St Ealing Police Station Sergent' and it reads, 'Beware there is two women I want here they are bastards. and I mean to have them my knife is still in good order [the card is date-stamped 29 October 1888] it is a students knife and I hope you liked the half of kidney. I am Jack the Ripper.'

The uneven handwriting and the smudges look authentic, so does the card itself, complete with lilac halfpenny stamp and postmark. But the wording itself is suspect. I have come across only one other mention of 'bastards' in the Ripper correspondence. The comment on the knife, the phrase 'I mean to have them' is straight out of the 1896 letter which forms the last surviving missive in the record. The reference to 'half of kidney' and the inference that students were involved is the result of a careful reading of the Lusk Letter controversy (see Chapter 15).

I hope the card is genuine and that the winning bidder feels his huge outlay is justified. Sadly, I do not believe it is. Welcome to the topsy-turvy world of Ripperology.

Chapter One

Jack's 'Funny Little Games'

The adjacent parishes of Whitechapel and Spitalfields in London's East End reached a kind of immortality because of what happened there in a four-month period in 1888; later called the 'autumn of terror'.

At the time, the area was known as 'the Abyss' and 'the Ghetto', a crime-ridden sink of poverty and corruption made all the more alien to Victorian polite society by the recent arrival of Ashkenazi Jews, driven from their Russian and Polish homelands by Tsarist pogroms. Writers like Israel Zangwill and, slightly later, Jack London, paint vivid word pictures of the teeming life in the Abyss where nearly half a million people struggled to survive.

The two great social evils of the period, drunkenness and prostitution, fused in the labyrinth of streets and alleyways, slippery with scum and forever, it seemed, shrouded in night. All of the victims of the man the press called Jack the Ripper were prostitutes. All of them were regulars in pubs and off-licences; at least two of them were probably alcoholics. Despite the fact that prostitution was illegal and that various governments had tried to limit the availability of liquor, the problems continued unabated. Charitable organizations tried their best. General Booth's girls of the Salvation Army went out from Angel Alley with soup, tambourines and an uplifting biblical verse. Thomas Barnardo opened up his homes for destitute children, left by profligate, useless parents to fend for themselves. The Reverend Samuel Barnett saved souls – and lives – from his headquarters at Toynbee Hall. But all this good work barely caused a dent in the vicious spiral of East End life. The police, undermanned and undervalued, turned a blind eye except when routine raids on brothels and places of assignation were among the orders of the day, usually prompted by middle-class sanctimonious pressure via the newspapers.

Violence was commonplace. 'So one is forced to conclude,' Jack London wrote in *The People of the Abyss* in 1903, 'that the Abyss is literally a huge man-killing machine.' The American writer cited a grim example he had come across; a man who had been out of work for eighteen months woke up one September morning and used his pocket-knife to cut the throat of his wife, Hannah, aged 33. Then he systematically slaughtered his four children in the same way: Frank, 12; Walter, 8; Nellie, 4; and Ernest, 16 months. Then he quietly waited with their bodies until the police came for him.

Edwin Pugh wrote of the Ghetto's young, 'Children are begotten in drunkenness, saturated in drink before they draw their first breath, born to the smell and taste of it.' He wondered particularly about the girls, for 'though she plays, the poor little girl of the London streets is never quite a child.'

Jack London described the finding of a body by the police in a doorway in Dorset Street, regarded by some as the worst street in London. 'Homeless, shelterless, sick, with no one with her in her last hour, she had died in the night of exposure … she died as a wild animal dies.'

The men of the Abyss, London noted, fuelled by alcohol, readily resorted to violence:

> They become indecent and bestial. When they kill, they kill with their hands … They gouge a mate with a dull knife … They wear remarkable boots of brass and iron and when they have polished off the mother of their children with a black eye … they knock her down and proceed to trample her.

Nicholas Charrington, heir to the brewing family, saw just such an incident outside one of his father's pubs. On the spot, he turned his back on his inheritance and formed a one-man crusade to combat the effects of 'demon drink', getting beaten up for his pains on more than one occasion.

And, to top it all, came Jack. The crimes of the world's most famous serial killer were altogether of a different calibre from the routine domestic violence that London, Pugh and Charrington describe. Polite society, unaware that such a place as the Abyss even existed, was appalled by the Whitechapel killings, but they came as no surprise to Canon Samuel Barnett. He wrote, 'The murders were bound to come; generation could not follow generation in lawless intercourse, children could not be familiarized with scenes of degradation … and the end of all be peace.'

One of the problems with any investigation into the Ripper murders is that experts disagree on the exact number of victims. For too long, writers on the subject have followed Melville Macnaghten's 'canonical five' – Polly Nichols, Annie Chapman, Liz Stride, Kate Eddowes and Mary Kelly. He did not join Scotland Yard until several months after the murders ended and his famous 'Memoranda', in which he named three possible suspects, is very wide of the mark, as recent research has shown. My personal preference for the number of killings is seven, based on similarities of MO, crime scene location and timing. The first was Martha Tabram, who also used the name Turner.

Her body was found by John Reeves, a dock labourer, on the first-floor landing at 37 George Yard Buildings, along a narrow alley off Wentworth Street. It was 4.45 am on Tuesday, 7 August 1888. Martha was lying in a pool of blood, her clothes rucked up and her legs splayed. Constable Thomas Barrett 226H was summoned and he in turn called Dr Timothy Kileen, whose surgery was along Brick Lane. The doctor carried out a post mortem in the Whitechapel Union Workhouse Infirmary, which was little more than a shed some distance from the workhouse itself and came to various conclusions.

One wound *may* have been inflicted by a left-handed person, but the other thirty-eight stabs to the body had been delivered from the right. The individual wound had been delivered by a different weapon – heavy and long-bladed – which *could* have been a bayonet. Over the years, Kileen's testimony has become garbled, especially since Martha had been seen in the company of a soldier on the night that she died.

Inspector Edmund Reid of H Division took charge of the case and interviewed prostitute Mary Connolly, known as Pearly Poll, who told him that she and Martha had met up with two squaddies and spent some time drinking in various pubs. At about 11.45 pm, Mary had gone up Angel Alley with her corporal and Martha vanished into the darkness of George Yard with his mate. Mary failed to identify any of the soldiers at either the Tower (the Grenadier Guards) or Wellington Barracks (the Coldstreamers). Reid was unable to shake the alibis of two likely lads (who, in effect, protected each other) and there the case foundered.

The inquest, before Deputy Coroner George Collier, was opened on 23 August. Siblings, friends and acquaintances came out of the woodwork to tell the authorities what they knew, which was not much. Martha was 39 at the time of her death, but looked much older. A Londoner by birth and the daughter of a dysfunctional family, Martha White married Henry Tabram on Christmas Day 1869. She bore him two sons, but by 1875 her heavy drinking had forced the family apart. Four years later, still trying to sponge off Tabram, Martha had taken up with William Turner, a street hawker. She often stayed out all night and drink remained a problem.

Once they had separated, Turner only saw Martha occasionally. The last time had been on 4 August near the Aldgate Pump when he gave her 1/6d to buy trinkets to sell. By this time, she was calling herself 'Emma', living in a doss-house at 19 George Street and selling her body. The pattern of downward spiral caused by drink was a common one and would be heard at several inquests over the coming weeks, as would the inevitable jury verdict, 'murder by some person or persons unknown'.

***

At this stage, there was no panic. Because violence was endemic in the Abyss, Martha Tabram's murder barely caused a ripple. In *Jack the Ripper: The Forgotten Victims*, Ripper experts Paul Begg and John Bennett have analysed a number of contemporary cases in a worthy attempt to pin down exactly how many women Jack killed. We will consider murders outside the immediate area later because they play a part in the central thesis of this book. Annie Millwood, a 38-year-old soldier's widow living in White's Row, was attacked on 25 February 1888 by a stranger with a clasp knife. Her death, on 31 March, was not linked to the assault, but attributed to natural causes. Three days before that death, Ada Wilson was stabbed in the passageway of her home at 9 Maidman Street, Mile End. A 30-year-old man with a sunburned face and blond moustache demanded money with menaces. When the cash was not forthcoming, he jabbed Ada twice in the throat with a clasp knife. Neighbours came rushing to her screams and she survived. Five days later, Emma Smith, another widow, was assaulted by three men in Osborn Street in the early hours of the morning. When she staggered to the London Hospital, Surgeon George Haslip discovered that her face was badly bruised, her right ear almost torn off and a blunt object, perhaps a stick, had been rammed into her vagina. She died from peritonitis on Wednesday, 4 April.

Many people were convinced that Jack was not a lone killer but part of a gang and several of the Ripper letters offer this as a solution. Modern psycho-profiling rejects this as being highly unusual and the evidence for the existence of such gangs is flaky. From various sources, there were the Whites Row Gang in Spitalfields and the Monkey's Parade outfit that operated out of Bow Road. Further afield were the Hoxton High Rips and the Limehouse Forty Thieves, but it is not clear whether they were all working at the time of the Ripper murders.

What Annie Millwood, Ada Wilson and Emma Smith had in common is that they were almost certainly prostitutes. Ada's occupation is listed as seamstress in the local press, but that was a well-known euphemism. The other common factor was probably robbery that went wrong. That was most obvious in Ada's case and the fact that *three* men attacked Emma led to the speculation that this was the work of professional street criminals, perhaps the Old Nichol gang, who operated in the neighbourhood.

The next credible attack by the man who would come to be known as Jack the Ripper took place in the early hours of Friday, 31 August. Charles Cross was a carman on his way to work along Buck's Row (now Durward Street) when he saw a body lying outside the locked gates of Brown's stable yard. He assumed at first that the woman was drunk – Whitechapel's streets at night were littered with down and outs – then realized that she was dead. Constable John Neil 97J turned up minutes later. Buck's Row was part of his beat and he had seen nothing suspicious half an hour earlier. With other officers now present, Constable John Thain 96J fetched Dr Rees Llewellyn, whose surgery was at 152 Whitechapel Road, and who ordered the body to be sent to the Montague Street mortuary where Martha Tabram had been taken.

Inspector John Spratling of J Division took charge of the case and noticed – as Llewellyn, astonishingly, had not – serious mutilations to the woman's body. Like Martha Tabram, the woman was photographed with a shroud covering the wounds. In a way that would be unthinkable today, *The Times* carried a detailed account of her injuries. Her neck was bruised, probably by manual strangulation, and her throat had been cut, down to the vertebrae. The lower abdomen had been slashed with a long-bladed knife, possibly by a left-handed killer. Llewellyn was of the opinion that whoever the perpetrator was must have had 'some rough anatomical knowledge, for he seemed to have attacked all vital parts'. The assault itself would have taken four or five minutes.

The dead woman was identified as Mary Ann Nichols, known as 'Polly'. She was 45 years old and 5ft 2in tall, the daughter of a locksmith. At the age of 19, Mary Walker had married printer William Nichols in St Bride's Church, Fleet Street. Five children later, by 1880, Polly's drinking had caused the all-too-common rift with her husband and she took to the streets. She was frequently admitted to Lambeth Workhouse or Infirmary and by the end of 1887 was 'carrying the banner' (living rough) in Trafalgar Square. She blew her chance for respectability when she stole clothes worth £3 10s from her employers, Samuel and Sarah Cowdrey of Rose Hill Road, Wandsworth. In the weeks before her death, she had been dossing at 18 Thrawl Street and she went, unknowingly, to meet her killer, saying to the doss-house deputy, 'I'll soon get my doss money. See what a jolly bonnet I've got now.'

Polly's inquest opened on 1 September at the Working Lads' Institute in Whitechapel Road; Edwin Wynne Baxter, coroner for the South Eastern District of Middlesex, presided. There were a number of adjournments while various witnesses were found, but by 22 September, the jury could only offer the all-too-familiar verdict - 'murder by some person or persons unknown'.

And by that time, Jack had struck again.

***

'Dark Annie', 47-year-old Annie Chapman, met her killer somewhere along Hanbury Street in the early hours of Saturday, 8 September. They probably agreed a price for a specific service and she led him through the passageway alongside Number 29 and out to the little yard at the back. There were three steps down to the ground and a wooden fence running around the area which housed a privy. Seventeen people were asleep inside Number 29, but in keeping with other Ripper killings, nobody heard or saw a thing. The yard was a well-known haunt for prostitutes and the residents had probably become used to it.

At about 4.30 am, Annie's killer grabbed her round the neck to silence her, forced her to the ground and cut her throat. He might have been trying to decapitate her. He then ripped her body with an upward movement, cleanly removing her uterus, part of the vagina and two-thirds of the bladder. He may or may not have been interrupted by John Richardson, a porter at Spitalfields Market, who was in the passageway of Number 29 on his way to work. When he had gone, the Whitechapel murderer slipped away unseen into the early morning ... and into legend.

Annie Smith, daughter of George and Ruth, had married John Chapman, a coachman, in May 1869 at All Saints Church, Knightsbridge. Their addresses until 1881 reflect Chapman's status as the employee of the well-to-do, including Bayswater, Berkeley Square and a spell at Clewer in Berkshire. The following year, however, Annie had taken to the bottle – perhaps over the sudden death of her daughter, Emily – and by 1886 was living in Spitalfields with a sieve-maker. Several of her friends knew her as Annie Sievey. Her temper was legendary and in the week before her death, she got into a fight with fellow dosser Eliza Cooper in Crossingham's doss-house, an altercation that continued into the Britannia pub and resulted in the bruising still evident on her face at post mortem.

Although the timing does not seem to be quite right, another prostitute, Elizabeth Darell, gave evidence at the inquest that she saw Annie talking to a 'foreigner' – the euphemism usually meant Jewish – at about 5.30 am on the last day of her life. He asked, 'Will you?' She said 'Yes' and may have been verbally signing her death warrant.

In common with the atrocities carried out by serial sexual killers in other times and in other parts of the world, the Ripper's mutilations were growing in number and ferocity. This was the case that provided a number of crime scene location clues that proved to be red herrings but have become part of Ripper folklore. A leather apron found in the yard of Number 29 turned out to belong to a resident and had nothing to do with the murder. Its reportage was enough, however, to lead to a search for – and the arrest of – John Pizer, a local whose nickname was Leather Apron. An envelope found near the body bearing the embossed crest of the Sussex Regiment had been brought there by Annie herself. She had found it on the floor of Crossingham's and used it to wrap pills she had been prescribed by the Infirmary. Small change scattered from the dead woman's clothing had landed haphazardly as the killer struck, but in Ripper folklore they were arranged in a straight line between Annie's feet, suggesting (supposedly) a Masonic ritual.

Once again, there were adjournments to the inquest that began on 10 September before Wynne Baxter. Once again, a series of unhelpful witnesses and the brick wall that obstructed many Victorian murder investigations. Only the verdict remained the same.

***

Of all Jack's crimes, the most contentious is that carried out on Elizabeth Stride – 'Long Liz' – around midnight on 29/30 September. The timing itself is debatable and, because of circumstances, the MO was different.

Louis Diemschutz swung his pony and trap into the narrow entrance to Dutfield's Yard, Berner Street, after a long day selling knick-knacks on the road. The animal shied at something on the ground and Diemschutz lit a match to see what it was. It was Long Liz and blood, still warm, was trickling from the gash across her throat. Diemschutz dashed up the stairs to the International Workingmen's Educational club, then in full swing, and it is likely that while he did so, Elizabeth Stride's murderer, hiding behind the gate, ran for cover.

When Diemschutz returned with the club members, they sent for the police. Rather tellingly, in an area known for its violence and increasingly in the grip of hysteria, two of them ran down and past a total of seven streets, shouting for the police all the time and finding no one. Club members who had run in opposite directions found two - Constable Henry Lamb 252H and Albert Collins 12HR (the Reserve). They in turn summoned Dr Frederick Blackwell of 100 Commercial Road. Elizabeth Stride's body was still slightly warm at 1.16 am when Blackwell arrived. A scarf around her neck had been pulled tight, probably to strangle her, and the gash to her throat had cut through the windpipe. The doctor placed the time of death to between 12.46 and 12.56 am; George Bagster Phillips, the police surgeon of H Division of 2 Spital Square, Spitalfields, more or less concurred. Exact times of death are notoriously difficult, depending as they do on temperature, weather conditions and much else. Even in the late Victorian period, we can only use these times as *very* rough estimates.

The contentiousness of the Stride murder lies in the fact that although the throat had been cut, there were no mutilations to the body or even attempts to do so. Was that simply because Diemschutz had virtually caught Jack red-handed and forced him to run for self-preservation? Or was Liz Stride killed by a copycat or even as the result of a street brawl? The evidence at her inquest which opened on Monday, 1 October before the indefatigable Wynne Baxter, this time at the Vestry Hall, Cable Street, brought to light an altercation that had been witnessed at the Dutfield's Yard entrance minutes before Diemschutz arrived. The evidence is confusing because it was dark and at least one witness, Israel Schwarz, had a poor command of English and may not *quite* have meant what he said. There were two men near a woman who may have been Liz. One was about 5ft 5in tall – shorter than Liz, who was 5ft 7in – and he was arguing with the woman before throwing her to the ground. To keep away from this incident, Schwarz crossed the road, into the path of a second man, taller and older than the first, who shouted 'Lipski', perhaps as a warning. Schwarz hurried away but felt he was being followed by the taller man for several streets. Israel Lipski had been hanged in August 1887 for murdering Miriam Angel with nitric acid. The term 'Lipski' had become underworld slang for Jew, which clearly Israel Schwarz was. Matthew Packer, who ran a grocer's shop in Berner Street, told the coroner that he had sold grapes to Liz and a gentleman on the night in question. He then retracted his statement, leaving the police and the inquest in a further state of confusion.

Long before the inquest began, however – in fact, a little over forty-five minutes after the murder of Liz Stride – a second woman died in the East End and this gave rise to an unprecedented panic over the 'double event'. We now know a great deal about Catherine Eddowes, usually known as Kate. A native of Wolverhampton, her father George was a tinplate worker who took his family to Bermondsey in 1843. Twenty years later, after minimal education and several spells in the local workhouse, Kate took up with Thomas Conway, aka Quinn, an ex-soldier of the 18th Foot. The couple had three children and travelled the Midlands in the 1860s selling chapbooks. Once again, drink became an issue as Kate hit the bottle, but it is likely that her teetotaller husband regularly beat her up. In 1881, she moved in with a market porter, John Kelly, a quiet, inoffensive man who was ill with kidney trouble.

For reasons that will become apparent, we have a clear picture of the last hours of Kate's life. On the morning of Saturday, 29 September, she and Kelly met up at the Shoe Lane workhouse and she pawned a pair of his boots in Church Street for 2/6d. She used the name Jane Kelly, which, bearing in mind Jack's next victim, has given the conspiracy theorists years of fun! Late morning saw the pair blowing the money on breakfast at Cooney's Lodging House in Thrawl Street. During the afternoon, Kate was in Bermondsey trying to scrounge money from her respectable daughter; she couldn't find her. By 8.30 pm, Kate was lying drunk on the pavement of Aldgate High Street and she was bundled into the Bishopsgate Police Station. Here, she gave her name as 'Nothing' and fell asleep. By 12.15 am she was awake, singing and demanding to be released. City Constable George Hutt 968 surely regretted his decision later, but he let Kate go, on the rather spurious grounds that it was too late to get any more drink. This was nonsense; the liquor establishments of the East End never closed. On signing out, she gave her name as Mary Anne Kelly with a fictitious address of 6 Fashion Street. 'Good night, old cock,' she called as she left. It would have taken her eight minutes to reach Mitre Square.

The square itself was very gloomy in 1888 with only one gas lamp. There were three ways into it, two of them narrow passageways. Tall buildings surrounded it and, in terms of privacy, it was a murderer's paradise. Whoever killed Kate Eddowes hacked her to pieces in one corner of the square, ironically outside an off-duty policeman's house and, as with Annie Chapman, took trophies away with him. Police surgeon Frederick Brown carried out the most detailed investigation of any of Jack's killings, both in situ and post mortem. He drew the body as it lay, with one leg raised and arms stretched out. He drew all the mutilations carefully and these were confirmed by the grisly morgue photographs later. Gone is the coyness of the earlier photos where only the victims' heads are shown. Kate's body was clearly hooked up against a wall and the entire body, naked, is on display in the ghostly sepia, complete with Brown's suture stitches with which he had sewn her up after the post mortem. The killer had slashed her lips, her ears and her eyelids; he had cut deep 'v'-shaped notches in her cheeks. There was a deep cut over the bridge of her nose. None of the other attacks had affected the face at all, except for bruising caused by strangulation; once again, the ferocity of the assault was increasing.

Kate's throat had been cut and she had been disembowelled. Her left kidney had been carefully taken out and could not be found. Brown judged that the killer had considerable anatomical knowledge, perhaps being used to working on animals rather than humans. Because of where the murderer carried out the mutilations, on the ground and to one side of the body, he would have very little blood on him.

Some of the blood, however, was found yards away by Constable Alfred Long 254A. The fact that he was from A Division, in the West End, is proof of the rising panic and the pressure on the police. Officers were being drafted in from the whole of London to catch Jack. Long was patrolling Goulston Street at 2.55 am when he came upon a torn and bloody apron dropped at a standpipe. The material, it was later established, came from Kate Eddowes; clearly her killer had taken it away to wash his hands and perhaps to carry the kidney.

The inquest on Kate Eddowes began under S.F. Langham at the Golden Lane Mortuary on Thursday, 4 October. Alone of the Ripper's victims, Kate had died in the precincts of the City of London, so that the City Force was now involved in the hunt for Jack. Langham was the City Coroner. There were therefore *two* inquests being held simultaneously, almost certainly enquiring into the same killer and, just to add to the hysteria, a limbless female torso was discovered in the foundations of the new Scotland Yard buildings along the Thames Embankment on 3 October. Although bizarre and never solved, the torso case was one in a series beginning in the capital in 1874 and was *not* the work of the Whitechapel murderer. At the time, however, such niceties were lost on the locals of the East End, forced to cope with a new horror in their lives; and on the West End, who scanned their newspapers avidly and feared that the mad fiend of the Abyss was coming for them. This, of course, was exactly what the media intended - ''orrible murder' sold newspapers.

***

And then, just when it seemed the hysteria could get no worse, Mary Jane Kelly happened upon Jack in the early hours of Friday, 9 November, Lord Mayor's Day.

If Kate Eddowes was different because she was killed in City territory, Mary was more different still, because she was twenty years younger than the other victims and died indoors. No. 13 Miller's Court was a one-room hovel at the end of a short alleyway off Dorset Street ('Dosset Street' at the time, because of the sheer number of common lodging houses). Mary was one of those people whose tall tales made serious investigation hell for the police. Going by aliases as different as 'Black Mary', 'Fair Emma' and 'Ginger', she claimed to have been born in Limerick, Ireland and moved with her family either to Caernarvon or Carmarthen in Wales. She married a miner called Davis who was killed in a pit accident in 1881 or 1882 and drifted to Cardiff, where she took up prostitution. In London by 1884, she became, according to her, a sought-after courtesan in a West End brothel and spent some time in Paris, then regarded as *the* centre of upper-class vice. She worked as a domestic servant in London, moving around regularly from St George's Street to Stepney. By 1886, after a series of short-lived relationships, she was in Bethnal Green with a plasterer called Fleming.

Mary met Joseph Barnett in Cooney's Lodging House in Thrawl Street in April 1887. She lived on and off with him, finally at Miller's Court, where the rent was 4/6d a week. She owed landlord John McCarthy £1 10s by the time of her murder. By the end of October, Barnett had left Mary, perhaps because she had a habit of inviting girl friends to the tiny room and Barnett felt squeezed out. Although she was drunk on the night she died, there is no evidence that Mary was an alcoholic. Her last known movements are not as clear cut as those of Kate Eddowes. In the middle of Thursday evening, she was at home with Lizzie Allbrook, a younger friend who was probably not on the game. Barnett called by for a friendly chat. Later she was seen with Barnett and another friend, prostitute Julia van Turney, in the Horn of Plenty pub on the corner of Crispin and Dorset Streets. By 11.45 pm another friend, Mary Cox, saw her with a carroty-haired man carrying a pail of beer. Between midnight and 1.00 am, Mary could be heard singing the schmaltzy 'Only a violet I plucked from my mother's grave' from her room in Miller's Court. She must have gone back out because at 2.00 am she met an unemployed labourer, George Hutchinson, who knew Mary and she tried to cadge some money off him. Hutchinson was broke but he watched as the girl picked up a foreign-looking man who seemed anxious not to be seen by passers-by.

Hutchinson heard laughter and the occasional snatch of conversation. 'You will be all right,' the man told Mary, 'for what I have told you.' He carried a parcel wrapped up with string and wore an astrakhan coat with an expensive-looking tie-pin. 'All right, my dear,' Hutchinson heard Mary say. 'Come along. You will be comfortable.'

At about 3.45 am, the residents or visitors in the cluster of rooms at Miller's Court – Sarah Lewis, Mrs Kennedy and Elizabeth Prater – all heard a scream of 'Oh, murder!' This was presumably Mary Kelly's farewell to the world.

Her body was found long after dawn by Thomas 'Indian Harry' Bowyer, John McCarthy's rent collector, who ran to Commercial Street Police Station to tell Inspector Walter Beck and Detective Constable Walter Dew what he had seen. By 11.30, Dr Phillips looked in through the broken window pane to make the obvious statement that Mary Kelly was beyond all aid and Inspector Frederick Abberline had arrived. There was a ludicrous delay because No. 13's door was locked and the police believed that bloodhounds had been sent for. At 1.30 pm, Superintendent Thomas Arnold of H Division CID turned up. There would be no bloodhounds and the door was forced. Phillips carried out a superficial examination of the ghastly corpse on the bed and the body was taken to Shoreditch Mortuary – not before at least two photographs were taken of the body in situ.

Abberline was back the next day, noting that a fire in the grate had burned so hot that it had melted the spout of a kettle on the hearth. The ashes also contained the remains of women's clothing, although whether these were Mary's was impossible to say. Perhaps the fire had been lit to enable Jack to carry out his mutilations. While this was going on, Drs Phillips, Brown and Thomas Bond (police surgeon of A Division) carried out a post mortem.

When the inquest opened at Shoreditch Town Hall on Monday, 12 November, Abberline took the jury to view the body and then to the crime scene. The usual array of witnesses was called – friends and acquaintances of the deceased and anyone who had seen her in her last hours. Dr Phillips' medical evidence was surprisingly brief. Mary had been attacked while lying on the right-hand side of the bed and pulled across. The actual cause of death was severance of the right carotid artery; Mary had bled to death. This lack of detailed evidence is germane to the thesis of this book as we shall see; the press, pushing the boundaries of what was acceptable in print, were now being reined in by the coroner.

We know the details from Dr Bond's very meticulous notes, partly published in the medical journal the *Lancet*. The original document was feared lost until its resurfacing in 1987. It is unfortunate that Bond made a mistake in the very first line – Mary was not found naked but still wore a chemise (petticoat), ripped and slashed though it was. He describes the body as he saw it in No. 13 and links this with the later findings of the post mortem. Mary's abdomen had been ripped open and its contents removed, most of them displayed around the corpse. Her breasts had been cut off – one was found under her body, the other near her right foot. Her face had been hacked beyond recognition and her throat cut to the vertebrae. There were long gashes to her arms and legs as if her murderer could not bear to leave any part of her intact. Mary's last meal had consisted of fish and potatoes and her heart was missing.

Thousands lined the route of Mary's funeral cortège on Monday, 19 November on the way to St Patrick's Catholic cemetery at Leytonstone. The funeral itself was paid for by Henry Wilton, the verger of St Leonard's in Shoreditch.

***

Many commentators today, following the 'canonical five' of Melville Macnaghten, Assistant Chief Constable CID, Scotland Yard, believe that Mary was Jack's final victim. So appalling were her injuries – the doctor believed that the killer had taken two hours to carry out the mutilations – that, they contend, he cracked up altogether and either left the area or committed suicide. I personally believe there was one more murder to come – that of 'Clay Pipe' Alice McKenzie on 17 July 1889. Alice, whose smoking habit gave her her nickname, was about 40 and had probably been born in Peterborough. Six years before she died, she took up with an Irish porter, John McCormack, drifting from doss-house to doss-house. She worked, when she was not on the streets, as a washerwoman for Jewish families.

On the last day of her life, she quarrelled with McCormack, who had given her 1/8d, part of which was the doss-house rent. One newspaper later contended that Alice had gone to the Cambridge Music Hall with a blind boy called George Dixon and that she had met her killer there. Of such 'fake news' are Ripper legends made! At 11.30 she talked to three friends along Flower and Dean Street, going in the direction of Brick Lane. Soon after 12.50 am, her body was found in narrow Castle Alley (in the opposite direction from Brick Lane) by Constable Walter Andrews 272H. The alley was cluttered with costers' carts and the body showed the tell-tale wounds that the Ripper usually inflicted. Her throat was slit, her skirt had been forced up and a gash ran from her left breast to her navel. There were seven or eight superficial cuts to her genitals.

The police chain of command kicked into operation and George Bagster Philips was again the police surgeon. Under her body, he found her clay pipe and a polished farthing, perhaps intended to pass, in the darkness, for a gold sovereign. There was considerable disagreement among the doctors over whether this was a Ripper crime or a copycat version. The wounds were not as vicious or extensive as in earlier cases but if, like Liz Stride, the murderer had been interrupted, that may have been explanation enough. The inquest, under Wynne Baxter on 17 and 19 July, adjourned until 14 August, returned the inevitable verdict.

***

What I have tried to do in this chapter is to build the detail of reporting exactly as it was done in 1888. Martha Tabram received relatively short shrift from the press, but as the killings mounted and panic gripped, newshounds cranked up the hysteria, creating the whole industry of today's Ripperology.

On 27 September 1888, the Central News Office received a letter. It had been written two days earlier, nearly three weeks after the murder of Annie Chapman and five days before the 'double event'. It was addressed to 'Dear Boss' and purported to come from the Whitechapel murderer. It prophesied that 'you will soon hear of me with my funny little games' and was signed, 'Yours truly, Jack the Ripper.'

Chapter Two

The Men Who Invented Jack the Ripper

The Whitechapel murderer was terrifyingly real, but Jack the Ripper was the creation of Fleet Street, then the newspaper capital of the country.

According to most accounts, the first letter purporting to come from the killer himself was dated 24 September and had a South East London postmark. It was addressed to Sir Charles Warren, Commissioner of Police at Scotland Yard, contained silhouettes of a coffin and a knife and was unsigned. We shall examine this self-confessional type of letter later, but it was eclipsed on the 27th by the famous 'Dear Boss' note, written on the 25th and addressed to the Central News Agency.

Today, news is everywhere and instant. Events happening thousands of miles away are beamed by satellite to all parts of the world and we can access it on our television screens, our computers or our phones. How much of it is accurate, how much of it is real as opposed to 'fake' is anybody's guess. In the Ripper's day, the prime movers of information were the press, local and national, who fed an increasingly literate society with what they craved – sensationalism.

The journalist William Stead, who would go down with the *Titanic* in 1912, summed up the power of the press two years before Jack struck. A newspaper editor, he wrote, sees

> Cabinets upset, ministers driven into retirement, laws repealed, great social reforms initiated, Bills transformed, estimates remodelled, programmes modified, Acts passed, generals nominated, governors appointed, armies sent hither and thither, war proclaimed and war averted.

As early as 1871, the media was referred to as the Fourth Estate, more important than the three that made up all Western societies.

The Central News Agency, with its offices at 5 New Bridge Street in the City, was founded in 1870 by the philanthropist MP William Saunders. Its purpose was to collect news reports from correspondents all over the world and it quickly built a reputation for 'scoops'. The information it collected, from breaking news to racing results, was telegraphed to newspapers the length and breadth of the country. When the 'Dear Boss' letter arrived, the natural response of the Agency was to treat it as a joke. In case it was not, the manager, John Moore, sent it to Scotland Yard. The covering letter was written by Moore's assistant, Thomas J. Bulling and read, 'The Editor presents his compliments to Mr Williamson & begs to inform him the enclosed was sent to the Central News two days ago & was treated as a joke.' Bulling had forwarded the letter to Chief Constable Adolphus (Dolly) Williamson as the senior CID officer at Scotland Yard.

The journalist George R. Sims, who wrote extensively on both London's East End and the Ripper murders, was the first to point out the salient fact about the 'Dear Boss' letter. In the *Referee*, 7 October 1888, he wrote:

> How many among you, my dear readers, would have hit upon the idea of 'the Central News' as a receptacle of your confidence? You might have sent your joke to the *Telegraph*, the *Times*, any morning or evening paper, but I will lay long odds that it would never have occurred to you to communicate with a Press agency. Curious, is it not, that this maniac makes his communication to an agency which serves the entire Press?

Sims goes on to make the obvious observation; either the letter is genuine and the Ripper really *is* a journalist or the letter is a hoax and its writer is a journalist. Most experts today plump for the latter.

Are we able to pin the 'Dear Boss' letter down to an individual? To do that, we have to understand what journalism was all about in 1888, to grasp what made newshounds tick and what sold newspapers.

In *The Ghosts of Fleet Street* in 1928, John Francis Gore described London's newspaper hub as 'a street of hasty judgement and elastic morality' and the phrase was equally true of the media forty years earlier when 'enterprising journalists' covered the Whitechapel murders. The country's first Education Act (1870) created the Board Schools and London, at least, appointed truant officers – 'kid catchers' – to force Britain's illiterate youth to the chalk face. How much effect this had by the time of the Ripper killings is debatable; further legislation in the 1880s tried to make schooling compulsory. Even so, the *notion* of literacy was accepted by that decade and the twin effects of the abolition of the stamp duty on newspapers and cheaper production methods using wood-pulp, meant that information was cheaper too and a readership of that information was growing. By 1888, both the 'classes' (polite society) and the 'masses' (everybody else) clamoured to read the news.

The cost of production of newspapers fell dramatically from the 1850s and the abolition of duty from 1860 added to the cheapness of London dailies and provincial weeklies. The invention of the electric telegraph meant that up-to-date information was disseminated quickly, so quickly in fact, that several commentators have taken the content of Ripper letters to be genuine, whereas they actually arise from the latest 'stop press' of the day. Most prominent was the rise of the Sunday papers – the *News of the World*, *Lloyd's Weekly* and *Reynolds's Weekly Newspaper* among them. By the time of the Ripper murders, the circulation of these Sundays was 1.5 million. Bearing in mind that most of the killings took place on Friday or Saturday, it was often the Sundays that carried the story first. Such papers were aimed at the lower middle and working classes (I believe the very group responsible for most of the letters) who could read them in pubs, coffee houses, libraries and barbershops for the readily available price of 1d.

Dozens of papers appeared and disappeared between the 1860s and the 1880s, each trying to outdo the other. Foreign correspondents, especially those covering wars, became national heroes in their own right. Kingston of the *Telegraph* and Dymond of the *Morning Advertiser* were with the Turks in their heroic defence against the Russians in 1877. Forbes of the *Daily News* and Villiers of *The Graphic* were with the other side. They were all dwarfed, however, by Henry Morton Stanley, who famously found Dr Livingstone in darkest Africa, and George Sala, who covered the American Civil War.

Journalists in the later Victorian era – and even more so their editors, who had to decide what could and could not be printed – had to walk the tightrope of contemporary morality. What went down well in the music halls or the tap room of a Bermondsey pub was not at all the same as acceptable fare over a gentleman's breakfast table, and that was without factoring in the sensibilities of his wife! Harriet Martineau and Emily Crawford both wrote for the *Daily News* but journalism was essentially a man's job and Fleet Street a largely male preserve. With so many papers competing for sales, it was not surprising that journalists were seen as nosey busybodies, inclined to pester people ad nauseam for the sake of a good story.

Into this dog-eat-dog existence, the New Journalism took national causes to new heights or sank them to new depths of depravity, depending on one's point of view. One of its leading lights, George Newnes, wrote to William Stead, 'There is one kind of journalism which makes and unmakes cabinets, upsets governments, builds navies and does many other great things. That is your journalism. There is another kind, which has no such great ambitions. That is my journalism. A journalism that pays.'

It relied on sex and violence to sell newspapers and although the mores of the time, as we have noted, imposed limits on this, the New Journalism essentially pandered to the ancient craving for 'bread and circuses' which exemplified Rome's mob and created the bloody spectacles of the arena.

Three weeks before what, I believe, was the last of the Whitechapel murders – that of 'Clay Pipe' Alice McKenzie in Castle Alley – an investigation of a very different type was under way, first by the Post Office police, then by Scotland Yard. It was July 1889 and a series of thefts from the General Post Office headquarters at St Martin-le-Grand led PC718 Luke Hankes to question Charles Swinscow, a 15-year-old post boy. What Hankes uncovered was a vice-ring based on a male brothel at 19 Cleveland Street. Several post boys were involved, as were a number of high-profile gentlemen, including Lord Arthur Somerset and the Earl of Euston. Chief Inspector Frederick Abberline, who had been working on the Ripper case until March of that year, was re-routed to lead this investigation. Hampered by the unassailable brick walls of the corridors of power, Abberline came up short and the titled miscreants got away safely to France.

With nothing resolved by November, Ernest Parke, the editor of the *North London Press,* finally lost all patience with the endless cover-ups and ran a headline on the 16th, 'The Distinguished Criminals who have Escaped', naming Lords Somerset and Euston and hinting at others. Euston sued, charging Parke with criminal libel. Two armed camps appeared: the one, spearheaded by the Prince of Wales and the aristocracy defending the establishment at all costs; and the other by freedom of the press agitators and virtually the whole of the working class. Ironically, the foreign press was free to print what it liked, especially when rumour put the name of Prince Albert Victor, son of the Prince of Wales, in the mix. 'The inbred crowd of royal stock of all Europe is becoming sadly deteriorated both bodily and mentally … whether England will ever have a king after the Prince of Wales is a matter of speculation.'

Parke's trial was held at the Old Bailey – perhaps to accentuate the supposed enormity of his 'crime' – and quickly became farcical. Various witnesses who had 'seen' Euston in Cleveland Street were discredited and the only reliable witness, John Saul, a homosexual 'rent boy' was held to be so obnoxious by the court that no one believed him. It speaks volumes for the twilight limbo of the press, even in the age of New Journalism, that *The*

Times refused to print the fact that Saul had actually had sex with Euston. The judge, Sir Henry 'Hanging' Hawkins, described Saul as 'a melancholy spectacle, a … loathsome object'. He harangued the jury for two and a half hours and, unsurprisingly, they returned a guilty verdict – 'libel without justification'. Parke went down for twelve months.

The importance of the Cleveland Street/Parke case lies in the attitude of the press. Far more so than today, Victorian newspapers were acutely class-conscious and made no bones about it. While the evidence heard in court, especially from rent boys, was 'unfit for publication', the *Labour Elector* wanted life imprisonment for Parke. As it was, his own paper collapsed.

But Ernest Parke was not the last victim of a priggish society determined to protect its own and the values they believed should be imposed on everybody. In the summer of 1885 William Stead, by then editor of the *Pall Mall Gazette*, bought a teenaged girl for £5 to make a point. Stead had jumped on the bandwagon of New Journalism, an initiative in which editors and journalists did not simply supply news, they espoused causes and exposed corruption wherever they found it. Today's recent phone-hacking scandal and the subsequent Leveson inquiry, testing that well-known journalists' excuse 'the public's right to know', is merely the same thing translated into the technology of the twenty-first century.

Back in the nineteenth century, what appalled most of society was the prevalence of child prostitution and Stead intended to use the *Gazette* to highlight the situation. Using an ex-prostitute as a go-between, the editor was introduced to 12-year-old Elizabeth Armstrong and her mother. A deal was struck and Stead and the prostitute, Rebecca Jarrett, took the girl to rooms – these could be hired by the hour, no questions asked – in Poland Street where Rebecca chloroformed Elizabeth and Stead arrived. No sexual activity took place and the girl was examined medically before and after Poland Street to prove the case.

Triumphant, Stead produced a number of articles in July 1885, by which time Elizabeth was 13, with titles such as 'The Violation of Virgins', 'Strapping Girls Down' and 'Where Maids are Picked Up'. His point was that what he did in a sort of controlled experiment, other men were doing for real. It all went horribly wrong. The girl's father had not given his consent; her mother came out with the implausible story that she thought that Elizabeth was going into service and she had the street-wise savvy to contact *Lloyd's Newspaper*, thereby exposing Stead and creating a circulation war among rival newspapers. Bow Street magistrates sent Stead down for three months. Of course, he capitalized on this, having himself photographed in prison slops complete with broad arrows, an identification number and shaved head. He played down the fact that he had books and a fire in his cell.

But the 'Maiden Tribute of Modern Babylon' which Stead wrote was only the start and for all his good intentions, the other side of the New Journalism coin was muck-raking and pandering to the public's growing appetite for sensationalism. The poet Matthew Arnold attacked him in the year before the Ripper struck, claiming that Stead 'throws out assertions at a venture, simply because [he] wishes them to be true'. Stead was an evangelical rebel, seeing himself as the mouthpiece of the working man destroying evil wherever he saw it; and he usually saw it in the corridors of power. It is largely because of him that we now have the media world as 'the fourth estate' without which no parliamentary party, church or police force can live easily for long. Such journalists tilting at windmills could of course have been seen as guilty of political naïveté; several contemporaries commented on Stead's childishness. But the bottom line is that, while Stead himself may have operated out of pure altruism, many of his fellow journalists did not. Incidentally, one Ripper writer maintains that Stead believed that one of his own copy-writers, Robert Donston Stephenson, was the Whitechapel murderer. Stead used the Ripper case to harangue the Metropolitan Police who were clearly getting nowhere in their investigations. It may have been from Stephenson that he got the notion that Mary Jane Kelly had been sodomized, for which there is no evidence at all. Fake news was not invented in the twenty-first century!

The newspapers that covered the Whitechapel murders operated at a number of levels. The nationals, not yet dailies, led by *The Times*, the *Telegraph* and the *Daily News* (London only) set the tone, with a reputation for integrity and honest, accurate reporting. *The Times* in particular was hugely influential and one of the oldest in the world. Unofficially known as 'the Thunderer', it railed against abuses and made governments tremble. Anybody who was anybody took *The Times* and wrote pompous letters to it. Under its previous editor, John T. Delane, it was a force to be reckoned with. Local papers tried to match the nationals' quality, but they usually fell far short. They were mostly biased, not strictly on party-political lines, but by class. Many of them had been established in the days of Chartism and showed varying degrees of liberal radicalism. In the 1880s, William Gladstone was their hero, the Grand Old Man who stood for the common man against the greed and indifference of Disraeli's Tories and the aristocracy. The finer points of politics – that it was Disraeli who had given many of their male readers the vote in 1867, not Gladstone, and it was Disraeli who had brought in a whole raft of effective social legislation in the 1870s – passed them by. There were increasing numbers of rags like this, funded by advertising (running a paper was – and is – an expensive business); between 1870 and 1900, eleven new ones were launched in Walthamstow alone.

And if the broad raison d'être of those papers was to provide a voice for the weak and oppressed, it was also to sell copy. What sold in the late nineteenth century? Sex and violence, exactly as today. The Victorians, of course, had a problem with sex. They did it, but they did not talk about it. Although generalizations are dangerous for an historian, the morals of the aristocracy/gentry and those of the working class were much more in accord with ours today. It was the middle class that provided the puritanism and the sense of outrage. And it was they who formed the bulk of the newspaper-reading – and buying – public. Stories of men being influenced by curving chair legs are nonsense, but a whole new level of euphemism was reached by writers anxious not to upset their readers. Underpants became 'necessaries', even in army circles; breasts were 'baby's public house'; legs were 'nether limbs'. It was tweeness writ large. When we read the details of Jack's attacks on his victims, the really gory stuff comes from the *Lancet*, an academic journal read only by the medical profession. Even so, a limited amount of violent description was not only permissible, it was actively welcomed. As long as Jack's targets were East End prostitutes, which they all were, the West End could allow itself a delicious shudder over their breakfast-table newspaper reports.

About thirty papers and magazines featured the Whitechapel cases regularly, most notably the *East London Advertiser* and the *East London Observer*. The *Star* was close behind, with its anti-police bias; but they were all left for dead in the prurience stakes by the *Illustrated Police News*. Herbert Ingram's *Illustrated London News* of 1842 *far* outsold any other publication. By the 1860s, it was selling 300,000 copies a week. Ingram had realized that pictures sell. They were engravings in those days – photography in newspapers would belong to a later generation – and people loved them. The *Illustrated Police News* took the hint and went into circulation in 1864. No doubt a number of readers assumed that the paper was actually printed by the police; after all, the Met in particular asked the public for help in the Ripper case via handbills. In fact, it owed much more to the earlier tradition, from which some papers had scarcely moved, of the Penny Dreadfuls and the *Newgate Calendar*.

The early years of the nineteenth century saw a growing fascination with ''orrible murder' and a people not yet fully literate did not care much whether such cases were true or not. William Corder killed his girlfriend Maria Marten in 1823 and he was transformed into a rasping stage villain, determined to bury the girl under the floorboards of the Red Barn. The case itself opened such floodgates that thousands flocked to his trial in Bury St Edmunds, tore up the crime scene for souvenirs and shuddered at Corder's dastardly deeds. His skin still adorns a prayer book in the local museum. Twenty years earlier, two families, the Marrs and the Williamsons, were butchered along the Ratcliffe Highway near London's docks. A sailor was put in the frame, without any real evidence against him, and he was found hanged in his cell before trial. Thomas de Quincey was moved to write his famous *On Murder as One of the Fine Arts* in response to those killings. Burke and Hare made a small fortune out of providing Dr Knox, the Edinburgh surgeon, with cadavers for his medical students, until they picked on Daft Jamie, a local who would be missed, and their game was up. Hare turned king's evidence and Burke hanged, to be dissected in turn as his victims had been. Thomas Greenacre killed his mistress, chopped her up and dumped her body parts all over London in 1829.

And as if these genuine crimes were not gory enough, Penny Dreadful writers created Sweeney Todd, the demon barber who just happened to live in Fleet Street, soon to become the newspaper capital of the world. Todd first appears under another name in fourteenth-century Paris, but that deterred no one. The murderous *folie à deux* of Todd who slashed men's throats while shaving them and Mrs Lovett, who converted their bodies into meat pies, gripped the public's imagination for ever. The *Newgate Calendar* itself, purporting to detail the crimes of murderers and other villains as they faced their (public) executions, sold thousands of copies, as did the handbills produced at hangings.

Executions were holidays until 1868, after which they took place behind locked doors in prison grounds. Literati such as William Thackeray and Charles Dickens went to watch, not the hanging, but the crowd. And their observations appalled them. There was a bloodlust in nineteenth-century Britain which showed itself in the leering, jeering faces of men, women and children who cackled happily while someone tried to snatch life for a few seconds more at the end of one of William Calcraft's ropes. It was not humane; it was not scientific. It was sheer murder.

All this was the newspaper background to the coverage of the Whitechapel murders. And because of those murders, circulation of all of them increased. To illustrate how wide of the mark they often were – and to prove that 'fake news' is not a new phenomenon – let us look at *Reynolds's*

Newspaper's version of the first potential Ripper murder, on Boxing Night 1887. Journalist Terence Robertson described in exciting, dramatic prose, using short sentences and word repetition, how a woman known as Fairy Fay took a short cut home from Mitre Square, where Kate Eddowes would die nine months later. The route she took 'cost her her life'. Two hours later, a constable flashed his bull's eye lantern into a dark doorway and was sickened by the sight. 'In its ray was all that was left of Fairy Fay.' There was an inquest; Inspector Edmund Reid of the Commercial Street police station took charge. The case led nowhere. In fact, Robertson wrote this article for *Reynolds's Newspaper* in October 1950, before what has become the Ripper industry took off and a number of otherwise sober crime writers took the Fairy Fay story as fact. The only possible reference to this murder comes from the *East London Advertiser*, 14 September 1888. 'Since Christmas week in 1887 nine women have been murdered in the East-end … An unknown woman found murdered near Osborne and Wentworth streets, Whitechapel.'

Note that the reference is dated six days after the murder of Annie Chapman, fifteen after that of Polly Nichols. The killer's speed was increasing and until he struck again, what better way for a paper to retain readers than by giving them a taste of murders past? So, according to some papers at the time, the complete list of Jack's victims reads as follows: Fairy Fay, 26 December 1887; Annie Millwood, 25 February 1888; Ada Wilson, 28 March; Emma Smith, 3 April; Martha Tabram, 7 August; Mary Ann Nichols, 31 August; Annie Chapman, 8 September; Susan Ward, 15 September; Elizabeth Stride, 30 September; Kate Eddowes, 30 September; Whitehall (Scotland Yard) torso, 3 October; Mary Jane Kelly, 9 November; Annie Farmer, 20 November; Rose Mylett, 20 December; Elizabeth Jackson, 4 June 1889; Alice McKenzie, 17 July; Pinchin Street torso, 8 September; Frances Coles, 13 February 1891. A grand – and newspaper-selling – total of eighteen!

The *Telegraph* also spoke of Fairy Fay's Boxing Day murder, but mentioned that death had been caused by the thrusting of a stick or iron bar into the body. This is clearly a confusion with the Osborn Street assault on Emma Smith in early April 1888 and does not say much for either the integrity or the accuracy of the press. The term 'fairy' was regularly applied by the working class to old female drunks.

***

While the papers continued throughout the 'autumn of terror' and long beyond, to confuse and even invent, they may have gone much further with the publication of the 'Dear Boss' letter. In fact, the *publication* of the letter was a police decision, in the hope that someone out there would recognize the handwriting. Because it has become so famous, it is worth quoting in full:

Dear Boss.
I keep on hearing the police have caught me but they wont fix me just yet. I have laughed when they look so clever and talk about being on the right track. That joke about Leather Apron gave me real fits. I am down on whores and I shant quit ripping them till I do get buckled. Grand work the last job was. I gave the lady no time to squeal. How can they catch me now. I love my work and want to start again. You will soon hear from me with my funny little games. I saved some of the proper <u>red</u> stuff in a ginger beer bottle over the last job to write with but it went thick like glue and I cant use it. Red ink is fit enough I hope <u>ha ha</u>. The next job I do I shall clip the ladys ears off and send to the police officers just for jolly wouldn't you. Keep this letter back till I do a bit more work then give it out straight. My knife's so nice and sharp I want to get to work right away if I get a chance. Good luck.
　　　yours truly
　　　　Jack the Ripper
Dont mind me giving the trade name.

At right angles to the above was written 'wasn't good enough to post this before I got all the red ink off my hands curse it. No luck yet. They say I'm a doctor now <u>ha ha</u>.'

Once the police received this letter via Thomas Bulling of the Central News Agency, they had to respond to it. There was no precedent. Later murders that attracted such 'confessions' have a body of literature and psychoanalysis attached to them; the 'Dear Boss' letter did not. Dolly Williamson no doubt discussed the contents with his senior men, especially Chief Inspector Donald Swanson who led the Whitechapel inquiry team until 6 October and was a key desk officer after that. What could they have deduced? If the letter was a hoax or prank, it could be ignored. If it was genuine, did it offer any clues as to the killer's identity? The science of fingerprinting lay just around the corner. It was Sir Edward Henry, who became Assistant Commissioner CID in 1891, who brought the new science to the Scotland Yard table, based on previous research by William Herschel and Francis

Galton. The envelope carried a penny lilac stamp with the 'classical' head of the queen and the postmark was suitably vague – 'LONDON E.C. 3 – SP27 88 – P.' Neither the location nor the date would be helpful. Whoever the writer was, he was giving his motive – 'I am down on whores' – which we will examine later. He was proud of his work – 'Grand work the last job was.' This was Annie Chapman in Hanbury Street. He regarded the murders as a mark of fame and apologized for the fact that red ink had had to stand in for blood. He kept his ears and eyes open as to what was being said about him and this almost certainly included following the various press reports now coming thick and fast. He was scornful of the police and the silly theories in circulation. 'Leather Apron' referred to the item found near Annie's body which was for a while believed to have been left behind by the killer. It had led to the arrest of the odd but innocent John Pizer, whose nickname that was, on 10 September. The medical angle – 'They say I'm a doctor now' – has either bedevilled the case ever since or is a genuine interpretation, depending on who Jack actually was.

It is the use of language which is most telling. The handwriting is very clear, unhurried, and shows no signs of the obvious psychosis of some of the later letters. The Americanisms are unusual – 'Boss', 'quit', 'fix me' – and they have pointed a number of researchers into a fruitless and erroneous quest across the Atlantic. The spelling is immaculate, with all the training of the National Schools in evidence, but the punctuation is erratic. There are no question marks after rhetorical questions and only occasional apostrophes. What is the writer trying to hide?

Sir Robert Anderson was Assistant Commissioner CID at the time of the Whitechapel murders. In 1910, long retired, he contributed his reminiscences (rather bizarrely called *The Lighter Side of My Official Life*) in serial form to *Blackwood's Magazine*. 'I will only add here that the "Jack-the-Ripper" letter which is preserved in the Police Museum at New Scotland Yard is the creation of an enterprising London journalist.'

He could not actually name the hoaxer, he said, because of the threat of libel. The fact that Anderson also claimed to know who the Ripper was but that those same laws of libel held him back, might give us pause in taking anything he says at face value. Retired policemen, especially men like Anderson who was at best a political officer with no experience of serial murder at all, are notorious for building up their part in their reminiscences and muddying the waters for future generations of researchers.

A reader of *Blackwood's* who referred to himself as 'a wide-awake East-ender' wrote in to the magazine to agree with the ex-Assistant Commissioner.

The 'Dear Boss' letter and others were the work of local penny-a-liners, in other words, hacks on a London newspaper.

Another retired copper who had a comment to make on the letter was Sir Melville Macnaghten. In *Days of my Years* published in 1914, he wrote, 'In this ghastly production I have always thought that I could discern the stained forefinger of the journalist.' By 1889, he was convinced that he knew who the author was.

We have already heard from George R. Sims, who pointed out as early as 7 October 1888 (in the *Referee*) that only a journalist would have the insider knowledge to post the letter to the Central News Agency. It did cross Sims' mind, of course, that the writer could be a news editor who was also a homicidal maniac, but he preferred to let that idea go!

In an internal memo, only discovered in 1993, ex-Detective Chief Inspector John Littlechild of Special Branch wrote to George Sims. It was September 1913 and Littlechild had been retired for twenty years. Even so, both men, engaged in their different ways in a quest for the truth, had shared the Ripper experience and in a sense, it never left them. Littlechild believed that the idea of the 'Dear Boss' letter was that of John Moore, the editor of the Central News Agency itself and that it was written by 'Tom Bullen [*sic*] ... [who] occasionally took too much to drink'.

Thomas Bulling was 41 in 1888 and his fondness for the bottle is hardly surprising. Newshounds lived by their wits then as now. They had to please their editors by finding stories that had to fit the criteria of the day. They had to work quickly, with ink-pens or the clumsy new typewriting machines and messy ribbons and had to frequent bars to pick up stories. Many of their informants were low-life and they all expected a hand-out, if not actual cash then at least copious amounts of alcohol. Men like Bulling hung around police stations, law courts and scenes of crime to feed the ever-hungry readership with sensation.

R. Thornton Hopkins, a former journalist himself and once a well-known ghost-hunter, described someone who was probably Bulling in his *Life and Death at the Old Bailey* in 1935. 'This poor fellow had a breakdown and became a whimsical figure in Fleet Street. He would creep about dark courts waving his hands furiously in the air, would utter stentorian "Ha, ha, ha's" ...' Hopkins believed that the Yard had their suspicions about him, especially Melville Macnaghten.

If not Bulling, how about Best? Frederick Best was 30 in 1888 and was sent, along with another journalist, Michael O'Brien, to investigate the Whitechapel murders for the *Star*. For reasons best known to themselves, various Ripper experts do not equate this man with the forename-less Best described by Nigel Morland in his 1966 book *Crime and Detection*. This seems to be straining credulity unnecessarily. Morland interviewed an elderly journalist in 1931 who covered the Whitechapel killings for the *Star*. How could it *not* be Frederick?

John Brummer, one of the *Star*'s shareholders, complained to O'Connor in no uncertain terms. 'Mr Best's attempt to mislead Central News during the Whitechapel murders should have led to an earlier termination of his association with the newspaper.'

Another possibility for 'Dear Boss' authorship is Harry Dam, a journalist born in San Francisco and educated at Berkeley University. In the middle of the 1880s, he was secretary to George Stoneman, the governor of California, and was caught up in a financial scandal selling pardons to ex-cons under the state's penal system. By January 1887, Dam was working for the *New York Times* and later in the year, moved to London to write for the *Star* and the *New York Herald*. The American libel laws were different from those in Britain and Dam created the legend of 'Leather Apron' as the Whitechapel murderer. 'Day after day,' journalist Lincoln Springfield wrote in 1924, 'Dam gave the public all the thrills it wanted.' The magazine *Fun* in 1897 referred to Dam as 'the historian of that shy but industrious person, Jack the Ripper.'

In an article written for the *New York Age* in November 1890, Dr Henry Monroe of St Mark's Episcopal Church in the city wrote:

> Few people in London believe in the genuineness of the 'Jack the Ripper' letters. They were simply the invention of some sensational fool or else a newspaper 'fake'. In fact, there is a suspicion that a *New York World* reporter might have been exercising his peculiar home talent, just to try its effect upon our British cousins.

When Harry Dam's name was specifically linked with this and he was accused by several American newspapers, T.P. O'Connor MP, the *Star*'s editor, rushed to his defence. Like so much else in the Ripper story, the jury on Harry Dam is still out.

The 'Dear Boss' letter, whether the work of Thomas Bulling or any other hack, was not written by the Whitechapel murderer. It did, however, create a mini-mystery in itself as to authorship and, far more importantly, give the killer a name that has gone down in legend. Few journalists can have that as their epitaph.

But one lingering doubt remains. In the 'Dear Boss' letter, written five days before the 'double event', the writer promises to 'clip the ladys ears off'. When Dr Frederick Brown carried out his meticulous post mortem on Kate Eddowes who had been murdered in Mitre Square, he discovered that the dead woman's right ear was mutilated; portions of the lobe and auricle fell from her clothing in the mortuary. Was this a case of murder imitating the art of forgery?

Chapter Three

'Letters written by him, but none by me'

Not all the Ripper correspondence has survived. The passage of time means that, inevitably, evidence has been mislaid, been stolen or otherwise gone missing. As Stuart Evans and Keith Skinner wrote, the surviving material is vast and transcription has taken several years. Their invaluable *Jack the Ripper Sourcebook* (Robinson, 2001) runs to a staggering 723 pages! Within that are numerous reports, letters and missives that are now generally too faded to read and key words that are illegible.

Documents that were sent to the police or compiled by them were housed first in the relevant divisional stations, like Commercial Street and Leman Street, then forwarded to Scotland Yard. As time passed, the bulk of these was transferred to the Home Office and then to the Public Record Office in Chancery Lane, later Kew. As with any chain of evidence, the best policy is to keep such material intact in one place so that proper analysis can take place. The problem lies in the name – the *Public* Record Office. Over the years, members of the public have 'borrowed' various bits and pieces and failed to return them. The in situ photographs of Mary Kelly's body in Miller's Court and Dr Bond's post mortem notes were victims of this. Not until 1987 did they turn up, posted anonymously to Scotland Yard. Who knows what else is out there somewhere and will never find its way back for real public consumption?

The letters and postcards relating to Jack add up to 222 – which, no doubt, numerologists and conspiracy theorists will find resonant – but there were once many more. Melville Macnaghten remembered, in *Days of My Years*, that one of the first things he found on the Ripper case when he took office read:

> I'm not a butcher, I'm not a Yid,
> Nor yet a foreign skipper.
> But I'm your own light-hearted friend,
> Yours truly, Jack the Ripper.

Almost all books on Jack cite this 'cheeky chappie' verse, but it is no longer among the original material in any archive. A similar rhyme was quoted by Edwin Woodhall, who joined the Met in 1907 and became an early Ripper expert:

> I'm not an alien maniac,
> Nor yet a foreign tripper,
> I'm just your jolly, lively friend,
> Yours truly, Jack the Ripper.

Macnaghten goes on …'at that time the police post-bag bulged large with hundreds of anonymous communications on the subject of the East End tragedies.' Where possible, this book factors in examples like this because, if accurately quoted, they are the raw data we need for analysis.

Various authorities give very different numbers of letters. Donald McCormick, one of the least reliable writers on Jack, guessed about 2,000 over a number of years. Others believed in October 1888 that the figure was 'upwards of 700'. Evans and Skinner cite the more realistic 208 (but they acknowledge that this is the current available figure for purposes of research) and Dirk C. Gibson, the author of *Jack the Writer*, suggests 244.

For the statistically-minded, of the 222 communications, 94 were sent to the police, 14 to the press and 22 'other'. Among the police, 24 were addressed to Sir Charles Warren, the deeply unpopular Commissioner of the Met at Scotland Yard. Fifteen were posted to the Yard itself without a named individual. Eleven were sent to James Monro, Warren's number two in charge of the CID. Eleven were addressed to various ranks – superintendent, inspector and sergeant – again, with no name. Of the detectives carrying out their enquiries on the ground, only Frederick Abberline received a letter. Leman Street, as one of the two police stations serving 'the Abyss', got twelve; other stations, scattered the length and breadth of the country, thirteen. Because Kate Eddowes was murdered in the City, Commissioner Sir James Fraser of that force received two.

The press was spearheaded by the Central News Agency, which received five. Next came *The Times* with three. All the others – the *Daily News*, the Press Association, the *Evening News and Post*, the *Surrey Comet* and the *Clapham Observer* – only got one. Interestingly, the papers that gave the killings the highest profile – the *East London Advertiser*, the *East London Observer* and the *Star* – received none at all.

It may be appropriate to examine the workings of the Post Office. In these days of emails and the internet, the traditional posting of cards, letters and parcels is becoming a thing of the past. In 1888, the General Post Office was highly efficient and the envy of the world. Rudyard Kipling, the 'poet of empire', wrote a poem extolling the virtues of delivery, even in the inhospitable mountains of Northern India – 'In the name of the Empress, the Overland Mail!' About 1,700 million letters and postcards were sent each year, a third of them in London. The system meant that every letter was stamped, showing the office from which it was despatched, the mail (there were up to twelve deliveries a day in London) by which it was sent and the operative who handled it. This meant that letters continued to arrive at various addresses from 7.00 am to 8.45 pm, an astonishing rate in comparison with today's half-hearted effort. The headquarters of the GPO was at St Martin-le-Grand. The nearest district office to Whitechapel was Commercial Rd East. There was no postal collection on Sundays and all offices were closed.

What do the statistics of postmarks give us? Is there a pattern? Infuriatingly, not. London, inevitably, dominates. Although the Whitechapel murders were publicized worldwide, the crimes attracted most attention in their own locale. Of the 222, 132 have London postmarks, East and West End, with no specific pattern within the capital. Birmingham is next, with three; then Dublin, Liverpool, Plymouth and Leicester with two each. Since Birmingham was Britain's second city in terms of size, the bigger number is not surprising, but the third city, Manchester, only produced one. Is it mere coincidence that Dublin, Liverpool and Plymouth all had busy docks and a large, if floating, foreign population? Actual foreign correspondents are important but rare. Boston, Massachusetts sent one letter. So did Philadelphia. Lisbon produced one as well, from '*Jack o estripador*' (Portuguese for 'ripper').

Eight missives were found, as opposed to posted, most of them in what today we would call Greater London. The most bizarre was literally a message in a bottle, floating with the tide onto the south coast between Sandwich and Deal in Kent.

As we shall see, the first Ripper letter was probably written on 17 September 1888, although there is some evidence that this is a forgery, written about 1966. If it is genuine, the 'Dear Boss' letter was the third in the sequence and its widespread publication by the Met led to the bulging postbag that Macnaghten refers to. There were seventy-five in October, sixty in November and then a sharp decline in the following month (eight) when the spate of murders appeared to be over. By the end of the year, 145 missives had been received. The first half of 1889 saw only single figures each month, with a peak of eleven in July – the murder of Clay Pipe Alice McKenzie, which may have been Ripper-related – and seventeen in September, when a torso was discovered under the arches in Pinchin Street; definitely *not* Ripper-related.

The last dated letter was written in October 1896, although fifteen of them were undated and it is difficult to place them accurately in context.

If we break the letter frequency down still further, we find five written on 4 October, the day on which various newspapers published the 'Saucy Jacky' postcard and the day on which the inquest on Kate Eddowes opened. There were six the next day and eight on 8 October. That day saw the burial of Kate Eddowes and the opening of the inquest into the torso found under the foundations of Scotland Yard along the Embankment, then referred to in the press as 'The Whitehall Mystery'. Two days later, seven letters were sent; there were five on the 15th and six on the 19th, by which time the most chilling Ripper letter of all, that addressed to Mr Lusk and postmarked 'From Hell' had arrived, complete with half a human kidney. Not until 12 November would the daily number reach six again, the day of the truncated inquest into Mary Kelly's death three days earlier. There were six again on the 15th and seven on the 19th, the date of Mary's funeral. After that, the missives revert to single figures.

We shall examine the psychology behind the Ripper letters throughout this book. For some, it was to do with ego. The film-maker Andy Warhol said that everybody is famous for fifteen minutes. Today's internet trolls and tweeters have the same compulsion. They are obsessed with the false cult of celebrity, itself created and sustained by a media intent on making money by any means. They long to see themselves on the screen, in print, their names and hashtags littering the superhighway of mediocrity. To this group belong the 65 per cent of Ripper letter-writers who claimed to *be* Jack. They were not, but they would have loved to have been.

To another group belong the finger-pointers. Ever since the enormity of the crimes of Jimmy Savile (a kind of Ripper for the twenty-first century) any male media personality is fair game for accusations, however libellous, however unfair. In our victim-ridden age, any female who has ever been patted, winked at or brushed past in the corridors of power or showbiz – and a great many who have not – believe they have the right to point an accusatory finger, especially if the finger is pointing at a rich and powerful 'predator'. We can find this group among the original Ripper letter-writers too.

Some were in it for the laughs. 'Funny little games', 'Ha, ha!', 'Saucy Jacky', 'Just for jolly', 'Your own light-hearted friend'; phrases like this litter the correspondence. Human nature being what it is, any disaster or catastrophe is fair game and can be turned into a 'joke'. While this book was in production, a prominent British politician told a Holocaust 'joke' – as if there could be such a thing – on prime-time television but was rightly ignored and shut down by a BBC presenter. In true crime, as opposed to crime fiction, there are no winners, merely losers; lives shattered by the lunacy of a killer who has no conscience. This does not and did not stop the letter-writers/internet trolls from winding up the authorities; 'Catch Me When You Can' was a typical and direct taunt against the police.

The darker side of all this is the thread of violence that runs through the Ripper letters. There are crude drawings of knives, coffins, body parts. There are blood smears. There is a profoundly disturbing, deep-rooted misogyny, especially in the pseudo-religious letters – 'I am down on whores' – as if Jack's victims were asking for their ghastly ends and nobody should be surprised by them.

So, where did it all start? Most commentators, even Stewart Evans and Keith Skinner in their landmark study *Jack the Ripper: Letters from Hell* contend that the first Ripper letter was written on 24 September 1888 and addressed to Sir Charles Warren, Commissioner of Police at Scotland Yard. But in fact, there may have been an earlier one, and although it cannot be said to have led to the avalanche that followed (the 'Dear Boss' letter did that), it is worthy of discussion. Dated 17 September, it reads:

> Dear Boss,
> So now they say I am a Yid when will they learn Dear old Boss? You an me know the truth dont we. Lusk can look forever hell never find me but I am rite under his nose all the time. I watch them looking for me and it gives me fits ha ha I love my work an I shant stop until I get buckled and even then watch out for your old pal Jacky.
> > Catch me if you Can
> > Jack the Ripper
> P.S. Sorry about the blood, still messy from the last one. What a pretty necklace I gave her.

We can now see the 'Dear Boss' letter sent to the Central News Agency in a different light. The 17 September letter was never published but it is likely that a journalist somewhere saw it and copied sections that appealed.

In general, the Met did not co-operate with the press and relationships worsened as the killings went on and the police seemed out of their depth. Even so, individual detectives worked with individual journalists on a need-to-know basis and who knows who showed what to whom? 'Dear Boss', 'gave me fits ha, ha', 'shant stop until I get buckled' and especially 'Jack the Ripper' are direct steals. There can be no other explanation; the handwriting of the two letters is clearly different, the first one less organized and well-educated than the second.

'Yid' of course refers to the 90 per cent Jewish population of Whitechapel and is a reminder of the latent hostility shown to the newly-arrived immigrants. As the Jews moved in, the Irish moved out and what was a flourishing weaving area on the edge of London 200 years earlier was now an appalling slum. 'Lusk' was George Akin Lusk, a builder and decorator who specialized in restoring music halls. His lot cannot have been a happy one because his wife, Susannah, died in 1888, leaving him to bring up their seven children. A week before the first letter was sent, Lusk had been elected chairman of the Whitechapel Vigilance Committee at a meeting at the Crown pub along the Mile End Road. These men were not vigilantes in the lynch-mob sense, but respectable rate- and tax-payers alarmed at what was happening in their neighbourhood and not impressed by the performance of the police. They urged the government to improve street lighting – all of Jack's victims died in relative darkness – and to offer rewards. During the time of the Whitechapel murders, neither request was honoured. The sixteen-strong committee included a tailor, a cigar-maker, even an actor; B. Harris was secretary and Joseph Aarons, landlord of the Crown, was treasurer. An upper room at the pub was made available and the committee advertised in the local press that officers were on hand daily to take down details from anyone who had information on the murders. Such ideas were no doubt well-intentioned, but they potentially opened the way to all kinds of malicious tittle-tattle that only served to waste the time of the police.

Crime historian John Eddleston raises the interesting issue of the letter's last line – 'What a pretty necklace I gave her.' This refers to the most recent murder, that of Annie Chapman in Hanbury Street. Eddleston conjectures that this refers to the ghastly mutilations in which the dead woman's intestines were thrown over her shoulder in the yard behind No. 29. Dr Bagster Phillips began his testimony at the inquest on 14 September, three days before the letter was sent, but it was not until he was recalled five days later that the intestine information was made public. Could the letter, Eddleston asks, be genuinely written by the killer in that he refers to something not yet in the public domain? Phillips' description of the intestines draped over both shoulders could indeed suggest a 'pretty necklace' in the eyes of a deranged killer. On the other hand, it could equally refer to the slash of the throat, which was already common knowledge by the time the letter was written.

***

The second letter, described by many researchers as the first, was sent on 24 September to Warren at Scotland Yard. It began formally:

> Dear Sir,
> I do wish to give myself up I am in misery with nightmare I am the man who committed all these murders in the last six months my name is [silhouette of coffin] and so I am a horse slaughterer and work at Name [blocked out] address [blocked out] I have found the woman I wanted that is chapman an I done what I called slaughtered her but if any one comes I will surrender but I am not going to walk to the station by myself so I am yours truly [silhouette of coffin].
>   – keep the Boro road clear or I might take a trip up there
> photo
[silhouette of knife]
of Knife
> this is the knife I done those murders with it is a small handle with a large long blade sharpe both sides.

Perhaps the most famous example of a killer weighed down with guilt and self-loathing was William Heirens, who left a message scrawled in lipstick on a wall at one of his murder sites – 'For heaven's sake catch me before I kill again. I cannot control myself.' Heirens is a classic sexual pervert, taught by his puritanical mother in the Chicago of the prohibition era that sex was dirty and women the spawn of Satan. His only sex life as a teenager and young man consisted of masturbating over female underwear stolen from clothes lines. Despite academic success at college, he took to burglary by night merely to enter a woman's bedroom. In June 1945 he was caught in the act by Mrs Josephine Ross and he stabbed her numerous times, nearly cutting off her head in the process. That was when he wrote his desperate plea, earning him the nickname the 'Lipstick Killer' in the Chicago press. He killed a 6-year-old girl after a ransom attempt backfired and he was finally caught six months later. He was sent to Joliet Prison for three life terms without the possibility of parole and died there in 2012.

Because Jack was never caught, we cannot analyse him in the way that Heirens was analysed. His sense of guilt and the inability to live with himself is common among serial killers and in the immediate aftermath of a murder. It does not last, however, and at any time, Heirens (and Jack) could simply have walked into a police station and confessed. That they did not speaks volumes for the complexity of a killer's psyche. They advertise the enormity of their crimes, paint themselves almost as victims, but do nothing about it.

In the context of the 24 September letter, if we take it at face value, the writer is confessing to the attacks on Annie Millwood, Ada Wilson, Emma Smith, Martha Tabram and Polly Nichols, even though the MO of all but the last two was different. There is a taunting quality about this letter, like the redacted files that reluctant governments grudgingly give out as a result of pressure via the Freedom of Information Act. The name and address are nearly there, but not quite. The description of the supposed murder weapon is unhelpful; various medical men argued long and hard over those grim weeks as to the exact nature of the knife and could only agree on the broadest essentials. Long before the country became hysterical about knife crime (largely in the twenty-first century), knives of all kinds were readily available to everyone, even children.

Most fascinating of all is the reference to the writer's occupation; he is a horse-slaughterer. When draft animals and army horses reached the end of their useful lives, they usually found their way to the abattoirs of large towns and cities. In London, the largest company was that of Charles Barber & Co., with major premises near the Thames at Battersea. A number of doctors giving their views on the Ripper murders believed that the killer had some anatomical training, but that he was unlikely to have been a surgeon. In my book on the Thames Torso murders, I conjecture that the killer in those cases was probably a horse-slaughterer. He would have had somewhere quiet and sheltered to take his eight victims and the skill to dismember them and distribute the body parts along the Thames and elsewhere. In all cases, the heads were missing. This, I believe, was because the murder method (so unlike Jack's) was a hammer blow to the head that would have shattered the skull. Horses died in the same way. Had the heads been found, the wounds would have left a clear trail to the knacker's yard. Instead, they were crushed in the huge grinding machines used to turn them to bone powder.

Tantalizingly, there is a link to Barber & Co. in the Whitechapel murders. One of their premises stood in Winthrop Street, just around the corner from the murder site of Polly Nichols. Constable John Thain had left his cape there before her body was discovered and went back to collect it. He must have told two of Barber's workers about the find because, moments later, Harry Tomkins and James Mumford turned up to gawp. Tomkins appears again in the story, testifying at Polly's inquest. The press described him as a 'rough-looking man' living at Coventry Street, Bethnal Green. Did he also have a warped sense of humour, revelling in the notoriety and did he pen the letter of the 24th?

There are two more points of note. The first is that the writer was specifically looking for Annie Chapman – 'I found the woman I wanted.' Does that mean that he knew her personally and perhaps had a score to settle? Or was she a physical type to which he was attracted, rather as, ninety years later, serial killer Ted Bundy would be drawn to murder pretty girls with long, straight dark hair? This supposes, of course, that the letter is actually from the Whitechapel murderer, which I doubt. The final point is the threat – similar ones would follow in due course – about an assault in the Borough Road in the near future. This attack never took place or, if it did, the police did not attribute it to Jack.

In the meantime, the *Star*'s attack on John Pizer, 'Leather Apron', was outrageous. As we have seen, it was probably the work of Harry Dam, quite prepared to smear anybody in his quest for a scoop. It was trial by media and would have resulted in criminal action today. The *Star* did not name him but to those who knew the sobriquet, that was more than enough. A number of people were accused publicly and the *Illustrated Police News* inevitably published a lurid, fiend-like caricature. Such 'photos', as we shall see, appear in the Ripper letters too. Needless to say, when the police found Pizer and cleared him – he was in custody when the murder of Annie Chapman took place – there was no hint of apology from the media at all.

In the context of the Ripper letters actually being the work of the killer, George R. Sims, as usual, made a salient point in the *Referee* that October. 'To imagine a man deliberately murdering and mutilating women and then confessing the deed on a postcard, is to turn Mr W.S. Gilbert loose upon the Whitechapel murders at once.' Gilbert was, of course, the libretto half of the hugely popular Gilbert and Sullivan, whose comic operettas were full of contrived plots, clever wordplay and 'topsy turvy'.

When a follow-up letter arrived, sent this time to the *Daily News*, the murder map of Whitechapel had changed and the hysteria was cranked considerably higher. The 'double event' had happened on the night of 29/30

September and that was when this second note was penned. Postmarked 'London E' and dated 'Monday', it read:

> I am so pleased to see another chance of ripping up a dear creature. I shall be in Buck's Row or very close to between 12 and 2 in morning on Wednesday I have got the girl set & I have been offered double money for her woomb and lower part of body mean to have them at any price I do like to find them nice parts. I do pity Leather Apron. I've got someone to write this for me,
> yours truly,
>   Boss
>   Ripper

The killer was threatening to return to the crime scene of Polly Nichol's murder, even giving the day and time. Although no one understood it at the time, the phrase 'I have got the girl set' implies a stalking MO, what American serial killer experts call the 'trolling phase', the selection of a suitable victim. Leather Apron was still topical but the notion of body parts for sale ushered in a new concept and was introduced by the coroner, Wynne Baxter, on the last day of Annie Chapman's inquest on Wednesday, 26 September.

Widely reported in the press, Baxter believed that Annie's uterus had been carefully removed 'by one who knew where to find it', someone used to a post mortem room; in short, a doctor. The coroner reported that after the publication of the morning papers, he had been approached by the sub-curator of the London Pathological Museum who told him that he had been contacted by an American who was collecting uteri and willing to pay £20 a time for them. He wanted them preserved in glycerine (as opposed to the usual spirits of wine) so that they could be shipped to the United States for his research. The American had already tried elsewhere and had been turned down, as he was by the Pathological Museum. Baxter commented grimly that 'there is a market for the missing organ'.

The medical profession was furious – the coroner had overstepped the mark – and the press pounced on it all gleefully. The *Telegraph*, then the largest circulation paper in the world, reported that University College Hospital regarded the whole thing as an unlikely and 'silly' story and the paper obliquely blamed the medical authorities for their contemptuous dismissal of the theory. The *British Medical Journal* admitted, on 6 October, that a 'foreign physician' (they do not say 'American') did indeed make such enquiries re his research but he had left the country, presumably empty-handed, eighteen months earlier.

The American press, of course, got wind of the story and the *Chicago Tribune* ran a number of articles, even interviewing Wynne Baxter on the subject. The description of the shadowy American has led some researchers to point the finger at the quack doctor Francis Tumblety, an eccentric self-publicist who was certainly in London at the time and prone to bizarre behaviour. As Baxter pointed out to *The Times*' reporter, he was not suggesting – and neither was anyone else – that the doctor with the peculiar request was actually the murderer.

In fact, the whole idea was preposterous. With what we now know about serial 'blitz' killers of Jack's type, financial gain is very rarely a motive. Burke and Hare killed for gain in the 1820s – the 'subject' victims they sold for anatomical dissection – but they actually murdered by asphyxiation and left the mutilations to the medical students!

The date of 1 October was something of a field day for letter-writers; the start of the trickle that would rise to a flood in the weeks ahead. The Central News Agency received a postcard and it appeared to have been stained with blood; the obsession with blood in the letters will be discussed further in Chapter 7:

> I wasn't codding dear old Boss when I gave you the tip. You'll hear about saucy Jacky's work tomorrow double event this time number one squealed a bit couldn't finish straight off. Had no time to get ears for police, thanks for keeping last letter back till I got to work again.
>
> Jack the Ripper

The *Telegraph* reported that the Central News Agency regarded this too as a hoax, but commented on the 'free, bold, clerkly hand'; the handwriting will be discussed further in Chapter 4. The Met now produced copies of both the 'Dear Boss' and 'Saucy Jacky' missives, hoping that someone could identify the writer. What they were in fact doing was to open the floodgates to the bizarre world of oddballs who saw a chance to make a dubious name for themselves. The *Star* was more aloof and took the opportunity to cock a snook at the *Telegraph*:

> … why does our friend, the D.T., print facsimiles of the ghastly but very silly letters from 'Jack the Ripper'? We were offered them …

and declined to print them. They are clearly written in red pencil, not blood, the obvious reason being that the writer was one of those foolish but bad people who delight in an unholy notoriety. Now, the murderer is not a man of this kind.

The article concludes with the bald fact that destroys the authenticity of almost all the Ripper communiqués – 'Thousands of Londoners had details of the crimes supplied in the Sunday papers.'

The people who wrote claiming to be the Whitechapel murderer had either not read the *Star* or refused to be deterred. Some 65 per cent of the surviving correspondence claims to come from the killer himself. Let us look at some examples. On 2 October, 'George of the High Rip Gang' drew heavily on 'Dear Boss' with his 'I am going to be heavy on the guilded [sic] whores now' but he has altogether a higher status in mind. What characterizes Jack's targets is their poverty. They lived a hand-to-mouth existence in and out of doss-houses and workhouses. 'George' had bigger fish to fry:

> Some dutchess will cut up nicely & the lace will show nicely … On to Brighton for a holiday but we shant idle splendid high class women there my mouth waters … My pal will keep on at the east a while yet. When I get a nobility womb I will send it on to C. Warren or perhaps to you for a keepsake. O it *is* jolly.

The High Rip gang was supposedly a group of thugs operating in Liverpool in the mid-1880s, but its existence has been called into question. No one was ever arrested as a gang member and, as with Jack himself, there is the suggestion that it was all a media creation to sell newspapers, in that case the *Liverpool Echo* and *Liverpool Daily Post*. We have a fascinating example of 'truth' distorting as entertainment with the recent television series *Peaky Blinders*, which portrays interwar Birmingham as a sort of Prohibition Chicago with funny accents!

What is fascinating is not only the writer's obsession with the aristocracy, but the implication that 'George' and Jack are a murderous double act, targeting both ends of the social spectrum. Sexual serial killers working in tandem are extremely rare. The 'best' example is that of Kenneth Bianchi and his cousin Angelo Buono, the 'hillside stranglers' who targeted women in Los Angeles in the 1970s. It goes without saying, perhaps, that there were no such attacks on well-to-do women either in Brighton or elsewhere and Charles Warren never did receive the uterus in the post.

The six letters sent on 6 October were posted not just in London but elsewhere. The theme of wombs was still there, even in Bradford where 'Jack the cunquorer' had arrived safely 'after a pleasant journey'. But there is an interesting line in this northern letter that speaks volumes for the kind of psychotic who confesses to murder. It reads 'the last letter was not from me'. A week later, a similar line is taken; this one from Colchester and addressed to Scotland Yard:

> Sirs, I am sorry that such a letter should be sent to you, viz, the one signed Jack the Ripper ... I can assure you it is nothing to do with us whatsoever ... I caution persons playing such tricks ... to beware of their Bodies for it's no joke.
> I am yours truly
> <u>Mr Englishman</u>

The language is educated and middle-class – 'viz' and 'persons' and the punctuation is excellent. Like 'George's' letter above, the writer uses the plural 'nothing to do with us'. Does he mean that Englishmen could not possibly be responsible for murders like these? Or that he *is* Jack but has at least one accomplice?

Three weeks later, a letter posted in the East End and addressed to 'the Inspector, Leman St Police Station' was written in block capitals and read, 'Those other letters were not written by me at all and has [*sic*] someone has been kind enough to give me the name of "Jack the Ripper" I'll accept it and act up to it. Look out for the next.'

The writer of the next relevant letter was still outraged when he wrote from Birmingham, specifically Rea St Lodging House:

> Dear Sir,
> I beg to inform you that I have read about that bungling affair yesterday morning in Whitechapel, this is to say that I have had no hand in it, but I think it must be one of my apprentices who has been practising while I have been away.

It was signed 'Old Original Jack the Ripper'.

The 'bungling affair' probably refers to the attack on Annie Farmer on 2 November. She was the right age for a Ripper victim (about 40) and a prostitute, but the Birmingham writer was right; she was not a victim of the Whitechapel murderer. She picked up a client and took him back to

Satchelles Lodging House at 19 George Street, where (unusually) double beds were available. Annie was well-educated and had three children whose father had done a runner when he discovered his wife's lifestyle. She knew her client and all was well until she woke up to find his knife at her throat. She screamed and the assailant fled before the doss-house deputy called the police. The long-suffering Dr Bagster Phillips stitched her wound and she was taken to Commercial Street police station on a stretcher. In a city still paralysed with fear over Jack's spree, the rumour spread that there had been another murder.

Tight-lipped as ever, the Met refused to comment to the press and denied journalists access to the injured woman. As one pressman for the *Evening News* wrote, 'One might as well try to obtain information from a sphinx.' Annie recovered and her attacker was never found.

On 28 November, 'the black Brunswick boy' wrote from Kilburn to say 'this is the first note you have had from the real man'. The writer was still furious at what he saw as a slight when he wrote to the *Evening News and Post* in Whitefriars Street. By this time it was September 1889 and the fifth of the Ripper murders had occurred more than a year earlier:

> Dear Boss,
> The Ripper scare this morning is an infernal scandal on me you know. I never do my ripping in that fashion.

Again, the writer was correct. The letter refers to the discovery of a female torso under railway arches at Pinchin Street and although this was almost certainly another victim of the Thames Torso killer, it was not Ripper-related. To be fair to the police and medical experts at the time, that was the view they held, but the newspapers sensed an opportunity to keep the Ripper scare alive and sales high. The usual 'red-tops' were involved, but a new one was added this time because a man calling himself John Cleary had gone to the London offices of the *New York Herald* to tell them that Jack had struck again. The real identity of Cleary was never established and the murder site he reported – Back Church Lane – had no body at all. Whether this was a garbled version of the Pinchin Street killing or whether 'Cleary' was a deranged hoaxer, the effect was to raise yet more awareness of the Ripper killings in America and to release a shower of letters to press and police.

The forensics of the Pinchin Street case – a neatly-dismembered naked torso – was so far removed from Jack's disorganized MO as to make any possible connection highly tenuous; not that that stopped the media speculating or the cranks from snatching up pen and paper.

On 8 October we have the same proprietorial theme again. Jack wrote vaguely to 'Chief of Scotland Yard' – 'The last murder was not done by me but by someone else …' The phrase occurs again on 8 November in what must be the most bizarre of all the Ripper correspondence. It is part of a four-page poem to which we will return later and sent to 'Superintendent of Great Scotland Yard, London' with an address of 30 Bangor Street:

> … In the papers you sometimes see –
> Letters by him, but none by me …

There was a proprietorial take on all this, smacking of one-upmanship. The Whitechapel murders were *so* spectacular, *so* revolting and had *so* caught the public's imagination that only one man could be responsible and all the others were sad hoaxers jumping on a bandwagon.

A letter on 16 October 1889 summed up the broad purpose behind all correspondence 'I hope you can read what I have written and will put it all in the paper, not leave Hall [*sic*] out.' We are back to Andy Warhol's 'famous for fifteen minutes' but motivation is infinitely more complex than that.

Chapter Four

'Two or Three Hands of Writing'

'P.S.,' said the letter sent to the Commissioner of Police on 26 July 1889, 'please excuse the writing, you shall hear from me again.' On 7 August 'Jack the Ripper catch me if you can', wrote from Victoria Docks, adding, 'I do shake writing these lines.' The 'shakey hand' was referred to again on 10 September when the Pinchin Street torso was found and the same letter warned, 'I can write a great many hands this is one far from detection.' We have already noted the missive of 16 October – 'I hope you can read what I have written … J. Ripper.' The 'poet' of 8 November admitted, 'I'm not a flashaway Belgravian swell. Although self taught I can write and spell.'

Over a year earlier and a week after the 'double event', the 'Jack' who warned the authorities that he was on the prowl in Kentish Town wrote, 'Now if you think you can catch me by the writing in the first letter I wrote. You cant, because I can write two or three hands.'

The letter found on 19 October 1888 in a letterbox at 37 West Ham Lane (the envelope carried a drawing of a postage stamp!) claimed he could write '5 hand writings' and went further – 'If anybody recognizes the writing I shall kill the first female I see in this house [presumably No. 37] or if there is no females I shall be down on the boss.'

It is notoriously easy to disguise handwriting. If the journalist T.J. Bulling *did* write the first 'Dear Boss' letter, he must have disguised his because he sent it with a covering letter of his own to Scotland Yard. Indeed, at one point, both were on display side by side in the Police Museum there. At its simplest level, making basic spelling errors and ignoring punctuation will do the trick. A right-handed man scribbling with his left hand is even better.

All the letters/postcards were written in black or red ink or pencil, all three of which were readily available at stationers throughout the country. Probably the most detailed research of any 'original' Ripper material was carried out on the now notorious Maybrick journal by experts after it came to light in 1993.

James Maybrick was a Liverpool cotton merchant who died, apparently of arsenic poisoning, in May 1889. His wife Florence was accused of murdering him (he was a bullying husband) and found guilty, more on the evidence of her adultery than the hard fact of murder. She spent fifteen years in gaol before emigrating to America, where she died in 1941. The story of the journal is tortuous and here I will concentrate on the evidence of the writing alone. It was written in a scrapbook with the first forty-eight pages removed – I have a Letts Diary for 1885 in my possession with similar mutilations; they are not difficult to come by. It formed a diary, signed by 'Jack the Ripper' covering the period April 1888 to May 1889, the month of Maybrick's death. Michael Barrett was given the journal by a friend, Tony Devereux, in May 1991 and Barrett, convinced that it was a) genuine and b) written by Maybrick, took it to the Rupert Crew Literary Agency. Shirley Harrison was commissioned to write a book on the subject.

The author turned to experts to authenticate it. The British Museum and Jarndyce's antiquarian books passed it on to others. In the context of handwriting, Dr David Baxendale and Dr Nicholas Eastaugh looked at the graphics, ink and paper. Despite the usual wrangling among forensic experts (for the 'prosecution' and 'defence') Eastaugh believed that the writing could be contemporary (i.e. 1888–9). A dye called nigrosin, which the ink contained, was available from 1867. The fact that the journal entries did not match Maybrick's signature on his marriage certificate and will was perhaps not that important; we have already met the boasting of several disguised 'hands'.

While Ripper experts quite rightly pointed to the numerous errors of fact and phraseology in the journal (there are at least twenty-one), the publishers Smith Griffon bought the rights in June 1992 and parties bidding for American and serial rights had further tests carried out. Warner Books team of Kenneth W. Rendell, forgery expert Dr Joe Nickell, Maureen Casey Owens (document-reader) and ink research chemists Robert I. Kurantz and Dr Rod McNeill went to work. The paper was genuine and the ink was genuine. What no one could determine was when the two had been put together; in other words, exactly when the journal was written. Maureen Owens in particular was unhappy with the writing slant and ink flow, giving the lie to the fact that the journal entries were supposed to have been made piecemeal over time.

The *Sunday Times* entered the fray in September 1993. *The Times* itself, of course, had already caught a million-pound cold over the authenticity of the so-called Hitler Diaries, accepted by historian Hugh Trevor-Roper as genuine. Their team – Dr Audrey Gilles of the Met's 'questioned document' section; Dr Kate Flint, lecturer in Victorian English at Oxford; and Tom Cullen, the author of several books on Jack and Victorian crime – were also dubious, although they had different views on the journal's authenticity.

Ripperologist Melvin Harris got hold of 'Maybrick's' ink samples and had them tested by Analysis for Industry, who found the presence of chloroacetamide, a constituent of Diamine ink, a type not available in 1888. Ergo, the journal was a forgery.

Other experts were asked to sort out the impasse. Shirley Harrison and Keith Skinner had the journal scrutinized by Leeds University in their department of Dyeing and Colour Chemistry. The ink was not Diamine and the whole fraught question was put to Professor John C. Roberts, head of Paper Sciences at UMIST who could only say that chloroacetamide was available in 1888, but he had never known it from paper samples. From there, the journal underwent further tests by Staffordshire University and the results were inconclusive.

In areas of research far removed from graphology and ink chemistry, Professor David Canter, one of today's leading authorities on the behaviour of serial killers, found the journal compelling; it was either genuine or the work of a literary genius who could get inside the head of a dangerous sociopath. With every respect to Professor Canter, it is merely what crime fiction writers do every day of the week!

The story of the Maybrick journal provides one very salient point: we cannot trust documents at face value and handwriting itself tells us little. Even so, we have to try.

Patricia Marne of the Graphology Society quotes the seventeenth-century French politician Cardinal Richelieu in her 1991 book *The Criminal Hand* – 'Give me two lines of a man's handwriting and I will hang him.' No doubt, there were several policemen in London in 1888 who wished that life was that simple. Graphologists themselves acknowledge that theirs is an imprecise science. Others claim it is not a science at all. Similarly, behavioural psychology only goes so far among certain police forces. Even with years of research into serial killers and sociopaths, only the broadest guidelines apply. There are always exceptions to the rule and in the case of multiple homicides – and, one might add, hoax letter-writing – the rule is notoriously difficult to pin down.

Handwriting analysis, graphologists contend, is studied on three levels. The upper zone covers the spiritual and intellectual aspects; the middle zone the everyday social interaction of the writer; and the lower zone the materialistic, emotional and subconscious elements. Age and gender cannot be determined by handwriting; of the only four people charged with hoax Ripper letters (see Chapter 12), one was a man. It is sometimes possible to guess that a writer is elderly because letters are formed slowly and shakily if the writer is suffering from deficient eyesight or a tremor-related condition. Without getting bogged down in technicality, a graphologist can make certain deductions from the size of the writing, the slant of the letters, spacing between words and lines, loops, margins, pressure and speech and so on. In the case of the Ripper correspondence, we have to factor in the quality of the paper/card available, the type of nib pen, the quality of the ink or type of pencil. We must also remember that literacy rates were nowhere near as high as today – in Britain now there are an estimated 2 million functional illiterates – and this shows itself in errors of spelling, punctuation and sentence construction. In at least one of the letters, the writer has used the common Victorian practice (popular in the armed forces on campaign because of a shortage of paper) of writing a letter in two directions, turning the page 90 degrees to continue. Deciphering this is surprisingly difficult.

In Britain, the law has been slow to accept graphological evidence, calling practitioners 'handwriting experts' which reduces their status to little more than circus side-shows. In 2009, a report by the American National Academy of Science questioned the legitimacy of such evidence and concluded that it could not, alone, be used in a court of law.

Patricia Marne's chapter on anonymous letter-writers is fascinating. Certain words are stressed in letters like these, written with a greater downward pressure than the others. This betrays emotion, anger and malice and is a clue to the motivation of the writer. Badly-formed letters are clearly the sign of poor education and also betray tension. Writing in capital letters to attempt to disguise handwriting does not get the culprit off the hook. For example, letters getting larger at the end of words is a sign of immaturity. Slants that fluctuate from left to right imply an unbalanced personality, hints of aggression and a sense of guilt.

As with the ink and paper forensic debate, so with the significance of handwriting. Thomas J. Mann believes that certain letters, most obviously the Lusk correspondence, were written by a semi-literate individual disguising their handwriting. C.M. McLeod's analysis of this letter is that it was written by a charmer with homosexual tendencies, backed up by the general misogynist tenor of all the correspondence. Sue Iremonger believes that the 'Dear Boss' letter and the threatening missive of 6 October – 'A WARNING at midnight – a woman will be murdered at the high level st'

– were written by the same person and that neither was written by Frederick Best's flattened Waverley nib. Using graphology, linguistic comparisons and content, Dirk Gibson believes that up to 119 of the letters are genuine.

Armed with the basics, what can the handwriting of various letters tell us? The 8 October 1888 letter, written in red ink, complete with 'blood' stains and artwork that will be analysed later, was sent to 'Detective Officers' at Scotland Yard and was posted in 'the slogging town of Brum' (Birmingham). Jack promised to kill three local girls he already had his eye on and the body count might rise to fifteen. After that, he would 'cheat the scaffold' by killing himself. Suicide among serial killers is actually very rare, despite the track record of two recent ones, Dr Harold Shipman and Fred West. Shipman, the 'Doctor Death' who remains Britain's most prolific serial killer, hanged himself in Wakefield Prison on 13 January 2004. West took his own life in the same way in Winson Green Prison in January 1995, guilty of the murders of nine girls, including his own daughter. The open-topped 'o' in the 8 October letter reveals a personality that is compulsive, needs to be with people and is very obstinate. The slightly inflated capitals show someone who seeks the limelight and has a built-in inferiority complex.

The same large capitals, though clearly in a different hand, appear on the postcard of 12 November and sent to 'Cheif [sic] Inspector Kings X Police Station', which had no direct links to the Whitechapel murders. The writer, who signed himself 'M. Baynard' claimed to be Jack's accomplice and the man himself would be leaving Liverpool for New York 'on Thursday next'. The left-sloping capitals in the 6 October letter from 'The Whore Killer' speak of deceit and vanity, which is probably common to all the hoaxers of the time and since.

The letter of 4 October that threatened to commit two murders in the Haymarket that night carries clues about the writer. The Haymarket was a well-known vice centre, well-dressed prostitutes promenading along the street on fine evenings among gentlemen on their way to the theatres and clubs. The loops of several letters, especially on the envelope addressed to 'Superintendent Scotland Yard' have been inked in, an indication of the touching up strokes which imply neurosis and a lack of decisiveness. Both 'murderer' and 'Whitechapel' have missing letters, which is not a symptom of speed; more a subconscious display of anxiety. The writing of such correspondence, likely to cause anxiety and distress, was, after all, a criminal offence.

The next day a letter was sent to Charles Warren commenting on the use of bloodhounds. Several missives refer to these hapless dogs because their ineptitude made a mockery of detective science and the police investigation in general. William Stead's *Pall Mall Gazette* cut to the heart of the matter on 9 October:

> Shall Jack the Ripper's arts avail
> To battle Scotland Yard forsooth?
> Quick – on the flying murderer's trail
> Unleash the bloodhound, Truth!

The dogs Barnaby and Burgho, belonging to Edwin Brough of Scarborough, were hired to track down the killer from his scent. Trials held in Regent's Park involved Warren himself as the target, but the animals failed to find him and, according to some reports, got lost. As sensible men were quick to point out, tracking a miscreant over the Yorkshire moors was a very different proposition from such a chase through the urban jungle of East London. The dogs were called off when Brough refused to risk them further; the bloodhounds were not insured. The letter-writer is clearly not a natural. He/she forms his/her letters carefully with no free flow and makes two spelling mistakes in seven lines – 'You can put as many bloodhounds as you like but you will never catch me ...' Prophetic words.

The sharp angles of the red ink letter of 5 October to the *Hackney Standard* show rigidity and compulsive behaviour. Such a writer has no concern for the views or problems of others and his spelling was almost certainly disguised – 'visit' has two 's's and 'luck' two 'k's. Bizarrely, it has a genuine address from the sender – 55 Flower and Dean Street, Whitechapel. This was Cooney's Lodging House, where Kate Eddowes often lived. She had breakfast there with her partner, John Kelly, on the day she died. The writer was almost certainly a local, referring to the journalists as 'my boys' and threatening to dump a corpse in the churchyard 'for the parson Sunday morning'. It was all going to be 'Glorious fun'.

A letter found in a letterbox at 37 West Ham Lane, written in pencil and addressed to 'the Occupier' was the one that boasted of 'five hands of writing'. As if to prove the writer's skill in that context, there seem to be at least three different people involved, with letters sloping (literally) left, right and centre. We shall return to this correspondence because it contains other clues to the writer's psychology. If the writing styles are not intentionally different, however, they can indicate irritability and a volatile temper barely kept under wraps. Easily stimulated, such people are emotionally unbalanced and can be decidedly dangerous. This one contained a threat to kill anyone at

No. 37 and 'I mean to have Charlie Warren yet even if I get him asleep poor old beggar.' Warren was actually 48.

The note of 10 November was not in 'joined-up' writing but in stark block capitals. This is the easiest way of all for someone to disguise their handwriting. By and large, the apostrophes are correct and the writer claims to have kept his word and 'done for the one I said I would'. Given the date, this is presumably Mary Kelly who was murdered on the previous day. Alternatively, block capitals are a classic sign of someone who is immature and uncertain of their literary abilities.

The 'Dear Boss' letter of two days later is again semi-literate. All 'i's are lower case and the purple-ink missive ends 'Signed Jack the Ripper'.

It was the letter written on 25 July 1889 that caused the greatest red herring in the whole Ripperology industry. Another 'Dear Boss' variant, it was postmarked West London and became a vital piece of evidence in the most famous of all books on the Whitechapel murders – Stephen Knight's *Jack the Ripper: The Final Solution* in 1976. 'You have not caught me yet you see, with all your cunning, with all your "Lees" with all your blue bottles …'

Robert James Lees was a 40-year-old Christian Spiritualist and clairvoyant who lived in Peckham, South London. As fascinated as everybody else by the Whitechapel murders, Lees offered his psychic powers to the police. Over time, police forces throughout the world have used such skills in their investigations, even though they are aware of the high risk of chicanery and that evidence obtained in this way has no authority in a court of law. Lees first went to the police on 2 October 1888 and the next day visited Berner Street, the site of Elizabeth Stride's murder, where he 'got trace of a man'. Both Scotland Yard and the City police were dismissive of him – the City force called him a madman and a fool – and at that point Lees, not surprisingly, seems to have given up.

That did not stop the *Daily Express*, in March 1931, naturally after Lees' death, coming out with a colourful story describing the clairvoyant's visions and his 'seeing' the Ripper while riding on a bus. The miscreant went into a West End Mansion which turned out to belong to a well-known physician. Stephen Knight, journalist that he was, built on this piece of uncorroborated nonsense to point the finger at Sir William Withey Gull, Physician in Ordinary to the queen. The story, involving scandal and cover-ups by 'the highest in the land' ticks all the boxes of the thousands worldwide who believe in conspiracies involving royals, freemasons and psychopaths. In fact, to some of these people, they are all the same thing! Knight's supposition stems partly from the fact that he was unfamiliar with Victorian handwriting. The reference later in the line 'all your blue bottles' (the River Police or Thames Division) gives the clue: 'Lees' is not Lees at all, but 'tecs', conventional slang for detectives.

There is only one letter that I believe *may* have been written by the Whitechapel murderer, not just for what it contained but the chaotic, erratic nature of the handwriting. We will analyse it later.

Clippings from newspapers are the stuff of crime fiction. They are the stock-in-trade of the blackmailer and kidnapper who want to stay in the shadows and keep their victims guessing. They were used in the Ripper correspondence too. With so many newspapers available in 1888 it was not difficult to obtain typeface. Such papers were cheap and scissors and glue readily available to everyone. Forensic developments years later would make use of such clippings risky for the sender; fingerprints and DNA would have ridden to the rescue of the authorities. As it was, in the Ripper's day, such correspondence was untraceable.

A prime example was a postcard sent from Glasgow on 19 November. This was ten days after the murder of Mary Kelly and judging by the speed of Jack's attacks, the country was probably holding its collective breath for the next one. The address – Metropolitan Police Office London – is made up of sixteen individual pieces of paper; 'Metropolitan' itself is in Gothic script on a blue background, clearly an advertisement for a company with that name. The text on the back reads:

> The Whitechapel Atrocities all on the wrong salvage! I am in a first class at Govan wanted young lady the 24th instant B God I shall clear Glasgow and Govan and Pollocshields of 16 English whore ladies and gentlemen the Lord will do his guaranteed work by Scutcher. 300 pieces regained. No clue.

'The Whitechapel Atrocities' and all place names are complete. Such was the coverage of the murders that 'Atrocities' appeared in every newspaper in the land at one time or other. The references to railways – 'first class' and 'salvage' – are odd. There is an element of religiosity here – 'the Lord will do his guaranteed work' – which we will discuss later. From the size and shape of the various fonts, there are at least thirty different sources. Some of the letters are glued on sideways and there is only a rudimentary attempt at straight lines.

The letter sent to the Thames Police Court magistrate Mr Saunders, one of three that he received, is a mix of handwriting and clippings. A neat copper plate reads:

Dear Boss,
Look out for 7th inst [December 1888] Am trying my hand at disjointing and if I can manage it will send you a finger.

It is written, not on plain paper but as a newspaper cutting. It is probably a London edition, but news items from Liverpool, Windsor and Donegal give it a national flavour. There was no shortage of oddball behaviour going on beyond the confines of Whitechapel. One of the articles refers to Henry Vaughan, a Liverpool businessman who, for a £100 bet, stripped stark naked (except for his top hat), smeared himself with lamp-black and strolled through the city centre until he was arrested by a patrolling constable. He was fined £2, presumably laughing all the way to the bank having collected the other £98!

Social reformers were at work in Brick Lane, Whitechapel, delivering lectures on the evils of the sweatshops where women and girls worked their fingers to the bone to provide cheap clothes. Olympia, on the other hand, was a paradise for children, with stalls and Punch and Judy shows. Their parents, in the same building, could enjoy the exotic colour of a Turkish bazaar. And, literally on top of all this, a possible madman was going to try a little dismemberment. This of course was the MO, not of Jack, but of the Thames Torso killer, who would claim his last victim nine months later in Pinchin Street.

Another 'combination' letter had already been sent on 10 October. The month was a quiet one in Whitechapel, perhaps because the killer was not in his murderous phase; perhaps because the month was unusually foggy. Contrary to almost all the fiction concerning the murders, especially films, Jack did not strike out of mist-shrouded streets nor disappear again into the dry-ice carpet so beloved of movie-makers. It had been raining on the night of the double event but fine by the time Liz Stride was attacked. All other nights were clear. The same fog that can hide a murder can also prevent the murderer from seeing an eyewitness or an approaching police patrol.

The cutting across the top of the page reads 'Have you seen the "Devil".' There is no question mark and below it, written first in black ink then in pencil, are the words:

If not
Pay one Penny & Walk in-side
Dear Boss I am Waiting every evening for the coppers at Hampstead heath you will find two or three of them gone before this week is ended I am lodging in Scratchem Park now the number I shall not tell you I mean Litchin st I Remain yours Jack the Ripper.

The missive is postmarked Hampstead but needless to say, the alternative addresses – Scratchem Park and Litchin Street – are fictitious. There was an 'Itchy Park', the churchyard of Nicolas Hawksmoor's Christ Church in Whitechapel itself where down-and-outs 'carried the banner' most nights. Although Hampstead Heath became notorious in the twentieth century as a haunt for homosexuals, its elite residents from its days as a spa meant that the area was always rather discreet. As one of the 'lungs of London', the Park drew large crowds from the capital on bank holidays, especially in the summer. The reference to the Devil (which we will explore in detail later) almost certainly refers to the penny gaffs, working-class entertainment of the lowest sort, usually performed in the back rooms of pubs or flimsy stalls erected along pavements. The East End was full of them. At one, virtually opposite the London Hospital in Whitechapel, Joseph Merrick, the 'elephant man' was exhibited as a freak before his rescue by Dr Frederick Traves. The gaffs were regarded by social reformers of the time rather as unbridled internet use is today, as corrupters of the young.

***

There are no typewritten letters in the Ripper correspondence. Although a gadget approximating to a typewriter first appeared in Italy in the sixteenth century, it was not until 1868 that the Americans produced a working model. Referred to as 'something like a cross between a piano and a kitchen table', it underwent several modifications before appearing on the market. The QWERTY keyboard was first used in America in 1874 and has remained constant, allowing for national variations, ever since. The term 'typewriter' originally referred to those who used typewriting machines and the new technology opened up a whole new career opportunity for women.

In 1888, most journalists probably still used longhand and pens, especially since they were usually under pressure to meet exacting deadlines. In the States, Mark Twain submitted a typewritten manuscript for *Life on the*

Mississippi (1883), though someone else probably typed it for him. Forensic identification of letters, based on the idiosyncrasy of keys, spacing, pressure etc., came with Arthur Conan Doyle in *A Case of Identity* (1891) and was taken up seriously by document-examiner William E. Hagan three years later.

The hundreds of 'Jacks' around the world were decidedly old school.

Chapter Five

'Dear Boss'

T he original 'Dear Boss' letter, whether we count this as that sent on 17 September or the 27th, has a great deal to answer for because it spawned so many imitations. It was clearly more an American salutation than British, but of course it was widely understood. In the context of the addressee, it could refer to any senior official in the police or the press, to whom most letters were sent. In Shakespeare's day, the term meant a fat woman, but in the modern sense of master, it was in written usage in America by 1806 and Anglicized for British consumption by 1850.

Of the ninety-five surviving letters and cards posted to the police, the lion's share specified Charles Warren, the Commissioner of the Met. We shall analyse these in a different way later, because there is an element of mockery in many of them, taunting the police and chiding them for their incompetence.

It is interesting that the second letter, of 24 September, in which the writer claimed to be in despair over his actions but threatening to do more, should be sent to Warren. The man had been in post for less than a year when Jack struck and the colonel of Engineers with a penchant for archaeology was hardly qualified to hunt, let alone catch, the Whitechapel murderer. As 'the boss' of course, Warren could not be expected to supervise every crime in the Metropolis himself, but as the killings mounted and the shortcomings of the force became obvious, he should have engaged more with his officers. His most high-profile personal involvement, testing the bloodhounds Barnaby and Burgho was, as we have seen, a PR disaster.

Today, commissioners of the Met have to be media-savvy if they are to enjoy the support of the public. The potential for disaster in a city as huge and cosmopolitan as London (still the biggest in the world in 1888) was correspondingly enormous. Warren fell into almost every trap. His main concern was to reform and modernize the force and, as a soldier, he was unused to working with committees. He gave orders and expected them to be obeyed. He quarrelled with A. Richard Pennefather, the Receiver, who was responsible for paying for the nuts and bolts of the force; rather ironic, in the context of the Ripper letters, that some of the brouhaha was about sheets of paper. He clashed with Henry Matthews, the Home Secretary who was the first Catholic in the Cabinet and accused him, rather unfairly, of interfering in police business. Later, at the height of the Whitechapel murders, he would go head-to-head with James Monro, Assistant Commissioner in charge of the CID before the assistant replaced Warren after his resignation. All these contretemps had two sides to them and the public knew little of the carping that went on behind the closed doors of Whitechapel. What brought Warren's name into perpetual disrepute was his handling of 'Bloody Sunday'.

Socialism came of age in the 1880s, the decade in which Marx and Engels' *Communist Manifesto* first appeared in English and 2,000 people, many of them the dispossessed of the East End, marched to the Mansion House to listen to tub-thumpers on 17 October 1887. But that was nothing to the 70,000 who descended on Trafalgar Square on 13 November. Warren was there, on horseback, as were 4,000 constables, 300 Life Guards and 300 Grenadiers. The infantry carried fixed bayonets and the cavalry had sharpened their swords. In the running battle that followed, 300 demonstrators were arrested and 150 people were taken to hospital.

In common with other flashpoints like this, before Warren and since, Bloody Sunday was a no-win situation. Although *The Times* praised the commissioner for his cool handling of a very fraught situation, it was not long before the reactionaries accused him of not doing enough; the riff-raff must be kept in check. For their part, the 'riff-raff' themselves saw Warren as the devil incarnate, a man only too willing to unleash the army and his own boys in blue against unarmed civilians merely expressing their opinion. The country had been here before, in St Peter's Fields, Manchester in 1819, when the Yeomanry had charged a crowd of weavers who had brought their families to listen to Henry Hunt, a leading radical of his day. The fact that Warren had sympathy for the poor disappeared in all that, especially when a grateful government gave him a KCB and the snobby Athenaeum Club elected him to its hallowed membership.

How closely did Warren follow the Ripper case? From the evidence that exists, very closely indeed but he was clearly no more aware of what made the Whitechapel murderer tick than any of his detectives. Two days after the first letter was posted, he sent a report to Evelyn Ruggles-Brise, private secretary to Matthews at the Home Office. A large number of officers were involved at that stage and Warren was hopeful. There were, on that day, three open lines of enquiry: Jacob Isenschmid, the 'mad pork butcher of Holloway', seen by the witness Mrs Fiddymont with blood on his hands; Oswald Puckeridge, a former surgeon released from an asylum in August and known to carry a knife; and an anonymous blood-stained man seen near one of the murder sites (this from an anonymous letter-writer). Isenschmid was in custody during the later murders and can therefore be ruled out. Puckeridge was not a surgeon but a chemist and was in and out of various mental institutions for most of his life. He had no link with the Whitechapel murders. The last theory was so vague that the police had to drop it. It may have been a genuine sighting, at least of a man covered in blood, but the brothel-keeper who reported it gave no name or address and the trail went cold.

We cannot blame Warren for any of this. Every report, however flimsy, had to be checked. The last section of the report to Ruggles-Brise is very telling and has echoes of this book's Chapter 2. 'Moreover the reporters of the press are following our detectives about everywhere in search of news and cross examine all parties interviewed so that they impede police action greatly …'

Because of that, Warren made the decision to give the media almost nothing, in contrast with the City force that sought their help. And so a feeling of mutual hostility grew up. It was not just that the detectives were not up to the job, but their leader was a narrow-minded martinet utterly out of his depth. Even letters not addressed to Warren referred to him. The 'Dear Boss' letter of 2 October 1888 offered to send a 'nobility womb' to him, as we have seen. And he was personally threatened – 'old Charles Warren *shall die*' – Jack ranted among the bloodstains two days later. Others were cocky – 'I am going to do another job under the very nose of the damned old Charley Warren', promised the letter of the 9th. The next day, Jack called the commissioner 'the biggest fool in London' and three days after that, accused him of being *too* officious – 'trust Sir C. Warren to make such a fuss'. *Mrs* Warren was not in the clear either – 'Sir, I don't know if you are married if so you had better look after your wife' – was written from Portsmouth on the 16th. Jack, 'a Poland Jew', wrote on the 19th, 'Dear Boss if you are the boss …' Was this a snide comment on Warren's leadership or did the writer genuinely not know who was in charge?

One writer claimed to feel sorry for Warren:

> Dear Boss,
> Just a line a I feel a certain amount of sympathy for you Placed in the Circumstances you are and I am also surprised at the so called Public that upbraid you of what you come not quit and call it quibbing I hope you will not lose your Billett though not being efficient enough to catch me.

If Warren received twenty-four letters, James Monro was next with eleven. The man who ran the CID as Assistant Commissioner was educated at Edinburgh and Berlin universities. He joined the legal branch of the highly-respected Indian Civil Service in the year of the Mutiny, 1857, and acted in a variety of roles with the Bengal and Bombay 'presidencies'. By 1884 he was at the Met and at the time of the Ripper murders was unofficial head of the detective service. A deeply religious man, looking forward to Christ's Second Coming, he was tough and popular, doing a great deal to stifle the operations of the Fenian 'dynamitards' who planted bombs in parts of London throughout the '80s. But if his men loved him, his equals and superiors found him abrasive. He was fiercely proud of his detectives – Monro's 'secret department' which morphed into Special Branch – and clashed with Warren and Matthews over it.

Interestingly, the first letter to Monro that has survived is dated 4 February 1889, three months after Mary Kelly's murder. He is referred to, wrongly, as 'City Superintendant of Police Authoritys':

> Dear Boss,
> Be on the look out. as I am coming to visit Mile-end and do for the rest to number 15 then I will give myself up to the Police Yours –
> Jack the Ripper returned from America.

This is typical of the threat-letter which constitutes the majority of those that have survived. We have met the American connection before and will discuss it in a later chapter.

The next letter to Monro was more articulate but contained a royal theme. It was sent on the same day as the American 'crusader' letter (see Chapter 11):

> Dear Sir
> I accomplished my eighth victim without interruption I shall now wait quietly till 27th when two shall fell the knife to celebrate the Royal wedding so to make more news for papers this week I am paid by a society abroad whose name wille not be mentioned I intend finishing my work late in August when I shall sail for abroad
> Believe me sir
> The Worlds Surprise
> Jack the Ripper

The 'society abroad' fed into the xenophobic beliefs of the day and will be discussed in Chapter 11. The wedding referred to took place in the private chapel at Buckingham Palace (the first time the venue was used) between Princess Louise, the Prince of Wales' daughter and Alexander Duff, the Earl of Fife.

On 12 September, the letter to Monro was personally threatening:

> Dear Boss,
> I shall certainly have your wife or Daughter of theirs leg Before another month she will be mutilated in a cruel manner But I can't help that.

On the same day, 'Birmingham Bill the Slaughterman' promised Monro that he would 'settle 4 more 2 in the east and 1 at Islington, at West end near Regent St some time next week for I have not got the right cow yet.' Needless to say, no such assaults took place.

Four days later, a correspondent claiming to be the Whitechapel murderer told Monro very courteously that he was changing his address and killing zone from the East End to Vauxhall. The 'Jack' who wrote on 30 September took to poetry, even though he could not spell Monro or commissioner and got the man's initial wrong:

> The police are bust looking for me I'm like a monkey up a tree not to be found as you will see While there is work for rippers three. This is the ninth murder we have done Yet it seems we have not begun But now the Evenings are getting dark With the loose Girls we'll rip up Not time for more Too Busy for more now

The majority of letters to the police were addressed to Scotland Yard. Twelve were to Leman Street, the headquarters of H Division closer to the murder sites. That sent on 9 October is typical:

> Dear boss
> I am going to do another job right under the very nose of the damned old Charley Warren You have had me once but like fools let me go Jack the Ripper.

This theme, of the killer having been caught or at least taken in for questioning, runs throughout the Ripper correspondence. It may be true because during the scare more than 200 arrests were made, none of them leading to charges because of lack of evidence. In the now infamous mishandling of the case of Peter Sutcliffe, the Yorkshire Ripper, in 1980, the suspect was interviewed nine times before he was finally stopped. As a result, at least three more victims died.

'J.T.R.' warned Leman Street on 5 November to keep 'a extra lookout in Whitechapel tonight. P.S. THERE IS ONE OLD WHORE WHO I HAVE GOT MY EYE ON SO LOOK OUT.'

The letter to Leman Street of the 12th was altogether more detailed. This was sent three days after the murder of Mary Kelly:

> Dear Boss
> Guess what make me fits and keep on laughing at the Detectives I shall make them Busy next Thursday A woman Jane Batemore in at place I may not explain as I may be prevented I mean to kill Packer the fruiterer in Berner St he knows me to well they can offer A hundred Free Pardons they will not catch me I mean to do 12 more I will do them How can they catch me Poor old Sir C Warren he is getting trouble if he likes I can put away wish me murdering him I am A Patentee of murdering The prostitutes I promised Kelly it 2/6 for to have A Fuck & she gave a Little scream but I act quickly by putting a chop in neck the Dear old knife who committed these murders is down the thames If Government will give me A Free Pardon I shall give myself up no, after doing twenty I tried to do one last week but was prevented.

Jane Batemore or Beadmore belongs in Chapter 13 of this book, discovering individual targets. 'Packer the fruiterer' was Matthew Packer, a Whitechapel local who ran a fruit and sweet shop at 44 Berner Street, very close to the Dutfield's Yard entrance where Elizabeth Stride was murdered. Contemporary drawings of him in the papers show an elderly man (he was actually 57) with side-whiskers and a peaked cap often worn by sailors or military men. Packer should have been a useful witness to the first atrocity of the double event but he quickly proved his unreliability. Questioned by Sergeant Stephen White of the Met, he said that because it was raining on the night of 30 September, he shut up shop early and witnessed nothing. He told a completely different story to Charles le Grand and J.H. Batchelor, private detectives who had been hired by George Lusk's Whitechapel Vigilance Committee. Now he claimed that he had sold black grapes to a couple at 11.45 pm on the night in question and that they had stood at the entrance to Dutfield's Yard eating them. The detectives took Packer to the mortuary of St George's-in-the-East where he identified Elizabeth Stride's body as the woman to whom he had sold the grapes. He told the *Evening News* on 4 October that no policeman had asked him any questions at all, even though White's detailed report is still available for scrutiny in the Public Record Office. So sure were le Grand and Batchelor that Packer had actually seen Jack the Ripper that they took him to the Yard where Assistant Commissioner Alexander Bruce made a report. Both Warren and Chief Inspector Swanson were dubious about Packer's timings, especially as Elizabeth Stride's clothes as he described them were not the ones she was wearing. The 'bloody grape stem' has found its way into Ripper folklore and derives from one seen on the morning of Sunday, 30 September by a local, Mrs Rosenfeld. There is nothing to say that the stain *was* actually blood or whether it had any connection with the murder at all.

Not content to let matters rest, Packer told the ever muck-raking *Evening News* that he had seen the man who had been with Elizabeth since, staring at him menacingly on several occasions and that he was approached by two men who believed that a cousin of theirs was the Whitechapel murderer. There is little doubt that Matthew Packer was every bit as much of a ghoul as the letter-writers, relishing his new-found notoriety. Whether he would have been so confident had he read the Leman Street letter promising to kill him is debatable.

None of the correspondence addressed to Leman Street or Commercial Street, the other station in the killing zone, has any specific reference to the immediate area except the one sent from Paddington on 20 November. It promised to take off the head and legs of a victim in Fashion Street, where Elizabeth Stride briefly lived with Michael Kidney. Needless to say, it did not happen.

The solitary telegram written to Inspector Abberline on 21 November reads like the scenario of a police thriller:

> Jack the Ripper wishes to give himself up will Abberline communicate with him at number 39 Cutter Street Houndsditch with this end in view Jack the Ripper. This is written with the *"Blood of Kelly"* all Long Liz's blood is used up.

As we know, Abberline was ordered back to the Ripper case from Scotland Yard because of his familiarity with Whitechapel. He had personally covered the Kelly murder, investigating the crime scene and interviewing witnesses. There is no record that he followed up on the Houndsditch offer. Cutter Street was mostly occupied by warehouses in 1888 and a Google Street View today shows 'massive marketspace' available for rent. Like all the other addresses in the Ripper correspondence, it constituted a huge red herring.

***

After the police came the press. Because the first 'Dear Boss' letter was addressed to the Central News Agency, a trend was established. Such correspondence fed the egos of newspapermen who could see 'scoops' galore in the way that today's tabloids claim victories in various causes that they espouse. The first of these, which we have discussed already, was sent to the editor at the *Daily News* office on 1 October:

> I am pleased to see another chance of ripping up a dear creature. I shall be in Buck's Row or very close to between 12 & 2 in the morning on Wednesday 1 have got the girl set & I have been offered double money for her woomb and lower part of body mean to have them at any price I do like to find them nice parts. I do pity Leather Apron. I've got someone to write this for me.

The notion of body parts, perhaps for research, is one that we have met before. Leather Apron (John Pizer) is already seen as the victim of a witch-hunt and the ultimate in handwriting disguises – finding a handy secretary – is a neat touch. Since the *Daily News* offices were in the City and the letter dated the day after Kate Eddowes' murder, a copy was sent to Colonel Fraser of the City Force.

The Press Association received a letter from Hull on 11 November:

> Sirs – this time
> I am not afraid of letting you know the whereabouts I am I can't help but laugh at the idea of Sir C. Warren and his bloodhounds It is of no use the police to be so reticent in the matter next time head clean off I have my eye on the next on the list there is plenty in Hull all good blood.
>
>   I have lost the real stuff. Take warning next time I carrie the head away with me in my bag the blood wont [illegible] I take good care of the uterus. I will give next one gip no Mersey
>   Jack the R –

Charles Warren had resigned two days before this letter was posted, but that fact seems not to have dawned on several writers who were still taking his name in vain weeks after the event. The 'real' blood, the collection of body parts, was rather old hat by November, but there are two elements of this letter worthy of discussion. Clearly, it is written by someone with a good vocabulary – 'whereabouts', 'reticent' and 'uterus' are not everyday words for a Victorian workman. The other point is the common theme that Jack's victims were on some form of pre-arranged list that the murderer was gleefully ticking off. The Whitechapel killer was a classic disorganized 'blitz' attacker, snatching opportunities to kill at random as the chance arose. He killed (with the exception of Mary Kelly) in the open and left the bodies in situ with no attempt to conceal them. The only organized skills he exhibited were in the murder weapon; he must have carried his knife with him and taken it away afterwards.

It can only have been a small feather in James Monro's cap when he read the letter sent to *The Times* at Printing House Square on 19 December:

> Dear Boss
> I have left London because it was too hot for me.
> Monroe [*sic*] made it too hot for me.
> I have come to Liverpool & you will soon hear of me
> Yours
> Jack the ripper
> PS some of the real stuff but I have to be verry sparing of it.

The editor of the *Surrey Comet* in 'Clearince' Street, Kingston upon Thames, got a Jack letter on 19 September 1889:

> Dear Boss
> I thought I would let you know jest to see if you could be clever enough to stop me as I mean to give you a turn I mean to commense business before the weak is out I have spotted one or two near kingston station as I was down there last night minippouse [?] the slops have got [missing] in there eyes some has
>
> They have up the old spo [missing] but if they intefier with me look out I got plenty of amineton [ammunition] & my long sticker is bleeding sharp I see by the papers you have yet 2 nice old strewbury nose top on the bench what price last one up the snook so good.

Much of this is incomprehensible today, but it contains authentic working-class slang. 'Slops' was Cockney back-slang for police, first recorded in 1859. 'Strawberry' was synonymous in Cockney-speak for red nose, but 'nose' is there too. It is far from clear what this phrase is all about. A number of Ripper letters warn that if cornered, the killer will defend himself but the mention of firearms is unusual; guns were expensive.

Some writers clearly hoped to see their efforts in print, rather as trolls do on today's social media. At the end of October 1889, the editor of the *Clapham Observer* was urged to 'Please insert this in your Paper', when the writer intended to come to Clapham on 8 or 9 November to 'have a turn at some of your Jews'.

This is a departure from the norm. Anti-Semitism was rife in the East End (the letter is postmarked London SW, however) because of the sudden arrival of a rush of Eastern Europeans in the 1880s. The actual *targeting* of Jews has nothing to do with the Ripper murders. None of Jack's victims was Jewish.

***

Some of the oddest addressees are personal. Sensation-seekers liked to think that the police were rattled and confused by their ramblings. They wanted to believe that their works would be printed in the papers because the first 'Dear Boss' letter was. Writing to an individual, however, makes little sense unless it was an act of spite or revenge. These cases will be discussed in Chapter 9, but there are some that effectively defy categorization. They are not malicious and would seem to have no direct relevance to the addressee.

The first of these appeared on 14 October and was addressed to 'the Woolwich People':

> Sirs
> Do you think that you can catch me and my pals if so say it at once and when you have said what you have to say why then we can lofe about, had to jump just now, thought you had next time I do anything it will be at the town in which I write this letter I remain your murdery friend J. J. Thompson alias Jack the Rippers NephewX PS Excuse bad writing JJT.

Five days later, Messrs Bensdorp of the City got a letter from Dublin:

Please send 1 Bottell whisky I intend to murder one in Dublin to night Good job I made of the last. Don't forget to meet me in Patrick st J the R.

The Bensdorp company, 'manufacturers of the Royal Dutch Soluble Cocoa' had their premises at 30 and 31 Newgate Street. Its directors promptly forwarded the Dublin letter to the City Police at Old Jewry, believing that the writer had got hold of one of their advertising postcards. These were plentiful and usually had happy pictures of smiling Dutch children printed on them. There is no record that they ever sold whisky!

'Jack the Ripper' thought the 'Head Postmaster' in London wanted to hear from him on 23 December. Writing from Limerick:

Dear   Boss
I am on leave now I will be all till after Xmas don't trouble London for me I want my holidays. I must travel all Ireland and Scotland the Police here are not of much use I have been happy to say I have been travelling with some of your Detectives which I met on the 15 in hollihead we was together as far as dublin when we parted on Sunday morning of the 16th.

There is no record of Met officers travelling to Dublin in the context of the Whitechapel murders, although the Irish press covered the case with enthusiasm.

Then there was the casual correspondence sent to the Standard Photographic Studios at 35 Buckingham Palace Road on 21 August 1889:

thinks [thanks?] old Pal but I don't want any taken this week I saw my Photo a short time ago in the Police News you know Johnny Rippers will give you a call in a day or two as you have a lot of in your district wants a look up yet. Mr one ready say Friday next what about 12.45 am where is Bird Cage Walk one of the old girls of Westminster yours
    Jack Rippers of nobles

The letter was written on the back of two special offer tickets from the studio, hence the declining of the offer. Buckingham Palace Road and Bird Cage Walk were upmarket addresses, miles away figuratively from Jack's

Whitechapel. Even so, the area, under C Division's supervision, had its share of prostitutes like most of central London. The misuse of the word 'photo' to mean drawing or illustration is common in the Ripper correspondence and will be discussed in Chapter 7.

The Controller of the General Savings Bank along Queen Victoria Street must have been equally surprised to hear from Jack on 6 December 1890. The trail of the Whitechapel killer had gone decidedly cold by this time, but the letters still dribbled in:

> I shall commence again very soon in Mile End (not Whitechapel) for that's rather too hot for me now. This will be my last one. The victim lives in Frimley St Mile End ...
> It was not that ... [illegible] Mrs Hoggs not Pearcey
>   JR
> This is some of Mrs Hoggs blood
>   Jack the Ripper
> [On the reverse] Not to be opened by anyone except The Controller Himself!

Mrs Pearcey was Mary Eleanor Wheeler who lived in Kentish Town. She had developed an attachment to Frank Hogg and had an irrational hatred for his wife, Phoebe. On 24 October 1890, Mrs Pearcey battered Mrs Hogg to death with a poker and stabbed her. There would have been plenty of blood from this attack to prompt the reference in the letter to the controller. Having strangled the Hoggs' baby, Mary Pearcey trundled both bodies in a pram through busy streets before dumping them on waste ground. She was arrested, her home searched and she faced Mr Justice Deadman a week before the controller received his letter. Found guilty, she was hanged at Newgate by James Berry, the executioner, on 23 December, without a murmur or hint of remorse. Frank Hogg sold various household items to Madame Tussauds to put the buck-toothed Mrs Pearcey centre stage in their Chamber of Horrors. The case was front-page news throughout December, no doubt sparking the letter. Other links, with Mile End and the General Savings Bank, seem to be non-existent.

If the controller was mystified, the headmaster of Desford Industrial School near Leicester was even more so. The letter he received, in November 1889, *may* have been threatening – perhaps the work of a disgruntled ex-pupil – but it is addressed to a genuine 'Dear Boss' and lacks specifics:

I write these few lines to you That the ripper is coming over on the
9th Nov. don't ? forget
       Mr Boss

Perhaps the oddest, but in some ways the most understandable, addressee in
the Ripper correspondence is that of General William Booth, the founder of
the Salvation Army. A now badly-faded pencil-written note (undated) was
sent to the man:

General Booth
dear sir Just a few lines to tell you when I am about to commit this
murder … chance to … and now Im about to do this I hear you are …
I'm about to commit this murder on the 16 of this … but bare [*sic*]
in mind you and your wife will be dead before the 17 of this month
I am yours very affectionate
       John the ripper amen

The religious theme of the letter is only apparent in the last word. I do not
believe that it threatens Booth per se: merely that the writer expects the man
to be dead by a certain date. Booth had set up the Christian Mission on the
Mile End Waste more than twenty years before the Ripper murders and was
regarded as little short of a saint by the desperately poor who were helped by
his 'Army'. In January 1890 he was charged by local magistrates for running
an unregistered lodging house to shelter the women of the Abyss. One of the
few men brave enough to discuss the evils of prostitution openly at a time
of middle-class hypocrisy on the subject, he never put forward his theories
on the Whitechapel murders. Contrary to the letter-writer's expectations,
William Booth lived on for another twenty-four years after the Ripper case.

Chapter Six

'Yours Truly'

A total of 146 Ripper missives currently in the Public Record Office are signed 'Jack the Ripper' with various spellings. The 'Dear Boss' letter has much to answer for, as do the Metropolitan Police who, by reproducing it in the form of handbills, clearly believed it was authentic. Not only did its creator dream up the most influential monicker in criminal history, he accurately described Jack's MO as well. Whereas most of the Ripper movies show the killer stabbing and slashing from above in a downward movement, the real wounds were created with an upward or horizontal rip.

It is the variants outside 'Jack the Ripper' that interest us here because they shed a significant psychological light onto the mindset of the writers.

The 1 October letter to the *Daily News* office in the City was signed 'Boss Ripper' – this was the one that alleged the sender had someone else carry out the actual writing. The next day, George of the 'High Rip Gang' wrote in red ink. He promised to be 'heavy on the guilded [sic] whores now', as we have seen. The High Rips were in the press in the mid-1880s not in London but in Liverpool, from where three Jack letters were posted. William Nott-Bower, Liverpool's Chief Constable who would later lead the Met, described the gang name as 'an invention which seemed to take the fancy of the press'. The Rips were largely unemployed riff-raff aged between 17 and 22 who jostled women and men alike and roughed up anybody who objected. Many of them carried knives called 'bleeders' and belts with sharpened buckles for stabbing purposes.

As we have noted, the attack on Emma Smith in April 1888 by three young men was the only hint at this sort of street violence. Jack's MO – a solitary sexual blitz attack – was very different from this.

Three days later, a letter came from Bradford signed 'Jack the cunquorer'. Presumably, his conquests were of women – 'I murdered a woman last night and have cut off her womb I shall sent it by parcels post.'

'The Whore Killer' wrote to Charles Warren at Scotland Yard the next day. The name itself is underlined and it reflects the fact that all of the

Whitechapel murderer's targets were prostitutes. Whereas ninety years later, the Yorkshire Ripper (Peter Sutcliffe) attacked *any* woman walking alone at night, Jack was more focused. He threatened to kill in Brixton, Battersea and Clapham and to spread his net further. Arguing against the precision of his pen name, he wrote, 'If I cant get enough women to do I shall cut up men, boys & girls. Just to keep my hand in practice.' He was also looking at Clapham Common as a useful murder site; an area of shrubs and bushes that could easily hide a corpse. In a high-profile case, Leon Beron's body was found there in 1911, his cheeks slashed, inexplicably, with the letter 'S'. Just as the Bradford letter promised a womb, this one promised a heart.

One of the four foreign letters to arrive was sent from Lille on 8 October and was addressed to 'Monsieur le Chef de la Police Angle[terre] Londres'. Roughly translated, it reads, 'While you are searching London for the author of the crimes against women, the assassin is, at this moment, in Lille. I will be back in […] to start again.' It is signed 'Isidore Vasyvair', one of the few specific names in the correspondence. Isidore, named for an obscure Spanish saint of the twelfth century, was not an uncommon name in France and Vasyvair may be a corruption of Vasvár, a region in Hungary. It is impossible after all this time to get any closer to the letter-writer.

'Bill the Boweler' wrote to the 'Head Boss, Metropolis Police' on 10 October, a month that would be mercifully free of Ripper killings. The writer sounds like a mad comedian, not only with the obvious 'Bill' for 'Jack' and 'Boweler' (actually, of course, disemboweler) for 'Ripper', but the letter's contents too – 'The Ripper will soon be on the task again, nose and ears he wants next as present for Boss. When he gets em will be able to write in blood, aha, aha, blood blood blood.'

The missive was in purple ink as if to underscore the insanity, and the themes of taking body parts from a crime scene are not only an accurate portrayal of serial killer behaviour, the posting of them is a common theme of Ripper correspondence.

We have already come across 'Mr Englishman' from Colchester on 13 October, on the surface of it following a standard belief at the time that no Briton could carry out such barbaric attacks and so the killer had to be a foreigner. We shall return to this theme later.

Several of the letters use a plural connotation. 'Mr Englishman' talks of 'us' as well as 'I' and 'J.J. Thompson alias J the Rippers Nephew', complete with x for kiss, wrote on 14 October 'Do you think that you can catch me and my pals …' which has led a number of Ripperologists to claim that Jack was part of a gang. The most famous instance of this is Stephen Knight's

1976 *The Final Solution*. This is the book that everyone knows because it involves the bizarre and convoluted theory of the 'highest in the land'. Briefly told, Prince Albert Victor, the Duke of Clarence, grandson of the queen and ultimately heir to the throne, met and married an East End shop girl, Annie Crook. Their child, Alice, with her half working–class pedigree, would in theory have become queen of England one day. Clearly this could not be allowed to happen, so Victoria turned in desperation to her doctor, Sir William Gull, who took matters, literally and bloodily, into his own hands. He employed coachman John Netley to take him by carriage to Whitechapel, not only to find Annie Crook, but her friends (the 'canonical five' listed by Assistant Commissioner Macnaghten) and to silence them all. Aiding and abetting him was Walter Sickert, the artist, who knew them all by sight and had actually introduced the prince to Annie in the first place. While Netley drove the getaway vehicle, Sickert kept watch at street corners and Gull went to work with his surgeon's knife.

While the plot is riddled with gaping holes and the whole scenario patent nonsense, it convinced thousands of thriller-readers that Knight had, at last, cracked the case. Gull, after all, had medical expertise and in top hat and cape, personified the murderous toff that the public hoped the Whitechapel murderer would be. It is much more likely that Jack was a local East Ender, killing women of his own class and had nothing whatsoever to do with royalty.

Not only that, killers of Jack's type do not work as a team or even in pairs. Research carried out in the United States, Britain and elsewhere over the last forty years has involved lengthy and painstaking interviews with murderers of Jack's type. He was an opportunist, a thrill-killer driven to murder by his own demons. The only organization he showed was the knife that he brought to the crime scene. Only Mary Kelly was killed indoors. The others died on the pavement and in alleyways open to passing members of the public. Jack made no attempt to conceal his crimes or hide the bodies. He simply took away his knife for next time and various bloody trophies to relive the moment of his kill. Double acts among serial killers are extremely rare. Perhaps the best-documented is that of Kenneth Bianchi and his cousin Angelo Buono, the Hillside Stranglers who struck in Los Angeles in the late 1970s. Between them, they killed nine women and girls aged from 12 to 28, sexually abusing and torturing them to death. Forensic science at the time was able to establish two sets of semen in one of the bodies and the killers were finally tracked down. As is often the case with killer couples, Bianchi and Buono fell into the grip of *folie à deux*, each goading the other to new heights of savagery they would not have contemplated on their own. There is nothing in the Whitechapel murders to indicate anything but a lone killer. If we are looking for a genuine Jack among the correspondence (see Chapter 15), we can discount any that refer to 'we' or 'us'.

Various sets of initials followed later in October. 'A.R.M.' said 'Good Bye' from Bristol on the 15th, threatening three murders there and perpetuating the myth of pluralism: '... I'll betray the whole gang'. The next day, a letter from Portsmouth was signed 'Yours respectfully, H.L.' but there was a continuation on the back, 'Sir I don't know if you are married [Warren was] if so you had better look after your wife' and there were yet more initials 'HTB'. Threats like this, against individuals or the police in general, we shall discuss later.

One of the oddest surviving letters in the Ripper correspondence was posted in Paddington on 12 November. It was one of a large number of letters genuinely trying to help the police with their enquiries which we will examine in a later chapter. 'Mathematician' was trying to analyse the Whitechapel murderer from the original 'Dear Boss' letter's linguistics:

> Reason for Supposing Jack
> The ripper a tailor from his letter.
> first (Ripper) is a tailors word.
> (buckle) is a tailors word
> they wont (fix) buttons
> (proper red stuff) = army cloth or suits
> (real fits) tailors words – good fit
> men generally – uses expressions
> borrowed from this trade.

This may have been a sincere attempt to be useful, but it achieved nothing. There were thousands of tailors in London and the words highlighted had other connotations; most obviously, the 'proper red stuff' was blood, not cloth. Above all, 'Mathematician' was working from the false premise of the hoax 'Dear Boss' letter in the first place.

The letter addressed to the police on the 16th is fascinating. The writing is chaotic, with scribblings out and bad art, posted in NW London:

> I know you are looking for me everywhere but you will never find me. I am chiefly in Hampstead Rd and Tottenham court Rd. Why I passed a Policeman yesterday & he didn't take no notice of me. Its no use you putting up those bills you wont find no partner. I'm on

the right side I do it by myself. Im not in any fishing smacks as you call them Im a private Gentleman. Look out for me on Saturday I intend to do some more murders. No one wont get no 1000 pounds I live in George St. very comfortable. Im 30 years old tall and dark if you cant find me your a lot of fools.

This is one of several letters purporting to give the killer's address. It is also typical of police taunting – Jack walks straight past the boys in blue undetected. The reference to the fishing smacks is the police theory that the killer came from the docks – again, the xenophobia that believed that no Englishman could carry out such atrocities – and all the docks were within easy walking distance of the killing grounds. The busybody Edward Larkins, a clerk in the Statistical Department of Customs and Excise went to the police four days earlier pointing an accusatory finger at Antoni Pricha, who resembled the police drawing of the dodgy character seen by eyewitness George Hutchinson talking to Mary Kelly on the night she died. When that did not pan out, Larkins fingered Portuguese sailors Manuel Cruz Xavier and José Laurenco as the murderers of Polly Nichols and Annie Chapman respectively. According to the excise man, Juan de Souza Machado had helped Laurenco, Hillside Strangler-style, and went on to kill Mary Kelly by himself. As late as July 1889, Larkins was attempting to put yet another Portuguese seaman, Joachim de Rocha, in the frame for the murder of Clay Pipe Alice McKenzie. It is a measure of the enormity of the job – and how hard the police worked – that all these men were investigated, both in London and Oporto. When they all turned out to be innocent, it was a pity that Edward Larkins was not charged with wasting police time. Today, he would be accused of hate crime!

What is really interesting about the 12 November letter is the signature:

Yours truly
Joe the cats meat man
    & woman hunter

Five weeks before this was sent, the inquest opened on a dismembered torso discovered in the foundations of Norman Shaw's Opera House, soon to become New Scotland Yard, along the Thames Embankment. This was the body of one of eight women, all of them disarticulated, that were found in or near the river between 1873 and 1889, stretching from Hammersmith Bridge in the west to Rainham in the east. Following the principles of 'murder-mapping', that a serial killer strikes first close to home in his comfort zone, I was able, in my book on this case, to suggest that the torso murderer lived or worked in the Battersea area. In all cases, the heads were missing and I concluded that was because it was the head that bore the brunt of the killing MO; the kind of blunt-force trauma with a hammer used to kill horses for slaughter. Where was the largest horse-slaughterer in London? Messrs Harrison, Barber and Co. in Garratt Lane, Battersea. A horse-slaughterer would have the medical skill to dismember his victims; he did it to horses on a daily basis. And horseflesh was the dish of choice for thousands of cats in the London area. Cats' meat men, like the 'Joe' of the 12 November letter, routinely wandered the streets in the early morning, with carts loaded with food for pets. What could be easier than using these daily routines to slip part-carcases into the river before it was quite daylight?

When I wrote *The Thames Torso Murders* I had not seen the 12 November letter and of course the whole thing may be merely coincidence. The letter, however, mentions Tottenham Court Road, where another dismembered body was discovered in dustbins in Alfred Mews nearby. Yet more were found in Bedford Square, a few hundred yards away. Messrs Harrison, Barber and Co. had premises not far away, near Euston Station. Had the killer been transferred there by October 1884 when these gruesome discoveries were made?

The medical/anatomical awareness that dominated the Ripper killings implied that the killer knew his way around bodies. Most doctors were horrified that the police and public came to believe that a medical man was responsible. But the far less honourable profession of horse-slaughterer fitted the bill perfectly. The 24 September letter, probably the second in the series and addressed to Charles Warren, said, 'I am a horse slaughterer and work at …' (the name has been blacked out). And of course, around the corner from the murder site of Polly Nichols in Buck's Row was Winthrop Street, home of yet another branch of Harrison, Barber and Co. Am I suggesting that the Whitechapel murderer and the Thames torso killer are one and the same? Emphatically no; the MOs are completely different. It is, however, possible that the cats' meat man who also butchered women and left their body parts all over London wrote 'To the Supt' on 12 November.

'The black brunswick boy' wrote from 'Kilburn lodging house' on 28 November. He promised to kill sixteen and had managed six by this date. He was coming west as the east (of London) was getting too hot for him. He had tried his luck in Hyde Park, a notorious place of assignation for West End prostitutes and their clients, but the 'nice little dears' got away because the moon was too bright. The Black Brunswickers were originally cavalrymen attached to the King's German Legion, stationed in England during the Napoleonic Wars. Their black uniforms and high reputation for efficiency endeared them to the public and a number of pubs around the country adopted the name. It is not known if there was one in Kilburn.

By January 1889, it looked as though the Ripper's murderous spree might be over. There were only three letters this month as opposed to sixty in November. 'Jim the Cutter' wanted everybody to be aware that he would soon be back in business in Blackheath: 'I have my eye on a few gay women [prostitutes].'

C Division of the Met heard from 'Jack Bane' on the 15th of the month. He claimed to have ripped up a little boy in Bradford and another in Slough. This widespread murder pattern is proof that the letters are not genuine. Since the highly mobile late twentieth century, it is possible to range far and wide in search of victims. Child-killer Robert Black operated between Oxford and Edinburgh, using his van to abduct his targets and dump their bodies miles from where he killed them. Despite the ubiquity of the rail network by 1888, most people were born, lived and died in one area, unless they emigrated. Even so, a reading of the Ripper correspondence gives us the impression that Jack was a travelling man. In reality, of course, it was simply a twisted individual who wanted to sow fear over as large a spectrum of society as possible and even to see their own locale as the focus of attention.

Bradford featured again on the 16th when 'Scarlet Runner' wrote from Alma Road, N London (probably Muswell Hill). The letter is bizarre:

> Dear Boss
> As to the Tunis scare I am still in London after my trip to Bradford.
> I shall remain still for a time I am preparing a draught, that will kill or leave no marks those I shall give it to will fall in various places, either being run over or die from its effects
> For the future I am Scarlet Runner should you wish for particulars of the Bradford mystery give me a corner in the echo (to Scarlet Runner
> I fear not your detectives as my disguises are as numerous as theirs
> I know I shall be caught one day, as I often rush against a boby in my haste
> Scarlet Runner
> Further particulars
> When I note corner

The letter was spread out over four pages in black ink. The Tunis scare almost certainly refers to the recent arrest of Alfred Grey in Tunisia. What a down-and-out from Spitalfields was doing in North Africa is a mini-mystery in itself. Conceivably, he might have got a billet on a tramp steamer from London docks. His arrest was in the context of burglary, but the links with the East End and a naked woman tattooed on his arm, as well as his vague similarity to eyewitness descriptions given to the police, put him in the frame briefly as a Ripper suspect.

The Bradford mystery was altogether more serious and disturbing. 'Jack Bane' was almost certainly alluding to the same case in his letter of the previous day. On Thursday, 27 December of the previous year, little John Gill was sent out to get some milk by his parents in Manningham, a suburb of the city. It was a few days before his eighth birthday and he was last seen alive hitching a ride on the cart of a milkman, 23-year-old William Barrett. When he did not return, his parents contacted the police and placed a missing person's ad in the local paper. John's body was found in a stable two days later and such was the ferocity of the murder that the local police, out of their depth against barbarity like this, believed that the Whitechapel murderer had come north. The press, of course, had a field day. Far from the Ripper trail having gone cold, he was committing atrocities 200 miles away.

The boy's leg, arms and ears had been cut off and internal organs were placed on his chest. A noose around his neck was made from an old shirt and his body was covered in stab wounds. His shoes had been placed inside his chest cavity. A local chemist, Felix Rimmington, had helped police with their enquiries before. An amateur forensic scientist years before professionals like Bernard Spilsbury dominated the scene, Rimmington concluded that the cause of death was stab wounds to the chest. The body had been washed and drained of blood and the killing did not take place in the stable. It had been partly wrapped in a copy of the *Liverpool Echo*, complete with a name and address: W. Mason, Derby Road. Despite this, police enquiries led nowhere.

The milkman William Barrett was twice arrested for the murder but there was no trial and little John was buried on 4 February. Was 'Scarlet Runner' (a type of bean) responsible for the boy's death? Unlikely, but we can assume that he read the papers diligently, especially the graphic *Illustrated Police News* whose comic-book drawings drew obvious parallels with the Whitechapel murders. Had Jack really gone north? No. Serial killers rarely change their victimology or their location. Whoever the Whitechapel killer was, he targeted prostitutes, mostly middle-aged; little boys were outside his sphere of interest.

A month later, using bad poetry, 'Augustus Robertson Raf[…] formerly of 24 Goulso[n?] Whitechapel, now of Vanbrugh Park Blackhea[th]' wrote to 'Chas Warren Esqre' at the Home Office. That had never been Warren's office, of course, and he had resigned three months earlier. 'Raf' or 'Raffa' (both names are used in the letter) touched a nerve perhaps with his mention of Goulston Street. This was the site of the greatest red herring in the whole Ripper case. On the night of the double event (29/30 September 1888) Constable 254A Alfred Long was patrolling this area and found a piece of bloody apron – later proved to be Kate Eddowes' – at a stand pipe outside 108-119 Wentworth Model Dwellings at the junction of Wentworth and Goulston Streets. On the wall nearby were the chalked words 'The Juwes are the men that will not be blamed for nothing.' Fearing a link with the events of that night and an anti-Semitic backlash in an area with a huge Jewish population, Charles Warren ordered the words to be removed. Consequently, with the hard evidence gone and not even much agreement as to the spelling or word order, all sorts of theories have been put forward. None of them bears scrutiny. The police wasted time trying to compare the Goulston Street graffito with various Ripper letters. Since no photograph had been taken at Wentworth Model Dwellings and only a handful of policemen had seen the original, such comparisons were pointless. In any case, writing in haste, using chalk on a brick wall is a very different proposition from putting pen to paper with all the time in the world.

'JMS Clarke' was definitely 'Not Jack the ripper', or so he claimed in his letter from London SW on 11 September 1889. He admitted to a recent near miss – 'PC passed me while I was carrying my deadly parcel to the arch off cable st or nere there.'

He is referring to the finding of the torso under the railway arches in Pinchin Street, probably the last victim of the Thames Torso killer. The police never believed the two cases connected, although the press of course were determined to keep the Jack legend alive. Constable 239H William Pennett discovered the severed trunk, wrapped in a thin chemise, as he made his routine rounds in the area in the early morning. The head and legs were gone but the police surgeon estimated that the woman, never identified, was between 25 and 40 years old. She was not a virgin but had never borne children and both elbows were discoloured, probably from leaning on them. Her hands indicated that she was not a manual worker. JMS Clarke was right in one sense, however. The woman was not killed under the arches, so someone must have carried her body there before dumping it.

The rest of the letter takes us into the murky underworld of a murderer's psyche:

> I can tell you I am miserable as one can be and shall be glad when my
> bloody work is over as I find it is reschard [wretched] at nite to sleep
> I have some dredfull dreames I do not care if i am cought or no …
> I bought a paper this morning red the news and wished I was ded.

Experts today cannot agree on this aspect of a serial killer's psyche. Such people do not willingly give up their murderous inclinations; neither do they usually surrender themselves to their local police station. We know, however, that in the various phases of the killing cycle as identified by the FBI's behavioural analysis team, the aftermath of a murder is usually full of depression. Is this mere coincidence? Or are we looking once again at a genuine letter from the torso killer?

The next day, Pinchin Street and slaughtermen feature again, emphasizing the unwitting role the media played in the creation of the Ripper correspondence. 'Brumigan Bill the Slaughterman' claimed not to be 'Jack the riper' either and he wrote to James Monro to tell him so. His predictions were very precise: he intended to kill four more, two in the East End, one in Islington and one near Regent Street 'some time next week'. He had nothing to do with Pinchin Street: 'I did not settle that one under arch way but I know who did.' This is one of the few letters that tackles motive:

> for I have not got the right cow yet. I have sworn to catch the right
> one that as Injured me … for they are all Brumigan Women, that I
> have settled for they have ruined many a honest man in their native
> town, and have come to Injure honest men but I intend to stop
> there little game.

For the record, the only Birmingham link for any of Jack's victims was Kate Eddowes who lived there briefly with an aunt as a child.

The notion of venereal infection leading to ruin was a genuine problem for the Victorians and at least one other Ripper letter alludes to it. On 8 November 1888, the day before Mary Kelly was killed, Jack wrote to Warren at Scotland Yard:

> I am still knocking about Down Whitechapel I mean to put to Death
> all the dirty old ones because I have caught the pox and cannot

piss I have not done any murders lately but you will find one done before long. I shall send you the kidney and cunt so that you can see where my prick has been up I am in one of the lodging houses in Osborn street ... You will hear from me a little later on that I have done another murder. But not just yet. Dear Boss if I see you about I shall cut your throat. The Old Queen is none other but one of those old ones I have Been up her arse and shot sponk up her.

Without doubt this letter was written by a seriously disturbed individual. His symptoms suggest gonorrhoea but the use of 'cunt' and anal intercourse with the queen went so far beyond the norms of behaviour as to be almost laughable. No pornography then available in England used language like that and equating the queen with the prostitutes of Whitechapel was clearly beyond the pale. The only book that came close in its use of vulgar terms was *My Secret Life* written by 'Walter' in the early 1890s. It was not intended for publication and, as far as the anonymous author knew, only six copies were run off, privately printed abroad because no British printer/publisher would touch it.

In the world of Ripperology, the idea that the Whitechapel murders were carried out as revenge is quite common. One of the earliest involves the otherwise unidentified 'Dr Stanley' put forward by Leonard Matters in *The Mystery of Jack the Ripper*, 1929. The story goes that Stanley's son met Mary Kelly on Boat Race night 1886 and caught syphilis from her. On the boy's death, Stanley went on the East End rampage, killing Kelly and her friends. Nothing of this makes sense. Even allowing for Kelly's unlikely attendance at an upmarket gathering like the Boat Race, syphilis takes *years* to show its fatal symptoms, not the twenty-four months alleged by the Stanley theory. Given the medical awareness associated with Jack's mutilations, of course, the 'mad doctor' theory has gained a considerable following in the Ripper community. The government's attempt to protect the armed forces from the ravages of sexually-transmitted diseases led to the controversial Contagious Diseases Act of 1868 which allowed the police to force suspected women (i.e. prostitutes) to undergo medical examinations. It was not successful.

None of the signatories, addresses or specific threats to murder at a particular time and place bore fruit. However contemptuous the Whitechapel murderer may have been of the police, he was not likely to give them actual information to work from.

Chapter Seven

'O Have You Seen the Devil?' or 'The Proper Red Stuff'

If we can learn something of a letter-writer's psyche from the formation of letters and slant of the pen, can we also gather data from artwork? In the surviving correspondence, there are twenty-five illustrations, most of them crude doodles that accompany the texts. Only one of them is by an accomplished artist.

The second surviving letter, of 24 September, has a silhouette of a knife accompanied by its description – 'this is the knife that I done these murders with it is a small handle with a large long blade sharpe both sides.' Various commentators have noted the phallic symbolism of the fifteen knife illustrations, but this is reading too much into too little. With obvious subtle variations, a knife is a knife and no more phallic than a spoon or fork. Medical experts at the time could not agree on the exact kind of weapon used. Two different ones were employed against Martha Tabram. The cause of death was a single thrust to the sternum that may have been the result of a bayonet. The other thirty-eight cuts, on the trunk and legs, may have been caused by an ordinary penknife. Since Martha had disappeared up 'Shit Alley' with a soldier, the fatal wound made sense and it was a serious failing by the police not to have found the culprit. Dr Llewellyn believed that Polly Nichols had been killed with 'a strong-bladed knife, moderately sharp and used with great violence.' Dr Phillips' testimony at the inquest into Annie Chapman's death makes no specific reference to the knife at all, although its slicing of her throat had ended her life. Likewise, the report on the death of Liz Stride does not focus on the knife either; merely on the fact that her throat was cut and there were no other mutilations.

Dr Brown carried out the most careful and detailed examination on the body of Kate Eddowes, found in Mitre Square. Her throat had been cut 'by a sharp instrument like a knife and pointed.' This was at least 6in long. Dr Thomas Bond, in his post mortem on Mary Kelly, makes no specific mention of the murder weapon in his report, but in answer to questions he described a very sharp knife about 6in long and 1in wide. This would include a clasp knife (the folding variety), a butcher's knife or a surgeon's. Oddly, Bond could not see any evidence of medical knowledge in the mutilations at 13 Miller's Court, so he presumably ruled out the last option, at least in his head. Surgeons' knives in the 1880s were far removed from the throwaway scalpels of today. They were often bone or ivory-hilted and were used for years in any number of operations.

'George of the High Rip' produced a drawing of a knife and there were crossed daggers at the end of the letter found outside 6 Vincent Square and addressed to Vine Street police station. Interestingly, it is headed 'Spring Heel Jack' in reference to the semi-legendary attacker of women in London, first recorded in 1837, who escaped because of his supposed demonic powers.

On 5 October, a knife and crossed bones appeared on the letter from 55 Flower and Dean Street, in the heart of Whitechapel's dossland. A week later, another knife appeared three times, once on the back of the envelope, in the text and again under the 'J the R' signature. Three days after that, 'Mr Smith' received a letter – 'for my knife is nice and sharp' – complete with a drawing and the word 'knife' on the handle in case there was any doubt. This is one of the personalized death threat letters that will be discussed in a later chapter. 'J.T.Ripper' who wrote to Charles Warren on 3 November promised to send 'the toes and earoles to you for supper' and added a hand holding a knife as a final flourish. Six days later another knife appeared on the letter to Warren claiming that the writer/killer was in Greenwich near South Street, Black Heath Hills. This was the day of Mary Kelly's murder.

'Not a very big blade,' said the letter posted on 22 July 1889, 'but o sharp.' Alice McKenzie had been murdered in Castle Alley five days earlier.

Two knives appeared on the letter of 7 October, again in a personally threatening letter addressed to 'Superintendent, Scotland Yard'. There is considerable overkill in this artwork. An obsolete percussion cap pistol is drawn in the top left-hand corner, next to a coffin complete with skull and crossbones motif, a bottle marked poison and the knives, one thrust into a heart.

In the two instances of skulls and crossbones, the anatomical correctness is laughable. One, with the letter written in red ink on 8 October from Birmingham, is drawn and blocked in in black ink with eyes still in the sockets and a halo above the cranium. To its left is a single-edged knife from which blood is dripping and what looks like a knife-sharpener. To the right is a coffin, complete with nails and a very approximate rendering of a skeleton.

The most fascinating examples of artwork with the Ripper letters are self-portraits of the killer. These are the Victorian equivalent of the 'selfie' and say a great deal about the egocentricity of the sender. By far the best is the head and shoulders that accompanied the letter of 12 November:

This is my photo of Jack the Ripper 10 more and up goes the sponge
Sig Jack the Ripper.

'Up goes the sponge' is a boxing term similar to 'throwing in the towel' and dates from the gruelling bare-knuckle bouts at fairgrounds all over the country where contestants slogged it out until one of them collapsed. The use of the word 'photo' appears again in another portrait letter. Studio photography was well-established by the 1880s and all classes were used to street photographers capturing scenes of everyday life. The sketch is clearly not a photograph, but I believe the word is used to imply a highly accurate likeness. Actually, it is not likely to be anything of the sort. The short, spiky hair and scarf are intended to show a working-class man. The unshaven muzzle and square jaw are reminiscent of the criminal types routinely drawn by artists like John Tenniel who drew for the satirical magazine *Punch*. It is the eyes that are the most telling, however. On 11 November, two days after Mary Kelly's murder, when hysteria was at its height in London, Dr William Holt, attached to St George's Hospital, was rescued by police from a crowd who were attacking him. Holt was the 'white-eyed man', using a variety of disguises, who was trying, vigilante-style, to catch Jack in the act. He was wearing glasses when he emerged from the fog of George Yard to terrify Mrs Humphreys who happened to be passing. That was not his intention of course – on the contrary, Holt was trying to *protect* the lady – it was merely that she misread the signs. It was the press who changed the humdrum spectacles into white rings painted around the eyes and this conformed to the accepted medical wisdom of the time. Anyone who carried out such atrocities had to be a dribbling maniac with mad, staring eyes and this was the sort of person the police should be looking for. Even as recently as the movie *Murder by Decree* (1979), the killer (in that case Sir William Gull) had terrifying blood-filled eyes; only when he was out and about in Whitechapel, of course!

From there the self-portraiture slides downhill rapidly. One of the poorest is a picture, not of Jack, but 'your portrait', written to 'Dear Boss' on 7 November. Chief Inspector Swanson noted that there was no envelope and it is by no means clear for whom it was intended. The sketch is awful, less competent than child art, of a bald man in profile with a battered coat and what may be a 'speech bubble' bursting out of his chest. The writer claimed to be a policeman – 'as I am a member of the force' – and the letter is personally threatening. The drawing may be intended to show a police tunic.

Six days later a slightly better portrait turned up, on the second page of a letter sent to Leman Street Police Station by a writer who 'Got no money to post it':

> Description of me Green & Black velvet coat and speckle trousers with 50 buttons down it & I carry a black bag.

The drawing actually shows an elaborate hat band too, stubble on the chin and a pipe. The number of buttons visible is actually thirty-one, but it is likely that this is an attempt to show the coster-monger's pearl-decorated clothes that had developed into the fund-raising pearly kings and queens by Jack's time. The first identified pearly king was the road-sweeper Henry Croft who attended charity events in the late 1870s.

On 16 November, another profile appeared, accompanying a dystrophically-written letter from 'Joe the cats meat man' – 'Look out old Charlie Warren. Heres my photo Im considered a very handsome Gentleman.' If the drawing is supposed to convey the tall and dark 30-year-old mentioned in the text, it fails spectacularly.

The best example of art imitating art was posted in Stratford (London) on 19 November:

> I am Jack the Ripper. Catch me if you can shall have one in Woolwhich This week Look out for me at Woolwhich.

On the same page was a rough drawing of a man wearing an astrakhan-edged coat that was clearly a poor copy of the description given by George Hutchinson of a man he saw talking to Mary Kelly on the night she died. It appeared on the 24th, although earlier copies may have been in circulation. Certainly the *written* description was available before that. The *Illustrated Police News* version is, in itself, an excellent piece of propaganda. Hutchinson saw the man briefly in the dark (albeit near a street lamp) and the man clearly did not want to be seen. Hutchinson's description is too detailed to be true and it is likely that he was describing someone against whom he had a grudge in the hope that the police would arrest him. Hutchinson described the man as 'Jewish' which the press altered to 'foreign', perhaps to avoid anti-Semitic trouble on the streets. The result is a caricature straight out of melodrama, where a wicked uncle, usually called Jasper, twirls his waxed moustache and plots the destruction of the hero and threatens the heroine with a 'fate worse than death'. We have the ubiquitous black bag for carrying the murder weapon, a fob seal as described by Hutchinson and the wild, staring eyes of a maniac. Of course a hard-bitten, streetwise girl like Mary Kelly would go with *him*!

In her anxiety to put artist Walter Sickert in the frame as the Whitechapel murderer, novelist Patricia Cornwell claims that many of the Ripper letters were written by him. We shall examine this from a linguistic/content point of view later, but here we are concerned with artwork. Ms Cornwell contends (p.17 of *Portrait of a Killer*, 2012) that 'art experts say that sketches in Ripper letters are professional and are consistent with Walter Sickert's ... technique.' She does not name the experts and, as a professional artist myself, I cannot disagree more. I copied examples of the art from the Ripper correspondence in the preparation of this book and can assure anybody that producing *bad* art is incredibly difficult! Since Ms Cornwell believes that Sickert is some sort of hybrid of Albert Einstein and the 'Napoleon of Crime', Professor Moriarty, then of course, he was able to disguise his artwork perfectly. The art experts cannot have it both ways – either it is the work of Sickert (in which case why did he do it?) or it is not (in which case, why make the claim?). If a man wants to taunt the police or boast of his murdering skills, he will surely want the world to know – or at least guess at – who he might be. For years, Banksy has produced his distinctive murals at various places all over the world. He has kept his identity secret for more than twenty years, although there have been many guesses by the media, but he never produced *bad* art; it is all extremely good. That, in itself, was his signature. If Sickert wanted to tease the police with a variety of art styles, how would that work? They never suspected him for a moment, either of being Jack or writing the letters. The first time that anyone linked the artist with the killer was Stephen Knight in *The Final Solution* and that thesis has long since been demolished. There is little doubt that Walter Sickert was a rather unpleasant character and appallingly arrogant, but to credit him, as Ms Cornwell does, with the authorship of a large number of Ripper letters, strains credulity.

***

'The proper red stuff' is first mentioned in the original 'Dear Boss' letter of 27 September:

I saved some of the proper <u>red</u> stuff in a ginger beer bottle over the last job to write with it but it went thick like glue and I can't use it. Red ink is fit enough I hope <u>ha ha</u>.

'Ha ha' appears in a number of letters and is indicative of the mocking purpose of them. The writer is enjoying him/herself, finding a gallows humour in the whole macabre enterprise of serial murder. 'Wasn't good enough to post this,' the letter goes on, 'before I got all the red ink off my hands curse it.' There are several clues in this letter which prove that the person (whether Jack or not) did not save blood in a ginger beer bottle or indeed in any other receptacle. Blood when stored in any vessel doesn't go 'thick like glue' – it separates into red cells (held in a clot) and plasma. This happens in a varying timescale depending on the physical make-up of the 'donor' but will certainly be complete within half an hour. The writer is clearly working from an experience of seeing blood from an injury – it could be something as trivial as a nosebleed – spattered on a surface. In those circumstances it does go thick before drying to a brownish stain. This is the other point when it comes to the letters written in 'blood'; blood does not obligingly stay a nice bright red when spilled. In fact, unless arterial, it isn't bright red even when first exposed to the air. Blood is a very dark red, almost purple, drying quickly to a dull brown. This is actually an obvious end product; the iron in the blood oxidizes and it very soon starts to look like rust. It therefore is not really necessary to discuss the practicalities of getting blood from one of Jack's victims into a bottle but assuming it was done, *how* was it done? Catching it as it flowed would be almost impossible, particularly considering the short time at the disposal of the murderer, working in the dark and in the open as he was. Scraping it off a surface would be even more difficult; murderers often go equipped with knives, not so often with a handy bottle and a spoon.

In the killings themselves, there was actually less blood than most people would imagine. Given the dreadful mutilations which increased in number and severity, the police and public at the time and since expected the killer to be covered in blood and therefore easily caught. On 8 September 1888, the day that Annie Chapman was murdered, Mrs Fiddymont, landlady of the 'Clean House' (actually the Prince Albert pub in Brushfield Street, Spitalfields) reported a customer who had blood on his right hand and below his right ear. This may have been Jacob Isenschmid, the 'mad pork butcher' of Holloway. He was all of those things, but he was not Jack the Ripper. During the later murders, he was penned up in Colney Hatch Lunatic Asylum. The blood on his hand almost certainly came from the sheeps' heads, feet and kidneys he bought at Spitalfields market.

The day after Mrs Fiddymont's sighting, William Piggott was arrested in the Pope's Head pub in Gravesend. He began quarrelling with women in the bar and the police were called. He had a bleeding hand which he said was the result of a woman's bite and had just walked from Whitechapel where the incident occurred, possibly in Brick Lane. His shoes appeared to have been wiped clean of blood and there were spots on a shirt in his travelling bag. Although Piggott was clearly unstable, there was nothing to link him with the Whitechapel murders and it is likely that he was sent as an inmate to an asylum.

There is little discussion at the inquest on Martha Tabram involving blood itself. A soldier who may have been with her on the night she died, Corporal Benjamin of the Grenadier Guards, came to the attention of the police. They checked his uniform and bayonet and found no signs of blood. This is hardly surprising – the checks took place two days after the murder and soldiers of all non-commissioned ranks routinely spent hours cleaning their equipment. Today's forensic science could have detected the presence of blood; a policeman's naked eye in 1888 could not.

In a move that would horrify crime scene officers today, a local threw a bucket of water over the blood at the murder site of Polly Nichols in Buck's Row. He was the son of Mrs Emma Green, who lived in the nearest house and the blood was in the gutter outside her front door. Dr Llewellyn, called to the scene earlier, reported little blood – 'not more than would fill two wine glasses or half a pint at the outside.' This was the version he gave to the press, no doubt to make it clear to a non-medical readership the volume involved. There was so little that it was speculated that Buck's Row was a dump site and that the murder had taken place elsewhere. Most of the blood had been absorbed by Polly's clothing. The doctor's findings made it clear that all the cuts were made with the woman lying down. If the killer knelt on her right side and cut her throat from left to right, the blood would flow away from him.

Annie Chapman's wounds were much more severe, with body parts removed. There were blood splotches on the back wall of 29 Hanbury Street and on the wooden fence dividing the property from next door. The blood on the ground came mostly from the throat wound, but again the left-right sweep of the blade would have meant that the killer would have escaped most of it. It goes without saying perhaps that the blood on the murderer's hands could easily have been disguised simply by shoving them into his pockets on his way back from the murder scene.

In the case of Elizabeth Stride, there was, according to Dr Phillips, 'an unusual flow of blood'. Most of this had trickled down the gutter outside the Working Men's Club in Dutfield's Yard. This time, the killer cut his victim's throat from the left side of her body and 'the murderer would not necessarily be bloodstained, for the commencement of the wound and the injury to the vessels would be away from him....' Such an attack, interrupted as it probably was by the arrival of Louis Diemschutz, probably took seconds.

If the timings of the police patrols are accurate, the murder and mutilations of Kate Eddowes took less than fifteen minutes. At 1.30 am on Sunday, 30 September, Constable 881 Edward Watkins checked Mitre Square and found it deserted. At 1.44, on his routine patrol, he saw the body of a woman lying in the square's darkest corner. There was a great deal of blood on the pavement, according to the careful observations of Dr Frederick Brown who attended the scene, but no spurting, indicating that Jack had not torn an artery. Since all the mutilations had been carried out post mortem, 'there would not be much blood on the murderer'. Jack was once again working from his victim's right side.

With Mary Kelly, Jack had no choice but to strike either in front or to the left as her room in Miller's Court was too cramped for any alternative. Dr Thomas Bond, as well as being the first man to offer what today we call a psychological profile of the murderer, not only carried out a post mortem on Mary, but re-checked the earlier cases too, coming to important conclusions:

> The murderer would not necessarily be splashed or deluged with blood but his hands and arms must have been covered and parts of his clothing must certainly have been smeared with blood.

Bond suggested that an overcoat or cloak could cover all this, playing into the hands of the 'lord-loving' devotees who to this day insist that Jack was a toff in cape and topper.

We know that Jack – and many of the serial killers who followed him – took away body parts from some victims as trophies. These can be humdrum items like jewellery or costume accessories or they can be visceral – Annie Chapman's uterus, Kate Eddowes' kidney, Mary Kelly's heart. These are fetish objects that give a killer a perverted reminder of the murders themselves and are a token of his skill. Notorious serial killers have taken this to bizarre lengths: John Christie sealed up three victims in a kitchen cupboard of his flat at 10 Rillington Place, London, as well as helping himself to cuttings of their pubic hair; Jeffrey Dahmer had heads in his fridge in his Milwaukee apartment; Ed Gein made 'furniture' from his victims and nailed their skin to the walls of his Wisconsin farmhouse. What is unrecorded, as far as I am aware, is the removal of *blood* from a murder scene, other than by accident. We have already noted its properties – it does not last in its red, fluid state and the act of transporting it implies a premeditation that we know Jack did not possess.

So, what of the blood on the letters? Most of it is red ink – the 'Dear Boss' letter apologizes for the poor substitute – but some of it may be actual blood. To the naked eye, there is no difference between human and animal blood and even under the microscope it is not immediately apparent unless the blood is non-mammalian (the most obvious being the use of chicken blood, which would be easily accessible to many of the letter-writers) because their red cells have nuclei, which human erythrocytes do not. Using species-specific antibodies, it would be possible to identify the species if it turned out to be other than human, but what would that prove? Most recipients of the letters purporting to have been written in blood would have been sceptical anyway, but going to the lengths of identifying species would have little purpose.

Blood groups were unknown in 1888; it was not until 1901 and the discoveries of Karl Landsteiner that the ABO system we know today was something that could be used forensically. Since then, of course, many sub-groups such as Kell, Duffy and the rest, not to mention the two types of A (A1 and A2) have been discovered and they have been used in the past to pin down bloodstains, before the discovery of how to separate and identify DNA in body fluids. Because no one could possibly have been 'typed' while the Ripper panic was at its height, work on the apparently 'blood'-stained letters now would not get us very far.

Crime fiction nowadays often hinges on DNA evidence and of course it was a major breakthrough, but with one obvious flaw: DNA profiles can only help if there is a suspect. Having details that are accurate to within one in millions can only help if there is the other half of the puzzle to hand. So, even with DNA, Jack would be as much a mystery as he is without it. DNA also degrades and of course it needs nuclear material. Even in a fresh sample, white cells (in other words, the ones with nuclei) are only about 1 per cent of the total volume. In a downstroke of a D, to take one example, there are not likely to be more than about twenty-five white cells, fewer if the letter is written in 'stored' blood because the white cells are more likely to be caught up in a clot matrix and so not be floating about to catch on a nib. It sounds like a challenge to a forensic scientist but it is a challenge not worth following up: with no suspect in the frame whose bodily fluids are handy and with nothing of the victims stored either, a DNA result would be pointless. As well as the scarcity of material and the inevitable ageing process, the letters have been freely handled throughout the 130 years since they were written so they are impregnated with skin cells, sneezes, coughs and incidental airborne DNA-bearing material, meaning that any results would be next to worthless.

George of the High Rip gang was writing in 'red ink but with a drop of the red in it'. Since this letter was received on 2 October, the blood could have been from Kate Eddowes or Liz Stride. The writer of the letter found outside No. 6 Vincent Square was 'in the crowd at Berners Street watching the blue boys wash the blood marks away'. There is a red smudge, clearly made by the side of a left hand alongside the skull and coffin drawings of the 8 October letter from the 'slogging town of Brum' and the writing is in red ink.

Nine days earlier, the 'Saucy Jacky' postcard to the Central News Agency caused quite a stir. Possibly from the same writer as 'Dear Boss', many people at the time believed them both to be authentic. The *East Anglian Daily Times* of 2 October reported, 'The card is smeared on both sides with blood, which has evidently been impressed thereon by the thumb or finger of the writer, the corrugated surface of the skin being plainly shown.' The paper hedged its bets as to whether this was actually from the killer or a practical joke.

On 17 October, a personal letter to 'Dear Parkin' from Croydon had a stain on the back labelled 'This is blood from the woman I done in Mitre Square I might have some of yours.' Two days later, 'Jack a Poland Jew' wrote to Charles Warren. He had lost his knife but promised to attack again in Birmingham on the 27th. On the fourth page is a brown smudge with the label 'A drop of Stride's blood'. Three days later, a letter from Brentford carried a large blot and smear which are probably blood. The almost illegible postcard sent from Rotherhithe on 10 November from 'Yours one who aint such a fool to sign his name' is written in brown ink. Evans and Skinner postulate that this might be blood. There may be blood smudges too on the letter of 15 November, from Tottenham, promising to send a bloody parcel to 'landlord McCarthy', Mary Kelly's landlord at Miller's Court where she had been killed six days earlier.

The letter to Leman Street two days after that was badly stained with what purported to be blood, making reading difficult – 'dear Boss I have ornamented the paper well so you can see I have got the proper stuff this time.' There were stains too on the 19 November letter sent to 'The Boss

Above: 8 October
1888, sent from
Birmingham – 'the
slogging town of
Brum'. Red ink,
signed Jack the
Ripper.

Right: 12 November
1888 sent from
London WC – 'This is
my Photo of Jack the
Ripper'.

Above: 13 November 1888 sent
from London EC to 'The Boss
Leman Street [police station]
Whitechapel'. The envelope
carried a drawing of a stamp as the
writer had no money to buy one.

Left: 19 November 1888 sent from
Stratford (London) E – somebody's
copy of the Hutchinson suspect.
The original was in the *Illustrated
Police News*.

7 October 1889 sent from Leith – 'These are for you you Doubly dyed villain.'

Above: Fleet Street – the newspaper capital of the world in 1888. The name 'Jack the Ripper' was coined here.

Below: The General Post Office, St Martin-le-Grand. The British postal system was the envy of the world.

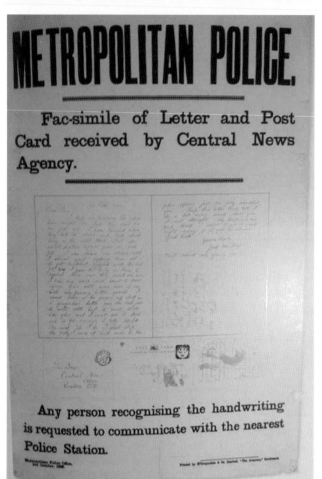

METROPOLITAN POLICE.

Fac-simile of Letter and Post Card received by Central News Agency.

Any person recognising the handwriting is requested to communicate with the nearest Police Station.

Left: The 'Dear Boss' letter, probably written by a journalist, gave the world a terrifying nickname.

Below left: The journalist George Sims, the first to expose the 'Dear Boss' letter as a fraud.

Below right: Sir Charles Warren, Commissioner of the Metropolitan Police, received dozens of critical letters, some of which threatened his life.

Above left: Chief Inspector Donald Swanson, in charge of the paperwork end of the Ripper enquiry, initialled and annotated many of the letters himself.

Above right: Matthew Packer, a fruiterer from Berner Street, claimed to have sold grapes to victim Liz Stride on the night she was murdered. His name appears in several Ripper letters.

Right: The *Illustrated Police News* version of the suspect seen talking to victim Mary Kelly by George Hutchinson. The description is too precise to be believed.

IS HE THE MURDERER?

Above left: George Lusk was chairman of the Whitechapel Vigilance Committee and received a Ripper letter and half a human kidney in the post.

Above right: Dr Thomas Openshaw, Curator of the Pathological Museum, examined the Lusk kidney. He was misquoted by an over-zealous press.

Above left: Robert Donston Stephenson is mentioned in more than one Ripper letter and has been accused of being the Whitechapel murderer.

Above right: Dr Forbes Winslow is mentioned in the Ripper letters as having 'a peculiar mind'. He ran a lunatic asylum and claimed he knew who the killer was.

From hell

Mr Lusk

*Sor I send you half the
Kidne I took from one women
prasarved it for you tother piece I
fried and ate it was very nise I
may send you the bloody knif that
took it out if you only wate a whil
longer*

Signed

*Catch me when
you can
Mishter Lusk*

The Lusk letter was perhaps the only one written by the Whitechapel murderer. Or was it a prank by a medical student?

Dr Neill Cream was a serial killer who wrote his own letters, intended to incriminate someone else.

The jury is still out on artist Walter Sickert. The evidence for his writing Ripper letters is flimsy at best; for being the Whitechapel murderer, it is non-existent.

Police Station Catton Bridge; 'Well my friend I have done another last night of which this is the blood.' Inspector Abberline received a telegram three days later in which the murderer offered to give himself up at 39 Cutter Street, Houndsditch – 'This is written with "The Blood of Kelly" all Long Liz's blood is used up'. 'Jim the Cutter' left what might be blood smears on his 8 January 1889 letter.

There is no doubt that the 'blood' letters were designed to shock. Much of the correspondence, with or without red ink, referred to the taking of body parts and sending them through the post, but there was only one actual example of this – the half-kidney sent to George Lusk 'from Hell'.

Chapter Eight

'Surely the Lord is in this House'

On 30 January 1889, the City Police received an envelope that carried a small piece of paper and the printed words, in red ink, 'Surely the Lord is in this House'. It was typical of the biblical texts routinely found in churches and chapels all over the country as well as religious foundations like schools and workhouses; this particular one is from Genesis 28:16. It sums up one clear theme in the Ripper correspondence – religious mania.

Prostitution was the 'Great Social Evil' and the Victorian middle classes used various euphemisms to describe what today we call by another euphemism – 'sex workers'. They were 'unfortunates', 'ladies of the night' and 'scarlet sisters' and whereas their numbers in the East End were considerable, polite society barely acknowledged their existence. All of Jack's victims were prostitutes, at once the most available and most vulnerable group in society. Henry Mayhew, writing his *London Labour and the London Poor* in 1851, divided such women into eight categories, although sociology was an infant and inexact science in his day and the category edges are rather blurred. Forty years later, General William Booth, himself the recipient of a Ripper letter, wrote *In Darkest England and the Way Out* in which he interviewed a number of working girls and discovered (a fact that feminists of today refuse to accept) that only 2 per cent of them took to the streets because of poverty. Many of them actually claimed to enjoy the life because it gave them friendship, clothes on their backs and a roof over their heads.

The danger came to those at the bottom of Mayhew's categories, who worked alone without the backing of a 'bully' or pimp, still less the relatively genteel comforts of a brothel. Because of the Ripper murders, a giant spotlight was trained on the East End and the friends and acquaintances of the victims talked (reluctantly) to the police and gave evidence at coroners' inquests. Mary Ann Connolly, known as 'Pearly Poll' and 'Mog' was a big, muscular prostitute with a gruff voice. She may well have seen her friend Martha Tabram's killer, but her evidence was shaky to say the least. She had to be tracked down by the police rather than coming forward of her own accord. Ellen Holland, who had seen Polly Nichols wandering the streets shortly before her death, was a 65-year-old flower-seller. She was frequently in trouble for being drunk and disorderly and using obscene language. None of this makes her a prostitute, but it is likely that she had been supplementing her meagre flower-selling income in this way for years. Lizzie Allbrook was 20 and lived in Miller's Court, visiting Mary Kelly on the night she was killed. She worked in a lodging house and may not yet have been 'on the game'. 'Whatever you do,' Mary frequently urged her, 'don't you do wrong and turn out as I have.' Elizabeth Burns was two years younger than Lizzie, living at Cooney's Lodging House at 55 Flower and Dean Street, from which a Ripper letter was sent on 5 October. 'One-armed Liz' had to be rescued by PC 866 John Johnson when she was attacked by Charles Ludwig, a vicious thug, on 18 September. Rose Mylett, 26, was known as both 'Fair Alice Downey' and 'Drunken Lizzie Davis'. Her body was found on 20 December 1888 in Clarke's Yard near Poplar High Street. Assumed for a while to be a Ripper victim, the medical consensus was that Rose died from natural causes, strangling, in her drunken stupor, in her whale-boned stiffened bodice. The list goes on …

Such women were targets because they were easy prey. Victorian society was a hot-house of repressed sexuality. Masturbation was considered dangerous, leading to mental collapse and mania. Whoever the author of *My Secret Life* was, he was clearly terrified of it. Polite society insisted that sex take place only within the confines of marriage. Any degree of nakedness was frowned upon: witness the all-encompassing bathing costumes at the seaside and even the long-shorted, long-socked kit of footballers. In the perverted, topsy-turvy world of the sexual serial killers, outlets for their pent-up aggression had to be found elsewhere. Street girls like Jack's victims would provide straight sex in alleyways, up against walls, but it was not specifically the sex that Jack was after; it was the thrill of the kill.

The religiosity of some of the Ripper letters does not reflect that. They express a horror and disgust of the very existence of prostitutes. 'I am down on whores,' said the first 'Dear Boss' letter, setting the pattern for dozens of others. The 5 October letter to the Central News Agency ranted:

> In the name of God, I swear I did not kill the female whose body was found at Whitehall [in the foundations of Scotland Yard]. If she was an honest woman I will hunt down and destroy Her murderer. If she was a whore God will bless the hand that slew her, for the women of Moab and Midian shall die and their blood shall mingle

with the dust. I never harm any others or the Divine power that protects and helps me in my good work would quit for ever. Do as I do and the light of glory shall shine upon you.

Moab and Midian, like Sodom and Gomorrah, were cities of sin in the Old Testament and generations in the country by 1888 had been brought up in the belief that every word of the Bible was 'gospel' and could not be challenged. The eminently sensible attack on the veracity of the Old Testament by scientists like Thomas Huxley, arguing against Genesis in the 1860s, were relatively new and such arguments barely reached the majority of people at all.

The letter was not written by the Whitechapel murderer but it is a workmanlike example of the sort of thing that would be written by a mission-oriented serial killer according to the FBI's psychological profiling. Classic among these was Peter Sutcliffe, the Yorkshire Ripper, still behind bars at the time of writing. Although he made no such pronouncements at the time of his arrest, having murdered thirteen women between October 1975 and November 1980, Sutcliffe tried to play the insanity card by claiming that he heard voices directing him to rid the world of prostitutes. He saw himself as the 'street cleaner', ordained by God to carry out his savage attacks. The ploy failed, especially as not all of his victims were actually prostitutes.

The letter sent to Charles Warren with a London EC postmark on 8 November cut to the chase as far as motivation for the Whitechapel murders was concerned:

> I am still knocking about Down Whitechapel I mean to put to Death all the dirty old ones because I have caught the pox and cannot piss.

We have discussed this letter and the seriously-disturbed writer before, but the lack of medical check-ups and the absence of an effective cure for sexually-transmitted diseases made such infection a genuine problem.

The contrast between 'good' and 'bad' women hinted at in the Moab and Midian letter was revisited on 19 November by a writer from Poplar:

> If you want a full description and a truthfull one, find the Good woman that took me across Hackney Common and through the Parks a fortnight ago. I had made up my mind to work that day on the first I met, we were in a dark place for it was foggy. But if I am the Devil I could not touch her. she is the only good woman I have

met in England I told her I was Jack the Ripper and I took my hat off and she is the only one that has seen my face.

There were a number of practical jokers and useless idiots on London's streets during the autumn of terror; some of them misguidedly (like Dr Holt, the white-eyed man) trying to catch the killer, others jumping out at women for a laugh. Two days before Mary Kelly was killed, a man accosted prostitute Sarah Lewis in a passageway in Bethnal Green. He was carrying a black bag and dramatically placed his hand into his coat as if to lift something out. Sarah ran. Such juvenile – some would add 'cruel' – behaviour did nothing but muddy the investigative waters of the police.

The moral indignation widened on 19 July 1889 in the letter sent to James Monro:

> I am a moral man and am determined to put down wholesale whoredom I am going for 'lady prostitutes' now and there are millions, then too some well known card sharper and other sports will be attended to ... I am a new god to reform abuses and advantage platers must be stopped.

This writer – Jack the rip – had it in for the 'swells', aristocratic layabouts who gambled, drank and fornicated their way through life – 'a word of warning beware and protect your low immoral pot bellied prince god has marked him for destruction and "mutilation".' The prince of course was Bertie, the Prince of Wales who would eventually become Edward VII in 1901. Although much of his philandering was kept out of the British press, other nationals had a field day, especially in France, where 'Rum-tum' was the darling of the demi-monde, as relaxed among the *grandes horizontales* as he was among the wives of his own admirals!

Even though there was no moral outrage in the 27 September 1889 letter to Commercial Street Police Station, the occupation was spelled out clearly enough:

> Now I shall tell you what I am. Clerk in holy orders. few years ago
> at St Pancras Church. Good morning Amen
> Refr J Ripper &c

One of the most bizarre letters – and the longest – written to Scotland Yard on 8 November 1889 covers a number of themes, but includes:

My blood boils and with indignation rages,
To perpetuate more bloody outrages –
Prostitution against which I desperately fight;
… destroy the filthy hideous whores of the night;
Dejected, lost, cast down, ragged and thin
Frequenters of Theatres, Music Halls and drinkers of
Hellish gin.

The tone of this and many other letters is pure misogyny but that was often conflated with an obsession with the Old Testament. Good women in the Bible are rare. The bad ones, like Eve, Salome, the Queen of Sheba, Delilah and Jezebel, were all the enemies of God. Perhaps Jack saw his victims that way; the writers of some of these letters certainly did.

Of the 300 letters written to the City Force over an eighteen-month period (1888–91), twelve have religious overtones. Bizarrely, John L. Bagg Jnr, writing from Corscombe Mills in Dorset, claimed he could see a hidden knife in an illustration of the Last Supper. Its relevance to the Whitechapel murders is not clear. William Gow of Alyth, Perthshire sent a booklet entitled *Apocalypse Unveiled*. M. Puddig of Thrawl Street, Whitechapel not only claimed to be Jack, but attributed his motives to religion. Mrs A.W. of Rendlesham Road, Upper Clapton had seen the murderer in Cavendish Court as well as a suspicious man exposing himself in the same area. Both letters are full of religiosity. W.G. was convinced, writing from Gloucester Walk, that the murderer was a religious monomaniac operating out of St Paul's cathedral. John Thompson of Southsea knew he was 'on the right track with God's help'. E.T. offered prayers. Louisa Gooding from Newton Poppleford in Devon wrote a sad letter saying that she was 'removed from the Asylum insanity has done its work'; the letter is rambling and incoherent but laced with biblical references. At the end of July 1889, an anonymous writer, again using religious terms, suggested that plaques be placed at the murder sites. Interestingly, without the religious overtones, there was a similar suggestion a few years ago, so that Durward Street would become Polly Nichols Street and Mitre Square would take the name of Kate Eddowes. It did not catch on.

Two of the letters mention a possible suspect: a religious maniac named Herbert Freund. One of them, John Bland of Sinclair Road, Kensington, wrote:

There is a poor lunatic called Herbert Freund who has been in the hands of the police several times for disturbances in St Paul's. I do not know anything whatever against this man, whom I have never seen, except that he was educated as a doctor and he went mad on the subject of religion.

A 'lunatic wandering at large' *and* a doctor – what a perfect combination for a suspect. Unfortunately (or perhaps fortunately for Freund) any enquires that were made came to nothing.

Chapter Nine

'Carroty Curs' and 'Double-dyed Villains'

The Whitechapel murders caused such a panic in the East End and boosted sales of newspapers so much that it was inevitable, perhaps, that some of the letter-writers should jump onto Jack's bandwagon. The letters in this chapter were all threatening, some against the police, others against individuals, named or otherwise, who had somehow incurred the wrath of the writer and deserved the same fate, in their opinion, as the Whitechapel victims.

In the surviving correspondence, the first of these was received on 4 October 1888 and addressed to Mr Voss of 115A Blackfriars, London – 'Prepare for thy doom,' thundered the letter biblically, 'For I mean to settle you You villain you've lived long enough.' Who Voss was and why this note should have been included in the Met's Ripper file is unknown.

The next day 'Dear Boss RIPPER' was threatening not one individual but a whole factory full:

> I hereby notify that I am going to pay your Girls a visit I hear that they a bragging what they will do with me I am going to see what a few of them have in their Bellies and I will take it out of them so that they will never had any more of it on the quite.

The Bryant and May matchgirls to whom this letter was addressed at Fairfield Road, Bow had famously come out on strike in July over the unfair dismissal of one of their colleagues. The campaigner Annie Besant took up cudgels on their behalf, especially as several of them suffered from the bone-eating 'phossy jaw' caused by handling yellow phosphorus in the making of match-heads. It was one of the milestone victories on the road to female emancipation.

Three days later, 'Jack' sent a letter with no addressee listed that threatened a potential eyewitness to murder:

> I know you know me and I see your little game and I mean to finish you and send yours ears to your wife ... I keep my word as you soon see and rip you up.

Whoever 'Jack Poras' was, the letter he received from New Cross on the 13th did not think too highly of him:

> This is to give you notice that I intend to rip your little fat belly up next week. A man so infernally conceited and such a liar as you are deserves no mercy at the hands of JACK THE RIPPER.

Two days later, it was Mr Smith's turn to feel the writer's wrath:

> A few lines to you to let you know that you will soon meet your death. I have been watching you lately and I know you must have money by you, therefore, I, Jack the Ripper will come and serve you the same as I did the other whores in Whitechapel I shall come quite unexpecet and I shant give you time to squeal.

'Dear Parkin' was warned that he would be Jack's next target, from Croydon on the 17th – 'I think you will suit my purpose a treat meet me at Thornton Heath Friday night at 8 oclock if you fail you will be a dead man...' All of this sounds like a lose-lose situation for Mr Parkin.

A letter found in a post-box at 37 West Ham Lane was addressed to 'the Occupier' in a formal way and threatened everybody:

> Dear Sir or Madam, I hope you are pretty well ... I shall visit you shortly in about 3 or 4 weeks time ... I shall kill the first female I see in this house or if there is no females I shall be down on the boss.

This is the uncharted territory characterized today by FBI profilers who refer to 'family annihilators', the murderers of entire households. The phraseology might be alien to 1888 but the crime was not. In 1811, two families, the Williamsons and the Marrs, were butchered in their beds by an unknown assailant along the Ratcliffe Highway near London docks. The incident encouraged Thomas de Quincy to write his spoof *On Murder as one of the Fine Arts*. Although a sailor named Williams was arrested for the crime, he was found hanged in his police cell before he could come to trial.

Albert Bachert of the Whitechapel Vigilance Committee had obviously upset someone because on 20 October he received a curt note addressed to 'Mr Toby Baskett' (an alternative spelling) that was clear in its message:

> Dear Old Baskett [he was 28]
> Yer only tried ter get yer name in the papers when yer thought you
> had me in the Three Tuns Hotel like to punch yer bleeding nose.

Bachert was perhaps the highest profile of the Vigilance Committee, writing to the papers frequently and campaigning on behalf of down-and-outs in the East End. He was German, from Mecklenburg, and that was probably enough to win him enemies in Britain in 1888. This is a rare letter in the Ripper correspondence archive because it refers to an actual incident. On the night of the double event, three weeks before this letter was sent, Bachert had talked to a shady character in the Three Tuns (or perhaps Three Nuns) pub in Aldgate. He was dark (which usually meant Jewish), wearing a morning coat and carrying the ubiquitous black shiny bag. He was asking specifically about prostitutes. The pair left the pub at midnight and parted company at the local railway station. Whether the letter-writer was actually the man in question is unknown, but Bachert claimed to be the recipient of other Jack-related letters up to 1892, by which time he had appeared several times in local and even national papers as a self-important troublemaker. No doubt the letter-writer felt that a punch on the nose was exactly what the man deserved.

We have already discussed the 'pearly king' artwork of the 7 November letter but its context is rather less jolly. There is no addressee other than 'Dear Boss' but whoever it was was a target:

> I think that my next Job will be to polish you off and as I am a member of the force I can settle accounts with you I will tear your liver out before you are dead and show it to you and I will have your kidneys out also and frie them with pepper and salt and send them to Lord Salshisbrury [sic] as it is just the sort of thing that will suit that old Jew and I will cut of your tows and slice of your behind and make macaroni soup of them and I will hide your body in the houses of parliament so you grey headed old pig say your prayers.

The writer claims to be a member of the force, and the notion that Jack was a policeman has haunted the Ripper case for 130 years. Henry Haslewood of Tottenham wrote to the Home Office, urging them to look closely at Sergeant William Thick, known to the underworld as Johnny Upright, both because of his bearing and his honesty. When the journalist Jack London wrote his brilliant *People of the Abyss* in 1903, it was at Thick's home that he stayed. 'I believe,' Haslewood wrote on 14 October 1888, 'that if Sergt.

T Thicke [*sic*] … is watched and his whereabouts ascertained upon other dates, where certain women have met their end, also to see what decease [disease] he is troubled with, you will find the great secreat.'

The Home Office response was the right one: 'I think it is plainly rubbish,' wrote clerk Charles Troup, 'perhaps prompted by spite.' It is possible that the 'old pig' referred to in the 7 October letter was Henry Matthews, the Home Secretary.

Hints of cannibalism occur here and there in the Ripper correspondence and as a fetish it is part of the mindset of some serial killers. Often referred to as the last taboo, it was by no means unusual in various primitive societies. In recent times it is mercifully rare. In Weimar Germany, Fritz Haarmann ate the body parts of his boy victims and sold leftovers in the local meat market. Georg Karl Grossman turned his female prisoners into sausages. Albert Fish killed little Grace Budd and ate her body parts with carrots, onions and bacon. Jeffrey Dahmer sampled various organs of some of his nineteen known victims, keeping others in his fridge and freezer for later consumption. There is no cannibalism associated with the Whitechapel murderer whatever the letters contend, but the fact that they do proves a sick element to Victorian society which rarely features in general histories of the period. There is something of an irony in referring to the prime minister, Lord Salisbury, as an old Jew; in common with many of the English aristocracy of the period, he was not overfond of the Chosen People.

Just as the Bryant and May workforce were in the sights of one writer, so were others. A letter to Kingslands Road Police Station on 8 November warned, 'first of all I am going to settle 4 of Barratts girls at Woodgreen next month.' The writer was very specific, targeting '2 boys and 3 girls between 14 and 15 years of age'. He then intended to emigrate to France. Exactly what problem he had with this particular workforce is unknown.

Jack ['Sheridan' deleted] wrote from Folkestone three days later, boasting of his growing success and promising to kill a woman and her daughter later. It was addressed to Mrs McCarthy at 28 Dorset Street. This was Elizabeth, the wife of John McCarthy who owned Miller's Court and a number of other properties in Dorset Street, including a chandler's shop at No. 27. A typical slum landlord with a reputation for bullying (which could, in 1888, refer to pimping), McCarthy inevitably hit the news over the murder of Mary Kelly.

'Jane Batemore' was mentioned as a possible victim in a letter to Leman Street Police Station on the 12th from a writer who claimed to be one of Mary Kelly's clients (she had been murdered three days earlier). Jane was the lover of William Waddle, a slag-breaker from

Gateshead, and she left him after a stormy relationship. Her body was found in a ditch near her home in the village of Birtley, Tyne and Wear, on 22 September 1888. Her abdomen had been slashed and her intestines exposed in a similar way to Annie Chapman. Scotland Yard sent Inspector Thomas Roots and Dr Bagster Phillips to the crime scene but Waddle had already confessed to killing Jane. Reading about the Whitechapel murders, Waddle said, had unhinged him. He was hanged by James Berry at Durham gaol on 18 December.

'Jacky the Ripper' from Ipswich clearly had it in for local women in his home town. On the 19th, he wrote:

> A friend of mine ... tells me this Polly wright living not far away from The Church at opposite mark with barracks Luisa Whitning may be the colour of her hair my short blade ...

He spoke of the Handicap race coming up the following week, and warned the Leman Street detectives to check the St Clements district, then the most populous and poorest part of the town, especially the 'Welcome Sailor Gardener's Arms & etc'. The Welcome Sailor stood along Fore Street in 1888 and has since been demolished. The Gardeners' Arms is still in business. An accompanying High Court of Justice Life Assurance form refers to the same pub and claims that a murder was committed in St Clements Road nearby on the previous Saturday. Ipswich would become notorious more recently as the home of Steve Wright, the 'Suffolk Strangler' responsible for a number of prostitute murders in 2006.

Mr MacKean of 6 [illegible] Hilldrop Crescent (the street later made infamous by the Crippen case) received a letter telling him that Jack would be visiting him shortly, either at home or in his City shop. Posted from Crawley, Sussex on 21 November, there are no further clues.

There was something personal (and non-Ripper-related) going on with the Shirleys of 3 Annerley Road, Junction Road, Upper Holloway on 6 December. That was when an anonymous letter signed '*no name*' tipped Mrs Shirley off about her husband:

> Madam, you are not aware of the way in which your husband carries on when he is out of your sight, but I can tell you he must look out for himself, as an outraged temper is determined to have revenge. For you, you saucy cat, it will not be your cheeks that will be slapped, but your heart-strings will be pulled before long. We are on your

husband's track the carroty looking cur, the sooner and better he carts himself and you out of this neighbourhood he will enjoy more his personal safety, for I tell you that either myself or some other member of my family, are waiting to take revenge. You can substantiate this that if he is clever at nothing else, he is a pretty good hand at getting children. Your eyes are closed for long enough, but I tell you they will be opened before long, it would perhaps pay you to watch the ginger looking swine a little closer, but the poor devil. I pity you.

The 'anti-ginger' remarks are fascinating and the letter is clearly from an educated and exasperated writer. What Mrs Shirley's reaction was and how her husband coped with the philandering accusation are unknown! There is, however, a rather more macabre follow-up, dated 21 December:

I have wanted to be your friend with mi letter i did not want to meet you it was to appear yours by a my the Bastard Riiper … one hart … i will rip you the first time meet ought to punish the Bastard.

This one is signed 'Jack the Ripper' and is so dystrophic as to make little sense. The spelling is chaotic but the reference to an earlier letter implies that this writer at least knew of the first, even if it was not from the same source. Like so much else in the Ripper case, we are left with a void.

A hapless maid who worked for a man on the top floor of a now illegible address, probably in Camberwell, got a shock six days later:

You to are the next I shall require. Beware – my next visit is Camberwell 'Ah Ah' slip me if you can Jack the Ripper I took stock of you last night and left you at your door my other victims have been whores and a change will [missing] though it is not money but blood blood blood I crave for.

Serial killers are of course stalkers writ large. In what American psychological profilers call the 'trolling phase', a killer selects his victim according to whatever attracts him. He then follows the victim, perhaps more than once, establishing his/her home, workplace and habits. Then, when he judges the time is right, he strikes. Who knows how many targets have walked free over the killing years, blissfully unaware that a monster was trailing them? It is most unlikely that the writer here was the Whitechapel murderer but the Camberwell maid may have got off lightly even so.

It was probably a genuine anti-police attitude that prompted the 'dark hearts' writer of a letter from Leith on 7 October 1889 to write:

> These [drawings of a pistol, coffin, poison bottle and pierced heart] are for you. Doubly-dyed villain. THIS IS NO JOKE.

'Jack' was temporarily in Edinburgh but promised to resume work in London soon.

Henry Matthews at the Home Office came in for his share of threats too. On 16 April 1890, 'Jack' wrote from Clifton, Bristol:

> Do you think yourself a man for if you do I dont in stead of young davis been hung you ought to have been hung instead let me ever put my eyes on you I will blow your brains out hav sure heard your name is what it is you are a bad carule [cruel?] fellow and no mistake about it I shall be close after your heals if I am hung You [missing] thing you done Justice if you do I dout it shant pass of how easy how you think so look out till I come back.

The Home Secretary was the 'man who rations mercy', with the power to overturn death sentences for life imprisonment if he felt the situation justified. This writer was clearly a supporter of 18-year-old Richard Davies, found guilty of the murder of his bullying, tyrannical father at Chester Assizes in March. His younger brother, George, 16, though equally guilty, was reprieved because of his age. Richard was hanged by the executioner James Berry who wrote later that the ghost of the young man often came back to haunt his dreams.

'Johnny ripper' promised to

> kill seven more women be the 23 of march next and shall kill 7 plocemen in may and for [four] soldiers gone so be on the watch … and cut of their tools eat the bugger so remember me to all the old plocemen I have treated for in edgway [Edgware?] in last December.

We shall look at the letter-writers' attitudes to the police in the next chapter, but the notion of eating body parts is alien to the Whitechapel crimes generally and remains one of the most shocking aspects of the correspondence.

A misogynist who wrote an anonymous letter with no date was clearly distressed by someone, and his focus seems *extraordinarily* vague:

To THE Occupier of THIS House. Fool? Ass? Duffer?? Woman??? Beware? the Avenger is on your track, and you had better make tracks for America if you want to save your bacon. Shall pay you a visit soon so beware???

'Jack the Invincible' wrote his exclamation marks as question marks and ends with a Biblical flourish – 'Be ye therefore ready to meet thy Doom Woman??? Amen.'

Another undated letter was equally broad in its focus:

Mrs somebody edwards lane Church St. Mrs I do not know your name but you may expect Jack any minit as I warn you because you are respectable person. If you want to know how many there are there are three of us Bill the Cutthroat Jack the Ripper and the grandson of Wainwright I am up stanfor A hill Signed DBJA.

Why Mrs Somebody should be a target of the Whitechapel murderer and why she should want to know who the killer(s) were is anybody's guess. We have already dismissed the notion of a serial-killing gang that does not fit any known psychological profile. The Wainwright referred to in the letter is Henry Wainwright, a reputable middle-class businessman who caused a wave of revulsion in Whitechapel in 1875. A temperance lecturer and family man with four children, he kept a mistress, Harriet Lane, at a house in Mile End and this caused problems. Running two households was expensive and Harriet was a demanding, loud-mouthed drunk. Luring her to premises at 215 Whitechapel Road, the company warehouse, Henry shot her three times at point-blank range and cut her throat. The foul smell emanating from the premises led to the discovery of Harriet's dismembered body. Wainwright was hanged by William Marwood on 21 December 1875. Aside from the nonsense of *three* Rippers, no one would be the right age to be a murderer *and* Wainwright's grandson in 1888.

In a way the personal letters in this chapter shed a unique light on the mindset of Jack's generation. Some, like the outrage over the hanging of Richard Davies, are the equivalent of trolling 'causes' on the internet today. Others, like the Shirley family's misfortunes, have featured for centuries in small communities where gossip is rife and people appoint themselves moral guardians. Still others are clearly intended to cause as much mischief as possible, written by people with a sick sense of humour.

Chapter Ten

'You can't catch me'

Most books on the Whitechapel murders focus at some point on the inadequacy of the police. This is justified, because there are glaring examples of sloppy police work and uniformed constables in particular being dismissed for drunkenness and unprofessionalism. We cannot criticize them, however, either for a lack of forensic awareness or their inability to grasp that Jack was a new kind of murderer: a blitz serial killer driven by what the German psychologist Richard von Krafft-Ebing called *Lustmord* (sexually-motivated murder). We now know a great deal about what makes serial killers tick, but we have the benefit of fifty years of one-to-one interviews with such people serving their prison sentences, mostly in the United States. No one hunting Jack in 1888 had that advantage.

The men who joined the Metropolitan and City police in Jack's day had to be between 19 and 45 years of age. They had to be 5ft 9in tall and strong, capable of walking at 2½ miles an hour around hard pavements in eight-hour shifts. Day duty covered 7½ miles; night duty 2. They were armed with a 14in wooden truncheon and carried a wooden rattle (until 1884 when it was replaced by a whistle) to attract attention and a 'bull's-eye' lantern for night work. They lived in block houses with other policemen and marched out from their local stations in pairs to divide later and patrol their beats. A sergeant checked on them regularly. Some had fixed points and they were not allowed to leave these, even in an emergency. Strict as discipline was, most coppers learned shortcuts very quickly, finding the cosiest corners and the friendliest coffee-stall-holders to while away the time, especially on night duty. Pay was poor and promotion slow.

The detectives, increasingly wearing plain clothes from the 1860s, were revitalized in 1878 by Howard Vincent's new Criminal Investigation Department (CID). As in all walks of life, their calibre varied. The chain of command in the Met meant that the officer who co-ordinated the day-to-day Ripper investigation was Chief Inspector Donald Swanson, who only appears in the correspondence under his initials, DSS, to show that he had read a particular letter. From 6 October 1888, Robert Anderson, Assistant Commissioner, was his superior and took a direct and personal interest in the case. Below Swanson came the officers of H and J Division, covering Whitechapel and Spitalfields, of whom Frederick Abberline, actually seconded from Scotland Yard, is probably the best-known.

At the top of the police establishment, the 'brass' were not generally impressive. Charles Warren, who comes in for considerable stick in the Ripper correspondence, was the Met's commissioner who eventually resigned on the day of Mary Kelly's murder. James Monro and Anderson had their own agendas and Adolphus 'Dolly' Williamson, who had been the doyen of detectives since the 1860s, had no direct links with the case at all. Several of them, in smug memoirs written years later, claimed to know who the Ripper was but have left no names and no evidence.

One of the most common themes in the correspondence is a cynical taunting of the police. Whoever the Whitechapel murderer was, he was extraordinarily lucky. In his brazen attacks in the area, he was raising two fingers to the law; the letters written in his name did the same thing. The mocking tone was there almost from the beginning. The 'Dear Boss' original began: 'I keep on hearing the police have caught me ... I have laughed when they look so clever and talk about being on the *right* track ... The next job I do I shall clip the ladys ears off and send to the police officers just for jolly ...' It was this attitude that led to extreme caution in the Met. If titbits and guesswork were being bandied about by the media (which they were), it was better to tell them nothing. The 1888 era is a long way from the routine press conferences offered by modern police forces who realize that the media can be used for the common good. The *Star* was the most virulently anti-police of all the tabloids, but it was by no means the only one. Of all the attempts used to catch Jack, the use of bloodhounds most caught the public imagination and several of the letters scoff at their uselessness. 'You can put as many bloodhounds as you like but you will never catch me' on 5 October 1888 is typical.

A number of letters boasted that, despite a close encounter of the constabulary kind, Jack had wriggled out of police traps – 'You will be surprised to heare that you had little Jacky in your Pub the other night. What fun to think the Police were Waiting for me at the East End ...' And: 'I am going to do another job right under the very nose of the damned old Charley Warren. You have had me once but like fools let me go.'

Since more than 200 arrests were made in connection with the murders and countless other people interviewed, it is entirely possible that this writer, to Leman Street on 9 October, is at least partly telling the truth. The same day 'Jack' wrote from Brick Lane, Whitechapel:

> You can offer all the reward you like but you wont catch me next two girls I will fetch their hears to the Police Station and lay them on the step of Leman Street ...

The next day saw a letter that targeted Charles Warren in particular:

> Dear Boss (you are the biggest fool in London) I am in Lester now for a holiday What a dance I am leading all those fools about London why I am passing them by dozens against Scotland yard way & don't laugh & say Damnd fools you work them too hard Poor fellows.

Delighting in the fact that anonymous letter-writers could walk past the police with impunity, Jack from London NW wrote on the 15th:

> I was passing the Houses of Parliament the other day & every police-man I did come across look at me especially number *1A*.

Westminster was indeed covered by A Division and all constables had their divisional letters and numbers displayed in white metal on their helmets and collars; presumably one of them had 1A on his.

Warren received another letter the next day that threatened his wife and was written 'to show you what a lot of idiots you London Policemen are'. And Jack surely had a particular copper in mind when he wrote to Warren from Bethnal Green on the 18th, even though he was talking about London's *other* force:

> To City Dedective, from the old Jewry [City Police HQ] – to day was wasting his time at Johnson's Gracechurch St looking at articles for today sale silks in particular & under garments – we do not pay our rate for the kind of thing – tall – fine – tall hat with band up – dark hair & countenance also one in the fact & I may add he parts his hair behind also.

Reporting this man for window-shopping when he should have been on duty seems petty, especially since Charles Warren had no jurisdiction over the City police. Perhaps the hint about women's underclothes was supposed to convey something even less acceptable about the detective's behaviour. The composer of the long, rambling poem of 8 November 1889 was not impressed by detectives either:

> The swellish flashaway Tecks I very often see –
> Treating whores and asking them for tea …

This was strictly against the rules; uniformed policemen were not even allowed into pubs. The reality of course was – and is – that the police had their narks and needed the co-operation of the public to make headway in a case. Buying a drink for a prostitute may have been officially frowned upon, but it could well yield results.

On 19 October 1888, 'An accessory' wrote to the City force with his own explanation of the murders:

> The crime committed in Mitre Square City [the murder of Kate Eddowes] and those in the district of Whitechapel were perpetrated by an Ex Police Constable of the Metropolitan Police who was dismissed the force through certain connection with a prostitute The motive for the crims is hatred and spite against the authorities at Scotland Yard one of whom is marked as a victim after which the crimes will cease.

The murder of Kate Eddowes brought the whole Ripper case within the remit of the City Police, whose boss was Colonel James Fraser. A former colonel of the 54th Foot, he had become chief constable of Berkshire before taking the City job in 1863. He was on leave when the Mitre Square murder occurred and received two letters. The first was actually a postcard, undated, and was addressed to 26 Old Jewery [*sic*], the headquarters of the force:

> Fraser
> You may trouble as long as you like for I mean doing my work I mean polishing 10 more off before I stop the game. So I don't care a dam for you or anybody else. I mean doing it. I aint a maniac as you say I am to dam clever for you
> Written from who you would like to know

Alongside various doodles analysed in Chapter 7 are the words 'poor annie' and 'rings I have those in my Possession'. What is curious about this is that it clearly refers to Annie Chapman's murder in the Met's jurisdiction and not to Kate Eddowes. It must have been written after 8 September (the Chapman murder date) but much more likely after the 30th (the night of the Eddowes killing) or why involve Fraser at all? The evidence that Dr Bagster Phillips gave at Annie's inquest on 12 September was that there were the marks of one or more rings on the dead woman's fingers but they had gone and a cut implied that they had been wrenched off by her killer. This is very much in keeping with the serial-killer mentality of taking trophies from a crime scene in order to relive the moment. The rings were almost certainly cheap brass – she had of course been married in 1869 – and were never found. It is possible that they were removed in the Whitechapel Workhouse Infirmary mortuary by the keeper, Robert Mann, or his assistant James Hatfield. Although robbing the dead was regarded with horror by the Victorians, mortuary attendants were woefully paid – Mann was a workhouse inmate relying on charity – and saw such acquisitions as the perks of office. Various witnesses at the inquest remembered Annie Chapman wearing rings: three on her wedding finger that she had bought from a black man. But since London and some provisional papers printed all the printable inquest details, knowledge of the missing rings was widespread.

Fraser himself was offering a massive £500 reward for information leading to the discovery and conviction of Kate Eddowes' murderer. This was in stark contrast to the Met, who had abandoned rewards four years earlier on the grounds that evidence so obtained could be tainted and easily overthrown in court. The press made it startlingly clear what the media – and presumably the public – thought about this. 'The metropolitan force is rotten to the core,' said the *Star* on 1 October. Henry Matthews, the Home Secretary, took his share of the flak too. The same paper called him 'a feeble mountebank who would pose and simper over the brink of a volcano.'

What is interesting is the umbrage the writer took in Fraser's claim that the Ripper was a maniac. It was a widely-used term in the press at the time and although unsatisfactory in terms of today's psycho-profiling, seemed to sum up the personality of the Whitechapel murderer perfectly. Altogether the City Force received 345 letters and postcards, which will be discussed in Chapter 13.

The policeman-as-murderer theme described in the 19 October letter is common in crime fiction because, on face of it, a policeman has the necessary inside information to steer an investigation in any direction away from him. Of the many police constables recorded as being involved in any way with the Ripper investigation, only four were dismissed from the force (*after* the murders) and none for consorting with prostitutes. In the endless game of hunting Jack, still being played conscientiously today, one of the most intriguing to emerge in the mid-1990s was that of the railway policeman, put forward by theorist Bernard Brown in the *Journal of Police History Society*. There were a number of Underground stations in the killing zone – Shoreditch at the northern end of Brick Lane; Whitechapel in the High Street; St Mary's (closed in 1938) only yards from Berner Street. Brown believes that it was tramway construction that caused a lull in the murders in October, so that far more horse-drawn traffic was on the streets than was usual, adding to the bustle of an already busy city. Brown cites two detectives – Inspector Richard Webb of J Division and Inspector Henry Moore at the Yard – who had experience as railway policemen, but neither of these fits any kind of profile. The likelihood is that 'An Accessory' was hoping to muddy the waters and cast aspersions on the police.

On 22 October, Jack claimed that he had killed two more women under the nose of a 'rather drunk' bobby; three weeks later, he boasted that he spoke to six constables a day and they were none the wiser. The idea of insider information hovers constantly: 'The police officers are not caught yet How can they when I am used to police work.' This one was personally read by Inspector Abberline. On 21 November, the writer was sarcastic in the extreme when he wrote:

> Being still at large – thanks to the energetic efforts of the Police to effect my capture, I take the liberty of writing to you to say that it is my intention of committing one or two outrages or murders in or near your locality – perhaps on the steps of your office.

Jack was 'all over Whitechapel and City' according to his letter on 26 November: 'Also see your brave worrors police I see them and they cant see me.' He got cockier still on 8 December:

> '... the police about here are fine looking fellows I had the pleasure of drinking with one this morning [*strictly* against the rules!] and asked him what he thought about my glorious work ...

And on the day before Christmas Eve, Jack thought the Head Postmaster would like to know that he had been travelling with detectives on the ferry between Holyhead and Dublin.

'Scarlet Runner' was not afraid of the detectives because his disguises are 'as numerous as theirs'. Chief Constable Williamson disapproved of disguises but we know that detectives of both the Met and the City force used them, a number of officers dressing in female clothing to act as decoys on the streets of Whitechapel.

A letter that showed that the writer was following the news closely was sent to the Yard on 19 July 1889, two days after the murder of Alice McKenzie. He threatened to kill twenty women, the next in two days' time near Castle Alley (where Alice's body was found):

> The police ant artfull enough for me … They searched all the barrows and carts Near the castle alley But they didn't search the one I was in I was looking at the police all the time.

Bearing in mind that the alley was only 15ft wide at the most (today it is a pavement's width) and full of costers' carts, it is inconceivable that a lurking miscreant would not be found.

Pointing accusatory fingers at individual officers continued. On 22 July, a letter from West London annotated with Swanson's initials urged 'Dear Boss' to 'Watch PC 60C light moustache Shaven clean rather stout he can tell you almost as much as I can …' Three days later, in the famous ''tecs' letter, Jack was threatening to target foreigners, especially Germans, and had been talking casually to the local force:

> . . . their eyes *of course were shut* & thus they Did not see my bag. Ask any of your men who were on duty last night in Piccadilly (Circus End) last night if they saw a gentleman put 2 dragoon guard sergeants into a hansom. I was close by & heard him talk about shedding blood in Egypt. I will soon shed more in England …If you want to know where Jack the Ripper is Ask a policeman.

There were six Dragoon Guards regiments in the British army, each one distinguished by the colour of their uniform facings (collar and cuffs). The 1880s saw a great deal of colonial activity in Egypt and the Sudan. The revolt of Arabi Pasha had seen the defeat of not one but two British-Egyptian armies, under colonels William Hicks and Valentine Baker respectively.

Jack was crowing again on 10 September: 'Oh, how I crack my sides with laughing when I read of dear Old Jack and to think the Shiny button [police] are baffled …'

The next day, specifically referring to the Pinchin Street torso, 'JMS Clarke Not Jack the ripper' wrote: 'I was as nere caught this morning as possible PC passed me while i was carrying my deadly parcel to the arch of cable st or near there ...'

On 8 October, the anonymous writer could assure the 'Chief of Scotland Yard' that the police were not and never had been on Jack's trail and 'I do not wish to waste a stamp to such useless dogs as you detectives.'

An interesting comparative letter from Jack arrived from Boston, Massachusetts on 30 October, addressed to the editor of *The Times*:

> Some of your police regulations are so absurd that I have to laugh at them. here [in Boston] the officers are armed and allowed to use their discretion ... I did not see it so much till I came here where such a series [of murders] would not be possible.

Bearing in mind the future of serial killing in the United States and the fact that Boston was until recently the drive-by shooting centre of America, there is a certain irony here.

Chapter Eleven

An American in London

More than twenty years ago, the United States led the way in the creation of serial killers and little has changed since – 76 per cent of the world's 'multiple murderers' (to use an older term for them) are American. Of these, 84 per cent are Caucasian. Ninety per cent are men; such a high proportion that some criminologists doubt whether the term serial killer can be applied accurately to women at all.

In the 1880s the concept of a serial killer was rare and the phenomenon often misunderstood. Today, thanks to cinematic successes such as *Psycho*, *Silence of the Lambs* and *Seven*, not to mention a whole raft of television crime series like *Criminal Minds*, we all know a great deal about what makes such murderers tick. Perhaps it is because we associate serial killing with America, there is a tendency to claim that Jack himself was American. As if the contemporary killer H.H. Holmes was not bad enough, in 1996, Ripper experts Gainey and Evans came up with Dr Francis Tumblety in *Jack the Ripper: The First American Serial Killer.* To be fair, the man suggested himself in the role and although he appears nowhere in the Ripper correspondence, he is worthy of study if only to get him out of the way.

Francis Tumblety was born the youngest of eleven children to James and Margaret Tumblety who moved to Rochester, New York when Francis was still a child. He became apprenticed to Ezra J. Reynolds aka Dr Lispenard, a venereal specialist. In his spare time, he sold pornography on canal boats and may have sold quack 'Indian' medicine in Rochester. By 1856, he was practising as a doctor in New York but this was an era, especially in America, when anybody could hang up a brass shingle and snake-oil salesmen with the gift of the gab like Tumblety could do well. Various writers recently have tried to paint the man as a successful herbalist in Toronto, if only because herbalism was no more 'quack' and dangerous than conventional medicine. A number of cases of irregularities and even causing the death of a patient are today written off as examples of police vindictiveness!

The outbreak of the Civil War found Tumblety in Washington, first as a doctor to President Lincoln's son Tad and second as part of the medical staff of General George B. McCellan of the Union Army. Neither story was true. The Pinkerton Detective Agency, then new, discovered that Tumblety was still peddling porn to the Army of the Potomac. There was some suggestion that he was the assassin John Wilkes Booth's doctor and that he was questioned by the government's authorities in the old capital state prison in Washington. As he swanned around San Francisco entertaining young men at various hotels, wearing ludicrous costumes and a vast moustache, Tumblety claimed to have been awarded medals by the French emperor Napoleon III, the Kaiser, Wilhelm I and had run an ambulance in the siege of Paris in 1870.

Three years later he was in Paddington, London, involved in various fraudulent activities and returned to New York, possibly for his own safety, two years after that. On 7 November 1888, two days before the murder of Mary Kelly, Tumblety was arrested in London. According to him, his arrest had to do with the fact that someone had said the Ripper wore a slouch hat (many Americans, Tumblety included, did) and that the police wanted the two valuable diamonds he carried in his wallet. He clearly disliked the police:

> Why, they stuff themselves all day with potpies and beef and drink gallons of stale beer. They can't help it; their heads are as thick as the London fogs … I never saw such a stupid set.

On 16 November, Tumblety was charged with eight counts of gross indecency against four men between July and November. He was released on bail. With his trial postponed until 10 December, Tumblety skipped bail and sailed for New York via France. After various brushes with the law over a variety of issues, he died on 16 May 1903 in St Louis. It is possible that the 'Dr D' referred to in a letter from Chief Inspector John Littlechild of Scotland Yard (himself once a Pinkerton detective) is Tumblety. The letter itself is fascinating, considering the theme of this book. He believed Tumblety to be a 'Sycopathia [*sic*] Sexualis' type, proving that Littlechild at least was abreast of current psychological thinking in that this was the thesis of the behaviouralist Richard Krafft-Ebing. Tumblety was a misogynist, much preferring the company of men. Whether he was the foreign doctor who tried to buy uteri from various London hospitals at the time is unknown.

In December 1888, Inspector Walter Andrews was seconded, along with Abberline and Chief Inspector Henry Moore, to Whitechapel to take charge of the Ripper case on the ground. Although he was vague about it himself, Andrews was sent out to Montreal. It is by no means definite that he went and if he did, a far more likely reason was as a follow-up to Fenian (Irish nationalist) skulduggery in Canada rather than chasing the louche self-aggrandisement of a man like Francis Tumblety.

As a suspect, Tumblety is highly dubious. His huge frame – he stood 6ft 4in tall and dressed flamboyantly – is reported by no one in the streets of Whitechapel on the nights in question. Neither is there any record of violence against women. He can be assigned to that very large rubbish bin of history – Ripper suspects who might have been.

But if Tumblety has no provable links with Jack, what about the other 'foreign correspondents' at work at the time? Perhaps the Americanisms of the 'Dear Boss' letter put people in the mood. There were plenty of Americans in London especially, mostly there on business at a time when the United States was flexing its muscles to outstrip Britain as the world's leading economic and industrial power.

'Spring Heel Jack' left a letter outside No. 6 Vincent Square, Westminster, addressed to Vine Street police station, the headquarters of C Division:

> I am an american I have been in London the last ten months [if accurate, since January 1888] and have murdered no less than six women I mean to make it a dozen now while I am about it I think I may as well have six men in blue to make the number as I see there is far too many knocking about the East End looking for me … I was in the crowd at Berners street [the Liz Stride murder] watching the blue boys wash the blood marks away … at night I have been sleeping in Bow cemetery one thing I have to tell you know [sic] is the policemen who has found the women it is those I mean settleing as they will not get the chance of giving evidence against me I shall shortly have to shift or shout my quarters from Bow cemetery as I have enlightened you a bit about I have written this on the Embankment near Waterloo … I will rip a few more So help my God I will.

Apart from the almost complete lack of punctuation, the vanity of the letter is extraordinary. What would be the point of killing the first policeman at a crime scene? The subsequent investigation was far more important.

'Spring-heeled Jack' made his first appearance in 1837, although this was possibly an extension of earlier urban ghost stories, mostly set in London. He was still reported as genuine in Liverpool in 1904. *This* Jack's first victim was a servant girl, Mary Stevens, who was assaulted while crossing Clapham

Common in October of the year that Victoria became queen. Enormously strong, Jack tore her clothes with his long claws, his hands cold and clammy, like those of a corpse. The next day, the same character leapt out at a passing coach, causing the horses to shy and panic and the coachman to be injured. Jack then disappeared over a 9ft-high wall, cackling and shrieking as he went. Other attacks, usually on servant girls, followed, Jack's terrifying appearance and speed of escape adding to the legend. He was linked in 1855 to the 'devil's footprints', a series of prints over snow-covered roofs in Devon in the bitter winter of that year. Although all this may well have begun as an elaborate hoax, the hysteria it engendered, about a woman-attacking maniac who could not be caught, had obvious parallels with the Whitechapel murderer thirty years later.

In October, Jack wrote from Philadelphia: 'Honorably Sir, I take great pleasure in giving you my present whereabouts for the benefit of the Scotland Yard boys.' He apologized for not having finished his work in London, but was currently in New York, bound for Philadelphia where 'I might take a notion to do a little ripping there.' However, there is no recorded outbreak of crimes of violence in the city at that time.

With no explanation, Jack wrote to the Central Police Station on 18 July 1889 from Leicester Races, a little miffed perhaps that people were accusing him of being 'an American butcher now. never mind ...' We have already noted the Boston letter of 30 October that found British police regulations absurd.

The undated letter from Jack talking of 'Saucy Jacky' and 'Charley Warren' has a cosy, familiar feel about it, but the opening sentence is pure American – 'I come from Boston You spanking ass ...' On the face of it, there is nothing outstanding about America's interest in the Whitechapel murders at the time. Although we could not match the States' potential, especially in national products like oil, gold and silver, Britain still led the world economically in 1888 and London was still the world's largest city. The world wars and the 'special relationship' lay in the future. 'Little Miss Sure Shot', 27-year-old Annie Oakley, was impressing audiences all over the world in Buffalo Bill's Wild West Show. The century's worst blizzards hit the States in the winter, with a cyclone killing thirty-five people at Mount Vernon, Illinois. George Eastman's lightweight camera – 'you push the button, we do the rest' – would soon make crime scene and mortuary photographs of the studio type obsolete. And in Chicago, America had its very own serial killer, the first recorded in the States: Herman Mudgett, better known as Dr H.H. Holmes. He was, like Francis Tumblety, a druggist and con-artist and he was in the process of creating 'the castle', an elaborate death house with false walls, secret passageways and trap-doors. 'I was born with the devil in me,' Holmes confessed eight years later. So, arguably, was Jack, but no one ever caught him!

On 3 October, the anti-police *Star* suggested a link that has become commonplace in Ripper folklore: that Jack was an American who had already committed murders across the Atlantic. The article cited the Atlanta *Constitution* which said:

> In our recent annals of crime, there has been no other man capable of committing such deeds. The mysterious crimes in Texas have ceased. They have just commenced in London.

The *Daily Telegraph* wrote two days later:

> The idea that the letters attributed to the murderer could have been 'a practical joke' or 'hoax' is quite untenable. It is inconceivable that any human being, even the most degraded, could joke on such a subject … The letters breathe the very spirit of such a murderer … His letters favour far more of American slang than of home. They are the exact reprint of the Texas rough's style and probably the Texas solution of the mystery is the true one.

Between December 1884 and July 1887, there were a number of assaults on black female servants in Austin and Gainesville, Texas and the murders of seven white women. If they were all committed by the same perpetrator, they are unusual. Most serial killers (and assailants) target victims of their own race, so it seems at least possible that one was a copycat of the other.

But the Texas link became at least a possibility. After a deluge of letters via the press, insisting that Jack *must* be a foreigner, the police questioned more than 300 people including 'three of the persons calling themselves Cowboys who belonged to the American Exhibition', who gave satisfactory accounts of themselves. This record is found among Superintendent Swanson's papers, but it is at least possible that the three were Lakota tribesmen, led by their chief, Black Elk, who had somehow been left behind in May 1887 when Buffalo Bill Cody's troupe left the country. They had wowed audiences, including the queen (called by Black Elk 'Grandmother England') and it is astonishing that Cody sailed without them.

***

Not to be outdone by the American connection, other foreigners put pen to paper. There were several from Ireland, which, although still part of the United Kingdom, was a place that bore watching. The disaster of the Irish potato harvests in the 1840s and the rise of the independence movement, the Fenians, gave rise to a Home Rule movement that was not merely confined to a talking-shop in Westminster. Before he was seconded to Whitechapel, Inspector Abberline had been heavily engaged in the 1880s against the 'dynamitards', determined assassins who placed bombs in the Tower of London, Clerkenwell Prison and even under Scotland Yard. The Irish were seen as dangerous and unpredictable and so the 'Jack' letters from across the Irish Sea perhaps carried more weight than was strictly necessary. As we shall see, the letter that many believe actually was written by the Whitechapel murderer, the 'Lusk letter', begins with the mock Irish 'Sor'.

The letter from Dublin sent on 8 October 1888 sounds very cosmopolitan. Jack promised to kill two more in Dublin itself, then try his hand in Calcutta! The Bensdorp letter discussed elsewhere also promised a killing in Dublin, urging the recipient to meet him in Patrick Street. What was perhaps particularly disturbing was the 3 November letter from Belfast, heavily stained with red ink:

> …at a meeting of the council of midnight wanderers of Belfast the following resolution was unanimously passed. That this Committee tenders hearty congratulation to "Jack the Ripper" on the grand success he has recently scored …

Presumably, this refers to the double event. The tone of this is exactly what would be printed in a number of newspapers and periodicals in our own time, posted by the IRA and similar terrorist organizations with an air of legality and respectability. In that the Ripper case undoubtedly rocked society and embarrassed the police, this was precisely the line that the Fenians would take. There was another Irish connection in the letter to Inspector Reilly at Bromley Police Station:

> Sir, I received your letter beware you are doomed Delaney will make it hot for you united U. F. Brotherhood If you will give me £1 0s 0d I will inform you where the Whitechapel Murderer Is hiding But if you dont chose then he will start work on some of the hores of Bromley.

This is perhaps the only Ripper letter to demand money with menaces, although how exactly it was to be paid – and precisely to whom – remains a mystery.

The Jack who wrote from Limerick just before Christmas 1888 to the Head Postmaster was rather more jovial. He was the one travelling with detectives en route to Dublin – 'I must travel all Ireland and Scotland' – and was on leave over Christmas itself. Alan Sharp's book *London Correspondence: Jack the Ripper and the Irish Press* (Ashfield Press, Dublin, 2005) points out the political propagandistic nature of the letters as well as many others sent openly to various Irish newspapers.

***

We have already discussed the French connection in the context of the writer styling himself Isidore Vasyvair. This letter was posted in Lille on 8 October and taunted the British police, claiming they were wasting their time looking for Jack in London. Four days later, probably more by accident than design, a 'suspicious person' was arrested at Boulogne. He looked like the line drawings produced in the *Daily Telegraph* which were in turn based on the description of Matthew Packer, the greengrocer who claimed that he had sold grapes to Liz Stride on the night of the double event. The man was arrested as a vagrant and wanted to go home to South Wales. A great deal of paperwork was generated in relation to the man who wanted to work in the Welsh coalfields but was actually American by birth. His story was that he had been working in mines in Scotland until the previous week. What possessed him to go to France is unknown as he did not even speak the language, but E.W. Bonham, the British consul, was not impressed by him. 'His manner was very unsatisfactory', especially as he seemed to be a drifter with no support and no papers. By 17 October, the Met were sure that the vagrant had no connection with the Whitechapel murders and the correspondence comes to an end. Red herrings like this litter the Ripper case. The whole thing was clearly a waste of time and effort but it shows, not only a foreign dimension to the crimes, but the meticulous lengths to which the authorities went to trace the killer.

It was nine days later that '*Jack o estripador*' wrote to Charles Warren, via the Police News Central Office. Two pages of red ink said very little, except that Jack was now in the Elbe-e-Guando area and sent his best wishes to his friends in the police. All very pointless until we factor in the obsessions of Edward Knight Larkins. Researchers Evans and Skinner kindly refer to this man as an 'early Ripper theorist'. I see him as an interfering busybody wasting police time. As we have seen, Larkins was a clerk in the Customs Statistical Department and, in common with a large majority at the time, could not believe that the Whitechapel murderer could be an Englishman. He wrote to the Metropolitan Police, the magistrate Montagu Williams and to the London Hospital with his ludicrous claims. Larkins had clearly read grisly accounts of the Peninsular War in which Spanish and Portuguese peasants had butchered French soldiers who were occupying their countries. Limbs were hacked off, penises removed and shoved into the mouths of their dead owners. The grim artwork of Francisco Goya covers some of this. In Larkins' rather peculiar mind, it followed therefore that the Whitechapel killer (or killers, as he believed) would probably be Portuguese and he had three in mind, working aboard cattle ships then in the Port of London.

He wrote to the Home Office on 11 January 1889:

> The theory I have formed is that the murderer is a Portuguese cattle-man who comes over with the cattle from Oporto ... in all probability he is a middle aged married man ... this monster contracted a certain disease by coming into contact with one of these unfortunates ... Finding himself in that condition and with the characteristic vengefulness of the Portuguese race he determined to wage war upon these fallen women.

The ship itself provided a safe haven for the killer who could simply lurk below decks until the time was right for his next attack.

Two ships in particular reached Larkins' attention, the *City of London* and the *City of Oporto*, and he went further by naming names. Manuel Cruz Xavier murdered Polly Nichols. His friend and copycat killer, José Laurenco, butchered Annie Chapman; this was because Xavier was not on board ship at the time of her death. Joao de Souza Machado had been Laurenco's accomplice in the earlier murders but he killed Mary Kelly all by himself. Machado was 41 and fitted Larkins' theory perfectly. He even noted that whereas all other cattlemen crew received 'very good' in reports on them, Machado only merited a 'good'; a clear sign of homicidal guilt if ever there was one! He spoke to Inspector Moore, Chief Inspector Dolly Williamson and Chief Inspector Donald Swanson, presumably boring them to death with his obsessions. Unhappy with their response, he drafted a seven-page report that was published by the *Daily News* on 20 February 1891 (no one could say that Larkins was not persistent). He even went to the lengths of describing the cattlemen, alongside the various murders with their dates. Working entirely on George Hutchinson's rather over-the-top description of a man in an astrakhan coat talking to Mary Kelly on the night she died, Larkins noted that Joao de Souza Machado had a black moustache too!

The point was that the ships and suspects did not match up, which is why Larkins' two original suspects had to become four in one of the most bizarre examples of copycat murder in history. By 1893, Larkins was accusing Dr Robert Anderson of conspiring on behalf of the Portuguese sailors. The Home Office had given up long before this:

> The most careful inquiry here has led to the same conclusion. I fear the man is a troublesome "faddist" & that it is idle to continue the subject with him. His recent letters are in a tone which renders further correspondence with him impossible.

Chapter Twelve

The Women Who Did

The vast majority of Ripper letter-writers, using the various pen-names we have looked at so far, got away with what was actually a crime. Only four did not and an examination of their cases gives us a fascinating insight, not only into their own motivation, but into contemporary attitudes of society.

The only male of the four is the least informative because his name is not given in the local or national press so we can only guess at his motives and circumstances. He was in a 'respectable position', said the *Bradford Citizen*, and clearly young. He wrote a letter signed 'Jack the Ripper' and the Glasgow police tracked him down. Exactly how they did this is unknown and it begs the question that if a relatively harmless example could be properly investigated, why were there not more arrests, especially for the twisted and downright vicious correspondence we have come across already? Presumably the Met and City forces in particular had bigger fish to fry. It is noticeable that all four cases took place outside London.

The unstamped letter read:

> Dear ol Boss – I am known as 'Jack the Ripper' and I am going to pay Glasgow a trip. I hear there are fair women in Saltmarket, Glasgow, so I am going to pay you a visit – Yours truly …

The red-ink letter ended up with Sub Inspector Carmichael who contacted Superintendent Orr at Glasgow's Central Police Office. The Saltmarket, ironically the site of the Courts of Justice, was once a fashionable district but by the Ripper's time it was a notorious slum crawling with liquor dens and prostitutes.

The terrified lad 'coughed' immediately and said he had written the letter 'for a lark'. In view of his youth and obvious distress, the magistrate took pity on him and he got off with a caution.

In December 1888, the *Torquay Times* carried the story of Charlotte Higgins, who was sentenced to three weeks' imprisonment for stealing ribbons. In the context of this book, however, her 'fame' rested on the Jack-style letters she wrote to the Reverend Samuel and Mrs Harvey of St Marychurch, Devon. Charlotte was a 14-year-old maid to the vicar and his wife, and in the letters claimed to be Jack and that his next victims would be the Harveys. Presumably her career with them ended rather abruptly!

Charlotte had written the letter at the end of October, but a month later the courts were not so lenient with another 'Jack'. This one lived at Penrhiwceiber, Aberdare, in the Rhondda Valley, at that time the heart of one of the largest coalfields in Europe. The Rhondda had sprung up quickly over a thirty-year period, with rows of cheap terraced housing for the miners and substantial villas for the mine-owners. It was chapel country with a reputation for teetotalism. Those who liked a tipple (men only) had to form working men's clubs where the drinking rules did not apply.

The *Cardiff Times* of Saturday, 24 November carried the story. Miriam Howells, wife of labourer James Howells, sent threatening Ripper-style letters to two neighbours, Elizabeth Magor and Margaret Smith.

> 'Dear Mrs Boss,' said Elizabeth's letter, with a clever take on the original, 'I mean to have your life before Christmas. I will play a _____ of a trick with you, old woman. I played a good one on the last, but this will be better. Arnt I clever? – Believe me to remain yours for ever, Beware. JACK THE RIPPER.'

Margaret's letter was similar:

> Dear Miss Boss, Before Sunday night I mean to have your life. I shall be upon you without your thinking. I will play a better trick with you than I did with the last one and that was clever – Yours truly, JACK THE RIPPER.

The ladies contacted the police and PC Luther Rees investigated. The details emerged at Aberdare police court the following Tuesday. Miriam admitted to writing the letters, saying that she had asked Polly Peak to post one and David Davies the other. Rees asked Miriam why she had written the letters and she told him she meant no harm; that (as with the Glasgow boy) she had merely done it for a lark. She regretted it, of course (having been caught), and hoped that the magistrates would let it all blow over. They did not.

Messrs W.M. North, R.H. Rhys and D.P. Davies took the threatening nature of the letters seriously, Mr Rhys in particular complaining that such conduct was 'most unwomanly'. Miriam was her own worst enemy in that she confided to hairdresser David Davies what was in the letter which she asked him to post on 16 November. They had all met up the following day and had a laugh about it, despite Margaret Smith being frightened up to that point. Polly Peak had posted her letter at the Miskin Post Office on the 15th. With Constable Rees giggling too, it looked as if the whole thing was a storm in a teacup. There appeared to be no animosity between the women, still less the implication of a long-running feud perhaps hinted at in the letters.

Somehow, the story reached the press and that was when it got ugly. Miriam was genuinely worried, burst into tears in the presence of PC Rees and asked him what was likely to happen. What *did* happen is that he arrested her two days later. Miriam had seen a copy of the *South Wales Echo* that contained a reference to Ripper letters and she had copied the style from that.

The magistrates found the case curious (although those in Glasgow regarded the offence as 'too common at present') and adjourned for a week to think about it. Miriam Howells was given bail of £28 and a surety of £26, no small sum in the Rhondda Valley in the 1880s; the equivalent today would be in the region of £3,000. As reported in the *Cardiff Times* on Saturday, 8 December, magistrate North gave his summation: despite the 'jokey' nature of the whole episode, the crime itself was very serious. Miriam had threatened to kill two women. The bench could have sent her for trial at the assizes and had she been found guilty, would have faced imprisonment for life. North was horrified that people should 'have made a joke of the crimes in London of a ruffian, who so far had not been found. She had made a joke of crimes of a most revolting character.'

The upshot was that a thoroughly chastened Miriam Howells paid 1 guinea to the Public Institute and the expenses of Peak and Davies were denied, since they were as guilty as Miriam. The Howells letters are typical of the personal type we saw in Chapter 9 involving 'Carroty curs' and 'Double-dyed Villains', but the letters received in Bradford and, more especially the personality of the writer, were altogether more chilling. Her name, with a grim irony, was Maria Coroner and, according to the *Jack the Ripper A-Z*, she was born in Canada.

Bradford was a thriving spinning and weaving town by the 1880s with a large German-Jewish community and an increasing number of impressive municipal buildings. On 22 October, Jack wrote, 'Talk about having caught a "Jack the Ripper" at Bradford, why I'm all safe and sound its all bosh.'

It was, and in this particular case we can assume that the writer was very keenly watching the press. That was the day that *The Times* reported the curious incident of 21-year-old Maria Coroner, born in fact in Oldham, who was charged with having 'written certain letters tending to cause a breach of the peace'. One of those, sent to J. Withers, Bradford's chief constable, read:

> Dear Sir – If the Bradford Police would like to make another gallant capture now is the time. I have arrived in town for the purpose of doing a little business. Bradford is the field that requires my labour. Of course knowing as I do that your men are so clevah it is not necessary to give my address nor yet to describe myself minutely. I will simply state that I am here and alone quite near to the Town Hall.
>
> I am, my dear sir, yours in the fight against wickedness J. RIPPER.
>
> P.S – Perhaps you would like my portrait, but you see I am in deep mourning for those ladies that I put to sleep and do not wish to have one taken.

The next day another letter with the same handwriting appeared in the *Bradford Daily Telegraph*:

> Sir – Would you permit me through the medium of your valueable paper to announce my arrival in Bradford. I would have wired you but you see the people would have gone to trouble and expense in order to receive me kindly, particularly the guardians of the peace; however, I shall start work as soon as possible as I have other engagements immediately that I finish here. Of course I have informed the Chief Constable by letter if [of] my presence in the town but I forgot to send my card with my name and address so that He might know to call when having a desire to see me, poor dear old Bobbies how very clever they are not so clever as my humble self, hoping that you will give this publication I am Dear Sir yours Etc J. RIPPER.

Maria Coroner's address was 77 Westgrove Street and, far from having just arrived in Bradford, she had lived there for two years. By trade, she was a mantle (cloak) maker, but there is something chilling in the formality of her letters that marks her immediately as middle-class. There is nothing crude or directly threatening in the letters, but the mocking tone and the 'signature' alone were enough to send some elements of Bradford society into hysterics. The police received umpteen complaints from women afraid to go out at night and from others who had been accosted by men. All this, of course, proved illusory – 'Jack' was never in Bradford – but the level of fear can be measured nearly a century later when the 'Yorkshire Ripper', Peter Sutcliffe, began his killing spree. He killed Patricia Atkinson in the city in April 1977 and attacked another woman in the same place on 10 July. In January 1978 he murdered Yvonne Pearson in Bradford and on 2 September killed Barbara Leach. His car was seen many times in the city's red-light district as he prowled the streets looking for victims. At the time, with a kill-count (thirteen) far higher than Jack's, Bradford and neighbouring Leeds were cities under siege.

With hindsight, Coroner's letters were clearly those of a woman, but had she not been caught, it is doubtful whether that could be decided for certain. The *Bradford Citizen* noted that the letters were written on mourning paper with black borders and stated, with no scientific evidence whatsoever, that 'The handwriting was obviously that of a woman.'

The police followed a number of suspects before getting what must have been a tip-off – the papers are suitably vague about this – and Inspector Dobson and Sergeant Abbey of the city's CID visited Coroner's lodgings. Here they found stationery of the same type used for the letters and while the sergeant collected the girl from her workplace, Illingworth and Newbolt of Westgate, the inspector searched her home in a way that would be illegal today. The evidence there was incriminating – exact copies of the two letters sent to the paper and the chief constable. There were other criminal memorabilia too, proving what an oddity Maria Coroner was. There were newspaper clippings on the Whitechapel murders, an envelope addressed to the governor of Strangeways Gaol, Manchester and part of a letter dealing with the recent murder of a warder there. Most chilling of all, perhaps, was the business card, with an elegant black flower design, of James Berry, executioner. Berry was a native of Bradford, living at Bilton Place, City Road. Perhaps the first of the 'scientific' hangmen who used the height, weight and physical characteristics of his 'clients' to get the length of the drop right, he went on lecture tours and wrote an autobiography later. We can be sure that Maria Coroner would have been there, asking the man to sign the book for her. Had Jack been caught, of course, it would have been Berry who would have hanged him. As it was, he hanged Ripper suspect William Bury who confessed to being Jack in Dundee in April 1889.

Confronted by the police and the incriminating evidence, Coroner confessed that she had written the letters but was 'at a loss' (according to the *Citizen*) 'to give any reason for her foolish prank'. She then said it was all a joke and could not see that she had done anything wrong.

Denied bail, Coroner appeared at the police court on 24 October. The place was crowded, mostly with women, who no doubt wanted to see what sort of monster could claim to be a lust murderer. Her defence counsel, Mr Atkinson, challenged the charges against her. If sending letters was a breach of the common law, he said, 'I should like to see the common law; it is so common I have not seen it.' Mr Withers, for the prosecution, outlined the details of the case and demanded that the woman be bound over. Inspector Dobson reported that Coroner had written the letters 'to create a sensation and *make the newspapers sell*' [author's italics] which is a fascinating indication of the close ties between the Ripper letters generally and the press of the day. The New Journalism thrived on sensation, reported and/or printed various letters and this in turn egged on morbid oddities like Maria Coroner to keep on writing them. Atkinson said that Dobson had believed all this to be a storm in a teacup, that there was no actual breach of the peace. Perhaps if Dobson had been an officer of the Met, struggling daily to cope with the rising tide of panic in London, he might have had a different take on the matter. With appalling arrogance, when asked why Coroner had written to the *Bradford Telegraph*, Atkinson said that the court had 'no right to ask her that. There were lots of letters sent to the "Telegraph".'

In the end, the magistrates decided that the peculiar Miss Coroner was more foolish than malevolent. She was bound over for six months on her own recognizance of £20. If she did not behave, she would go to prison.

There is no doubt that the confident and attractive mantle-maker won the hearts of the old fogies on the bench. She smiled in court and found the whole proceedings rather amusing. Today, Maria Coroner would be a vicious troll on the internet, using her anonymity to cause who knows what kind of murder and mayhem. Some 200 years before the Ripper, the powers that be in Bradford would have stripped her to the waist and whipped her at the cart's tail before kicking her out of the city.

Chapter Thirteen

'Just a Few Lines ...'

In the autumn of 1888, at least 301 people wrote to the City Police with suggestions as to who the Whitechapel murderer might be and how he could be caught. As Evans and Rumbelow say in *Scotland Yard Investigates*, 'They range from the sensible to the eccentric to the apparently insane.'

Most people were perfectly willing to submit their names and addresses; several of them wrote more than once, especially if they felt their earlier correspondence had not been dealt with properly. Henry Armitage, a retired copper living in Penzance, wrote six times. Almost half of them, as is to be expected, came from London (130). Sixteen came from various states in America, with similar numbers from Bedfordshire to Kent. Australia sent six, Italy two, Ireland five, Holland three and France and Germany two each. The point of course is that the murders fascinated everybody and the world's press carried details almost as regularly as their British counterparts.

Those who were not prepared to use their real names hid behind some interesting aliases. 'Revelation' (who also gave a name, Delia Bass) was a 'see-er' who wrote on Christmas Day 1888. She had the psychic power to catch the killer and thirty-six letters carried a religious or spiritual tone. R. Barraclough's children were table-rapping in Bradford early in October and discovered that the killer was Tom Totson of 20 Wurt Street WC. The late nineteenth century was obsessed with spiritualism, although it was in something of a decline since its heyday in the 1850s. Briefly told, two teenaged sisters of the Fox family in Hydesville, New York, claimed in 1848 that they could communicate with the dead by a series of knocking sounds that formed a code. Various experts examined the girls and discovered that the sounds came from their ability to dislocate their knee joints at will. Despite this obvious fraud, the idea caught on and seances became the trendy thing among the middle classes in particular, first in France, then in Britain. Literally hundreds of spiritualist circles sprang up overnight and clairvoyants, mediums and 'sensitives' were hired to conduct conversations with the recently – or not so recently – departed.

By Jack's time, the Society for Psychical Research gave all this nonsense an air of gravity and respectable science, although to be fair to the SPR, they spent most of their time debunking the whole thing and catching the frauds. The Barracloughs' table-rapping was a variant of the Fox girls' knees and who Tom Totson was is anybody's guess. Such is the ongoing interest in Jack that there are still 'psychic' books on the Whitechapel murder in print today; for example, *Jack the Ripper: A Psychic Investigation* by Pamela Bell (Arcturus, 1998).

Mrs Melinda Bate of Friendly Street, Deptford had a 'presentiment' that there would be other murders after 13 October when she wrote, and Sarah Golding of the High Street, Lincoln had a mesmerist friend who might be able to track Jack down. Mesmerism had vague links with the spiritual movement; named after the Austrian doctor Franz Anton Mesmer (who was kicked out of various European courts as a charlatan and fraud), it was actually hypnosis. The Reverend William Harrison put his faith in dreams, years before Sigmund Freud used them for analysis purposes. He dreamed that Jack was two people, Pat Murphy and Jim Slaney, who lived at 22 Graham Street. Not to be left out of any religious take on the murders, Mary Kidgell, writing from Turin, Italy, thought the murderer might be a Buddhist, one of the mildest and least murderous faiths in existence.

In terms of motive, E. Ballon of Tenth Street, New York, believed that the killer was a religious monomaniac. This theme, which would surface again in Peter Sutcliffe in the 1980s, was commonly held. Such was the prevalence of vice in London's East End that murder, in the mind of the deranged, must seem the only solution.

In a community dominated numerically by the Jews, it was perhaps inevitable that fingers would be pointed in their direction. J.W. Causier of Yetminster, Dorset believed that Jack was part of 'a sort of minor priesthood holding a license to kill from the Chief Rabbi.' We are, here, in the dark realms of mysticism and Freemasonry apart from the nonsensical James Bond-style phraseology. 'Have the offices connected with the Great Synagogue, the one in Bevis Marks, been searched?' Causier wondered. Bevis Marks was, after all, around the corner from Mitre Square. It was precisely this sort of bigoted hounding that had prompted Charles Warren to have the Goulston Street graffito removed.

But still, the Jewish connection would not go away. Alese Brown of Caledonian Place, Aberdeen wrote to the mayor of the City of London that Jews believed that prostitutes should be put to death:

Now, a Jew, if a monomaniac, would naturally reason that he was doing according to that law, if he was clearing the streets of these unfortunates …

'Justitia' was a London Jew who believed, on 16 October, that a recent fire in Hooper Street may have been Jack burning his bloodstained clothes. Fires in the East End were not uncommon; there were two of them at London Docks on the night that Polly Nichols died, both of which drew huge crowds. 'Nemesis' from Dumfries suggested, along with many others, the use of bloodhounds, better than the much-maligned Barnaby and Burgho, and that every police officer should have one. Mrs Luckett of Somerford Grove agreed. Eight such dogs should be placed in pairs at police stations at the four compass points because clearly, Jack would never strike again in Whitechapel. He did, at least twice more. 'Nemo' ('Nobody') believed that Jack enticed his victim with the lure of sweets. The theme was taken up by 'saccharine' from West Ham who was convinced that the killer worked in a sugar factory because there was one in Hanbury Street (Annie Chapman) and Berner Street (Liz Stride). The idea may have originated from the fact that Liz's body was found with a packet of cachous (breath-fresheners) in her hand.

'Scotus' from Southampton believed, along with many writers, that Jack was a diseased medical man working at a local hospital:

My theory of the crimes is that the criminal has been badly disfigured by disease – possibly had his privy member destroyed. He is now avenging himself on the sex by these atrocities.

The disease he had in mind was phagedena, rapidly-spreading destructive ulceration associated with syphilitic sores.

The most obvious hospital was the London, along Commercial Road. The hospital was first set up as early as 1740 and moved to its present site twelve years later. A medical college was founded there in 1785 when Whitechapel still had green fields that led to Limehouse and the river. Inevitably, because of its location (only 150 yards from Buck's Row, the murder site of Polly Nichols), the institution has several links with the Ripper. Dr Thomas Barnardo worked here while setting up his home for the street urchins who slept rough in the alleyways and under arches. He met Elizabeth Stride in the days before she died and has, of course, been 'fingered' for her murder by a recent spate of Ripperologists. A patient at the London, Robert Donston

Stephenson, is another possible killer. He was in the wards in 1888, suffering from neurasthenia, a psychosomatic disorder, the chief symptom of which is fatigue. Stephenson was himself a letter-writer to the City Force. On 16 October, commenting on the cryptic chalk message left at the entrance to Wentworth Model Dwellings in Goulston Street, he wrote that the spelling 'Juwes' is actually 'juives', French. Not only was the message written by the killer, Stephenson contended, but he was giving away his nationality as well. There is, of course, no proof that either is true.

Stephenson as a Ripper suspect first emerges in the 1920s when the first books on the Whitechapel murders were being written. The problem with the man (rather like Dr Tumblety) is that he was an eccentric fantasist. The son of a mill-owner from Hull, he claimed to have studied at German universities and served as an army doctor with Garibaldi's red shirts, at the time when the hugely popular rebel general was fighting for Italian independence in the Risorgimento (1860). The census of 1861, however, has Stephenson still living in Hull with no medical qualifications at all. He claimed that in the 1860s he learned occult practices in Africa, citing examples he probably read later in H. Rider Haggard's *She*. In reality, he was fired from his Customs job in Hull, suffering from meningitis and consorting with prostitutes; either of these were 'sackable offences' in Victorian England.

Revelling in links with black magic and spiritualism, Stephenson was admitted to the London Hospital in July 1888. While there, he became convinced that the Whitechapel murderer was Dr Morgan Davies, a house surgeon at the hospital, because he retold the story of the murders to a mutual friend in a graphic way. Patients on the Curie Ward were not allowed out at any time, so the notion of Stephenson 'nipping' across to various murder sites on the nights in question seems unlikely. He went to Scotland Yard on Boxing Day to explain his case against Davies. There, Inspector Thomas Roots described him as a man who led a Bohemian life and used drugs to stave off the delirium tremens of acute alcoholism. It was in the 1890s that the novelist Mabel Collins and Baroness Vittoria Cremers became convinced, through various bizarre and not very convincing 'evidence', that Stephenson was Jack. No one seriously shares their views today.

One story that the press did not get wind of was the fact that Inspector Abberline was trying to trace three insane medical students from London in late October. If true (Major Smith of the City Force was carrying out a similar investigation), it is an example of the desperation among the police at the time. The notion that Jack was a doctor was commonly held then, but only one such student can be identified. He was the son of an Indian army surgeon who became mentally ill in 1881. By 1887, he was incarcerated in Holloway Asylum in Virginia Water, thereby eliminating him from any list of suspects.

In the context of the 'helpful' letters, 'a thinker' wrote on 3 September 1888 that the murderer probably had venereal disease. This idea surfaced from time to time in the original police enquiries and has since, most notably in the case of the fictional 'Dr Stanley'. Leonard Matters was one of the first writers on Jack and put the idea forward in *The People* newspaper in 1926. Stanley was supposedly a doctor at Charing Cross Hospital with a practice in Portman Square. His son contracted syphilis from Mary Kelly, whom he met on Boat Race night 1886. Stanley killed Mary and her friends as an act of revenge. There are so many things wrong with this theory it is difficult to know where to start. A street girl like Mary would hardly be present at what was actually an upper-class event. Syphilis that affects the brain takes far longer than two years to develop and there is no hard evidence that Jack's victims knew each other at all. Half a million people lived in the East End, so the odds are that they did not.

The ongoing problem of prostitution was highlighted in the City letters by 'A Well Wisher' appalled at the number of loose women in Brixton, about whom the police did nothing. It was just as well that the writer of 4 October called herself 'A Sane woman' or we might have thought otherwise! She had seen a suspicious-looking man in Bond Street the previous week who, being 'un-English' in appearance, might well be the Whitechapel murderer. 'Mary-Bee' from Edinburgh was convinced that the killer lived at 29 Fleet Street. 'andy-Handy' thought along similar lines. His 'Jack' lurked in Fleet Lane and on 5 November was reported as 'carrying a bag with a head and two feet in it!'

'Feather Few' had a workable suggestion that thirty-five other letter-writers agreed with and that was to dress policemen as women and give them steel collars to wear. Collars had first been suggested in the 1860s when the garrotting craze struck. Based loosely on the Indian cult of thuggee in which victims were ritually strangled with wire, street criminals took up the idea which briefly terrified everyone. While one assailant looped a noose around a victim's neck, another helped himself to wallet or purse and was gone in seconds. Since Jack's MO was strangling and throat-cutting, the steel collars made sense. The cross-dressing idea was more complicated. Since the average East End prostitute was *over-* rather than *under-*dressed (a list of the clothes worn by Kate Eddowes makes this clear), it was not so far-fetched as may first appear. In his autobiography *I Caught Crippen*, Walter

Dew remembered plainclothesmen dressed as women regularly patrolling the streets. How realistic they were is anybody's guess, but the Yard used a wide range of disguises and most senior officers set great store by them. One officer who actually did this was Detective Sergeant John Robinson of G Division. On 9 October 1888, in full female fig, he accompanied another detective (dressed as a man) following up enquiries about a possible Ripper at large in Clerkenwell. Identifying himself as a police officer, he was attacked by a cab-washer, William Jarvis, who tried to slash him with his knife. Robinson remains the only known recorded example of disguise of this type in the Ripper case.

Cross-dressing appears in another way in the letters. 'An observer' pointed out, this time to Scotland Yard, that a drag act, the Conway Brothers who performed at Dauntless Main Hall in Marylebone, certainly bore watching. Tom Conway used the alias Eliza Armstrong (the name of the little girl 'bought' by William Stead three years earlier) and in company with others, wore his female clothing off stage and at all hours of the day. 'Baby Kate', 'Esmerelda', 'Poll', 'Alice the Betrayer' and 'Madge Wildfire' were all wolves in sheep's clothing. The Bolton and Park case of the previous decade, although outraging polite society, was thrown out of court; there was actually no law against a man dressing as a woman. 'Observer' clearly had an axe to grind and the cross-dressing 'Vine Street Gang' had no links to the Whitechapel murders whatsoever.

On 9 October, 'One that has had his eyes opened' was critical of the police, especially because they were 'advertising your doings in the Papers'. While it is true that the media's reporting of the 'Dear Boss' and 'Saucy Jacky' letters achieved nothing but a wave of copy-cats, sensible, balanced reporting could be useful. The City Force did this well, but the Met, under instructions from Sir Charles Warren, gave away as little information as possible. The idea that the police acted in response to every nuance of press reportage was brilliantly lampooned by the satirical magazine *Punch* on 22 September:

A Detective's Diary à la Mode

Monday – Papers full of the latest tragedy. One of them suggested that the assassin was a man who wore a blue coat. Arrested three blue coat wearers on suspicion.

Tuesday – The blue coats proved innocent. Released. Evening journal threw out a hint that deed might have been perpetrated by a soldier. Found a small drummer boy drunk and incapable. Conveyed him to the Station House.

Wednesday – Drummer boy released. Letters of anonymous correspondent to daily journal declaring that the outrage could only have been committed by a sailor. Decoyed petty officer of Penny Steamboat on shore and suddenly arrested him.

Thursday – Petty officer allowed to go. Hint thrown out in the Correspondence column that the crime might be traceable to a lunatic. Noticed an old gentleman purchasing a copy of *Maiwa's Revenge* [a novel by H. Rider Haggard]. Seized him.

Friday – Lunatic despatched to an asylum. Anonymous letter received, denouncing local clergyman as the criminal. Took the reverend gentleman into custody.

Saturday – Eminent ecclesiastic set at liberty with an apology. Ascertain in a periodical that it is thought just possible the Police may have committed the crime themselves. At the call of duty, finished the week by arresting myself!

In fact, on 19 October, 'An accessory' went further than Saturday's entry above and named a specific ex-officer of the Met who had been dismissed. The City force was not immune either. An anonymous letter sent to Sir James Fraser contended, 'There was a man in your force, at Seething Lane for some considerable time ... When he joined, I am possitive there was a screw loose with regards a child.' Since this officer knew the Aldgate area very well, it was obvious that he was the Mitre Square killer.

'One of the public' thought, on 12 November, that the murderer was a caretaker in one of the City's many offices and two other writers specifically point their fingers at George Morris, a witness at Kate Eddowes' inquest. Morris had served as a regular soldier for four years and did two stints as a constable with the Met, finally retiring in 1882. On the night of the double event, he was nightwatchman at Kearley and Tonge's warehouse in Mitre Square and was asked by beat officer Edward Watkins (881 City) to heat up a can of tea on his stove. This was about 1.30 am. Morris left his door open and heard nothing outside until an agitated Watkins came back fifteen minutes later. 'For God's sake, mate, come and assist me!' Morris grabbed a lamp and followed the constable across the square. 'Here's a woman cut up to pieces,' Watkins said. Morris took one look at Kate's mutilated body and ran out of the square to Aldgate where he found Constable James Harvey (964 City) already running towards him, having heard Watkins' whistle. Various scraps of evidence suggest that Morris was authoritarian and unpopular (which possibly goes with a career in both the army and the Met), but it was not until 2007 that he was put forward as a possible Jack. Other than being in Mitre Square at the time, there seems no evidence against him at all.

If not Morris, how about Watkins? In the context of murderous policemen, men with the insider knowledge to beat any enquiry system, an anonymous writer from Trowbridge in Wiltshire named him as the killer of Kate Eddowes. 'Watch him,' the letter warned. It made a sort of sense to implicate Watkins in that Mitre Square was part of his beat. The route, along Duke Street, Creechurch Lane, Leadenhall Street, Mitre Street, Mitre Square and St James's Place took him fourteen minutes at the traditional speed of 2½ miles an hour. Watkins joined the Met in 1870 but transferred to the City Force the following year. There is nothing untoward or exceptional in his conduct and he retired in 1896.

'Qui Vire' ('Who grows') wrote from Liverpool on 24 July 1889, a week after the murder of 'Clay Pipe' Alice McKenzie, to suggest that the killer may be a simple man living alone, probably a butcher or a shoemaker. An unsigned letter of the previous November concurred – the murderer was a butcher living in or near Buck's Row. What is fascinating about these two letters is their accuracy and similarity to modern behavioural profiling and 'murder-mapping' techniques. In 1988, to mark the centenary of the Ripper killings, the FBI at Quantico analysed Jack from the scientific/psychological viewpoint. John Douglas, responsible for the work, came to the same conclusions – the murderer was single and a loner, able to come and go without attracting attention. The butcher theory was hardly new, but that Jack had *some* anatomical awareness cannot be denied. If we assume that Polly Nichols was the first of Jack's victims (personally, I believe it was Martha Tabram), then the close proximity of Butcher's Row (now Vallance Road) to Buck's Row (now Durward Street) fits absolutely the geoprofiling of today's 'murder-mappers'; a serial killer will strike first close to his home because he knows the area so well. Only with subsequent attacks, emboldened by his success, will he venture further afield.

And there were even more realistic attempts to plot Jack's movements. The *Pall Mall Gazette* published a map of Whitechapel soon after the double event with all the murder sites marked, including those of Emma Smith and Martha Tabram. At that stage, the sixth victim, Kate Eddowes, had yet to be identified. A modern geoprofiler can read a lot into a map like this but 'Observer', writing to the *Daily Telegraph* on 1 October, believed that the murder sites formed the shape of a dagger. Although this is a huge red herring, William Dickinson of 27 Zetland Street, South Bromley, wrote to Inspector McWilliam of the City Force with a map of his own which included Jack's likely escape routes, something that modern geoprofilers still do. The murderer, Dickinson was sure, lived near Chicksand Street Board School (schools overlook many of the murder sites) and he was following press accounts closely. He was a local, who was well-known to the women of the area, so he would arouse no suspicion whatsoever.

Major General E.R.C. Wilcox of Ashburnham Road, Bedford named Thomas Conway and his brother as the murderers. Conway was the common-law husband of Kate Eddowes and had served as a private in the 18th Foot (the Royal Irish) where he used the surname Quinn. He had lived with Kate in her native Wolverhampton since 1864 and the couple had three children. He wrote chap-books which he sold to the public on street corners. By 1880, the marriage had broken down, she being over-fond of drink and Conway given to wife-beating. They had been separated for some time by the date of Kate's death. But the major general's motivation is bizarre. He describes Conway as 'missing' (he had left Kate in 1881) and suggested that the husband was an impostor, pretending to be the real Conway in order to draw his army pension. He killed Kate because she could identify the original.

Staying with the military theme, one of the oddest letters was a 'dead' one, i.e. a letter that could not be delivered because the addressee did not live there. Her name was Jane Bromley but the letter itself was from a man to his son, an army officer. The father believed that 'General Brown is the Whitechapel murderer'. The official sources hint that nobody knew quite what to do with this and it was passed around Whitehall like a hot potato. Charles Warren confirmed that General Brown had been interviewed and that, because he operated on horses for racing, this horrified a passing lady who 'jumped to the conclusion that he would not shirk at anything'. As with so many examples of hysterical reactions, it is difficult to explain the leap of logic from a horse castrator to the Whitechapel murderer. Incidentally, there were two General Browns in the army at the time. This one is not likely to have been the national hero, a VC who invented the Sam Browne belt, because cutting up women with only one arm would have been very difficult!

Six letter-writers suggested that science should come to the aid of the police, but only one got it right. Five suggested that the dead women's eyes be photographed in the morgue as there was a widely-held belief that the last thing seen by the living victim would be Jack, suitably close up with knife in hand like an unbelievably clear CCTV image! There is a rumour that this was actually done in the case of Kate Eddowes, with the obviously disappointing result.

The only one that made sense was an unsigned letter sent on 2 October, suggesting that a thumbprint be taken from the 'Saucy Jacky' postcard to catch the sender, presumed by many at the time to be the murderer. Although fingerprinting was known to the Chinese centuries earlier, used on official documents, in the West only a handful of scientists paid any attention to it. William Herschel used the technique in India and Francis Galton took up the study seriously. Interestingly, five years before the Whitechapel murders, the American writer Mark Twain's *Life on the Mississippi* had a chapter called 'A Thumb Print and what Became of It'. Galton's work would not appear until 1892, however, and it was not until 1901 that Assistant Commissioner Edward Henry introduced a comprehensive system at Scotland Yard. Although each fingerprint is unique in its pattern of loops and whorls, it is of course only useful if such prints can be matched against a particular suspect. In 1888, this was impossible.

Many of the 'helpful' letters talk of generic medical culprits, butchers and slaughtermen and of course anyone who looked foreign *and* suspicious was fair game in the xenophobic Britain of the 1880s. There are, however, twenty-six individuals who are listed by name as potential Jacks, apart from the Conways and George Morris referred to above. No doubt much of this was malicious; a chance to make life difficult for someone by subjecting them to police and/or press scrutiny. Sarah Fremlin of Maidstone blamed 60-year-old John Davis, a retired doctor down on his luck, partially because he was known locally as Jack! James Malcom was a hotel guest, bigamist and butcher, according to John S. Gordon of Bridge Street, Aberdeen; it stood to reason that he was the Whitechapel murderer as well. Dr Sass or Sassy sounded foreign enough to interest N. Hollander of Kensington, especially since the man was a surgeon.

'M.P.' and Mrs Luckett, of whom we have heard before, had probably been to the Lyceum Theatre to see *The Strange Case of Dr Jekyll and Mr Hyde* which ran from 4 August to 29 September 1888. Its star was the American actor Richard Mansfield, who, despite the terrifying portrayal, was running the tour at a loss and was never as popular in Britain as he was in New York and Boston. 'M.P.' wrote:

Now these Horrible Murders are being Committed, I think it the
duty of Everyone to let the Police know if they Suspect anyone ...
When I went to see Mr Mansfield Take the Part of Dr Jekel and Mr
Hyde I felt at once that he was the Man Wanted.

His speed of make-up change, 'M.P.' believed, would mean that the actor
could disappear in any disguise he chose. The City Police did not agree and
there was no follow-up. Mrs Luckett, however, went further. Conscious that
Mansfield was merely playing a role, she enquired about the play's author.
In a letter to London's mayoress, Lady de Keyser, she asked, 'Is he a capable
or likely individual to be the perpetrator of dire offences?' Since he was
Robert Louis Stevenson, this is possibly the first example of what is now an
international pastime: putting celebrities in the frame for the Whitechapel
murders.

Two letters in October, one from A. Blandy, Chief Constable of the
Berkshire Constabulary, refer to the same incident – the 'strange story of
the cabman's shelter'. This was well covered in the London and provincial
papers early in the month and was investigated – and dismissed – by
Inspector Abberline of the Yard. Cabman Thomas Ryan told the story of
a stranger who shared a meal with him and other cabbies in their shelter
in Bayswater, London on the day after the 'double event'. Inevitably, the
conversation turned on the killings and the stranger, recently returned
from India, confessed to the murders. Since all the cabbies (bizarrely) were
teetotallers, the rest of the conversation was all about the perils of the demon
drink and the stranger, clearly under the influence, ended up signing a
ledger – 'the pledge' as it was known – in which he wrote 'J Duncan, doctor,
residence Cabman's Shelter 30th Sept. 1888'. Various Home Office papers
show that Duncan had two convictions for assaults on women in Newcastle
(where he admitted he lived before going to India) and that his real name was
George Donkin. He was 28, 5ft 8in tall, had an old wound on his left cheek
and had been born in Morpeth, Tyne and Wear. Abberline, in his interview
with 'Donkin' concluded that his real name was John Davidson, that he
could not have been the Newcastle assailant and that he could account for
his movements on the night of the 'double event'. It is interesting, however,
that the second letter from Captain St G. Rathbone of Reading claims that
he met 'Duncan' in Bombay while serving there. It is not clear how the
Duncan/Donkin/Davidson confusion came about, but it is a good reminder
of how complex the police enquiries were and how the slightest rumour
could lead to hours of official enquiry. Just to add more complications to

an already tortuous tale, J. Trustram of Harpenden, Hertfordshire believed the cabman's doctor to be Dr MacDonald who had escaped from Leavesden Asylum the previous year.

Edward Smith of Upper Grange Road was convinced, at the same time as the cabmen's shelter story, that the murderer was Professor Reynolds, an 'electre biologist' (whatever that was) who also went by the name of Andrade. Contrary to today's psychological profiling, which implies that Jack was a Whitechapel local of the same social class as the women he killed, the idea of a rather exotic intellectual, no doubt complete with cape and top hat, had a wide appeal even then. Smith believed that Reynolds/Andrade 'put the poor pesons [victims] under his influence while speaking to them'. This, no doubt, would explain the lack of screams in all the attacks except, arguably, that on Mary Kelly. He had seen Reynolds/Andrade, who may have been two different people, lecturing on the theme of electre biology at various London halls. Since he thought that Andrade was a part-time stallholder in the Metropolitan Meat Market, it not only gave him a working knowledge of the area but access to sharp knives and a rough knowledge of anatomy into the bargain.

W.J. Smith offered two possible Jacks from his home in Red Lion Passage, Holborn. He was either a Hungarian (the usual xenophobic approach) or he was a Mr MacSweeney, but the story was more complicated than that. Smith was shaken by recent events. Bloody Sunday of the previous year and now a series of atrocities by a maniac who evaded the police like a will o' the wisp led him to believe that the whole thing was a political attempt to demoralize the police force, pressurizing Salisbury's Conservative government to resign and bring in Gladstone and his Liberals, which would ruin the Empire and achieve the Liberals' goal of a Republic; 'God Forbid!' The catalyst for all this was a Hungarian anarchist who was a radical book importer with an antipathy to both Jews and women. A number of other people were involved, connected to the Hungarian club opposite the British Museum, one of whom was Mr MacSweeney, who was educated as a doctor at University College Hospital and, having lived for a while in America, called people 'Boss'. At a stroke, Smith had ticked all the boxes of motivation. Bomb-planting dynamitards, be they Irishmen or Middle Europeans, were anathema to right-thinking Englishmen. The Whitechapel murderer was clearly a doctor and he used Americanisms in his letters to press and police. Smith clearly chose to ignore the fact that the Liberals had no leanings towards Republicanism at all. In fact, Gladstone was intensely fond of and loyal to the queen, even if she could not stand him!

William Onions was altogether more likely. The unsigned letter of 13 November said that he was 'late of Colney Hatch and Wakefield Asylums'. In an earlier book I wrote on the Thames Torso murders, there is a chapter called 'Men Behaving Madly'. There seems to be an extraordinary preponderance of disturbed people, mostly male, in the area at the time, usually referred to in official parlance as 'a lunatic wandering at large'. This is because of police procedure and general thinking at the time. 'Experts' like Dr Havelock Ellis who wrote *The Criminal* in 1890, believed that criminal types could be identified by facial characteristics. The Italian criminologist Cesare Lombroso agreed. The 'habitual homicide' (Victorian-speak for serial killer) had eyes that were 'glassy, cold and fixed; his nose is often aquiline, reminding one of a bird of prey … the jaws are strong; the ears long; the cheek-bones large; the hair dark, curling and abundant; the beard often thin; the canine teeth much developed; the lips thin …' More than that, Jack would have a weak chest, heart disease and probably genital peculiarity.

A watered-down version of this would have passed down to the Met and City beat coppers who would be on the lookout for a dribbling, wild-eyed lunatic. This explains the arrest of so many of them. So Aaron Davis Cohen, who may have been the Whitechapel suspect favoured by Dr Robert Anderson, Assistant Commissioner at Scotland Yard, was constantly being picked up by the police, sent to asylums and released. Rather abruptly, the official line in various reports on him is 'Single; Tailor; Insane; Hebrew'. Thomas Hayne Cutbush was another. He prodded women's bustles with a knife and wandered the Whitechapel streets at night. Jacob Isenschmid was the 'mad pork butcher' of Holloway, blood-stained because of his trade and behaving oddly; he ended up in Colney Hatch. Joseph Isaacs, interrogated by Abberline, threatened women and was heard pacing around his room on the night that Mary Kelly was killed. Oswald Puckeridge threatened women too and Sir Charles Warren mentions him as a suspect in a letter to Evelyn Ruggles-Brise, private secretary to Henry Matthews at the Home Office. Puckeridge was a chemist (not a surgeon, as Warren supposed) who had been released from an asylum in Shoreditch on 4 August. The police failed to find him. Charles Ludwig, Aaron Kosminksi, William Piggott; the list goes on. All of these men and, no doubt, many more were disturbed and disturbing but not one of them could be linked with the Whitechapel murders. Onions was simply one in a long line.

Mixing all kinds of stereotypes, R.C.N. from Bristol wrote in on 6 October that Jack was an American doctor called Sequah who dressed as a cowboy. We have the commonly-held medical link, Jack as a foreigner, as well as links with Buffalo Bill's Wild West Show, hugely popular with British audiences. The idea of a cowboy walking unnoticed through the streets of Whitechapel is laughable. 'Sequah' appears twice, in slightly different contexts, in the letters. R.C.N.'s letter describes him as fitting the description given to the police by Matthew Packer, of a man seen with Liz Stride on the night she died. He had long hair, stood 5ft 7in and was in his late twenties. On 3 October, however, John S. Gordon of Aberdeen wrote to Charles Warren in connection with 'a Dr Hartly, here selling a patent medicine named Sequah or Indian medicine'. It seems extraordinary that the same man, with an American connection, should be operating in two cities far apart within three days. On the other hand, I am surprised that no one has made a link with Dr George Sequeira, who was called to view Kate Eddowes' body in Mitre Square. His name appeared in the press the day before the 'Sequah' letters were sent.

The alienist Dr Stewart Lyttleton Forbes Winslow holds a unique place in this chapter as being both a correspondent and a suspect. Writing from his home address in Wimpole Street, he telegraphed the City Force offering his expert services on 2 October, when the capital was still reeling from the 'double event'. The very next day, C.J. Denny, medical officer for the Hartley Wintney Union Rural Sanitary Authority of Farnborough, Hants, accused him of the murders as he 'has a peculiar mind and one who is possibly suffering from incipient form of insanity himself, wd go to any lengths to prove his case'. Forbes Winslow believed, not unreasonably, that the murderer was a 'homicidal lunatic'. Since he ran an asylum himself and was an ardent campaigner for the reform of lunacy laws, we can assume he was in the position of a true expert, as opposed to many writers who were not. After the discovery of the Pinchin Street torso in December 1889, Forbes Winslow gave an interview to the London office of the *New York Herald*. In it, he made the extraordinary assertion that not only were the torso killer and the Whitechapel murderer one and the same (the media had always believed this; the police had not), but that he lodged in the area, had disappeared suddenly after Pinchin Street and had left behind a pair of rubber-soled, bloodstained boots, which Forbes Winslow had in his possession. 'I know for a fact,' the *Herald* quoted the doctor, 'that this man is suffering from a violent form of religious mania' and that he had an accomplice.

On 23 September, Chief Inspector Donald Swanson, in charge at the 'desk' end of the Ripper enquiries, interviewed Forbes Winslow at his home. The doctor claimed he had been misquoted by the *Herald*'s reporter but told Swanson that he believed the murderer was a Canadian, G. Wentworth Bell

Smith, who lodged with friends, Mr and Mrs Callaghan of Finsbury Square. Bell Smith kept odd hours, often returning to his rented room in the early hours of the morning. He was appalled by the scale of prostitution in London, believing that 'low women' should be drowned in the Thames. He wrote long religious tracts, had blood-stained clothing and boots (which Forbes Winslow showed to Swanson) and kept three loaded revolvers in a chest. He was 5ft 10in tall, had a peculiar splay-footed gait and well-trimmed beard. His teeth were probably false and he spoke several languages. Bell Smith worked for the Toronto Trust Society and planned to spend several months in London working for them. His peculiar behaviour led Mr Callaghan to report him to the police, but neither Swanson nor Abberline could find any record of this. The *Penny Illustrated Paper* at least regarded Forbes Winslow as an irritating nuisance in that he was constantly writing articles. In a spoof letter from Robert Anderson to Major Henry Smith, Acting Commissioner of the City Police, the *Penny Illustrated* wrote, 'Keep to Ripper stories and the worse you will do will be to make Dr Forbes Winslow rush into print.'

Forbes Winslow, in his *Recollections of Forty Years* (1910) reproduced a letter he had received from 22 Hammersmith Road, Chelsea. It was dated 19 October 1889, by which time the Whitechapel murders seemed to have ceased, but it has been altered to 1888, possibly by Winslow himself:

> Sir, I defy you to find out who has done the Whitechapel murder in the Summer not the last one You had better look out for yourself or else Jack the R may do you something in your house to before the end of Dec mind now the 5th of Nov there may be another murder so look out old mr Sir pluril fonk funk Tell all London another ripper open will take place someone told me about the 8th or 9 of Proximo not in Whitechapel but in London perhaps in Clapham or at the West End Write to the Poste Restante Charing X address to PSR tonigt.

The handwriting is dystrophic, with one commentator believing that 'tonigt' is actually 'Luigi'. If the 1889 date is correct, the summer murder refers to Alice McKenzie (19 July) and the 'last one' to the Pinchin Street torso (8 September). Bearing in mind that Forbes Winslow ran an asylum, this letter has all the hallmarks of one of his disturbed patients. Hammersmith Road, incidentally, is not in Chelsea.

There is a curious reference to 'old funk' and Hammersmith Road in the bizarre four-page poem sent to Scotland Yard on 8 November 1889. Although

Forbes Winslow was constantly in the limelight, the Hammersmith Road letter was not published until 1910. The writer of the poem was probably the author of the first letter too. 'Funk stupid Fool, believes me to be insane.' There are references to his dark good looks and his boots that Old Funk has got. And he contends, 'the letter addressed to 22 Hammersmith Road was written by some vulgar toad.' Interestingly, in the context of Jack as a top-hatted toff which for so long has hampered a real understanding of the case, he writes:

> Old Funk thinks me a flashaway swell
> A first rate man and in a fine house I dwell.
> A fourpenny doss I have at a Common East End Doss House
> And do not dine on aristocratic grouse.

Not to be outdone, Florence Forbes Winslow, wife of the above, also rushed into print in a letter to the City Force on 26 October. Jack, she knew, lived in North London and she saw him getting on a train! Men behaving badly on trains have a history nearly as old as the railways. At least two murderers, Percy Lefroy and Frederick Mueller, had killed victims in railway carriages and Colonel Valentine Baker of the 10th Hussars had tried to force himself onto a young woman in 1876. Mrs Forbes Winslow, clearly as obsessed with Jack as her husband, quoted a woman terrified in a carriage on 25 October by a man with the already ubiquitous top hat and Gladstone bag.

There again, George West of Hereford alleged, the killer of Mary Kelly may be Mad Jack Ryan. With a name like that, how could it be anyone else? No wonder the police got nowhere.

One or two of the City letters are definitely weird. The murderer escaped through the sewers, wrote Fred Allinson of Plaistow, and indeed there was – and still is – a labyrinth of tunnels under London's streets known to only a few. Josiah Boys of Commercial Street had seen a message from Jack written on a wall of toilets in the Guildhall. Jack was an Irishman, specifically Charles Stuart Parnell, leader of the Irish Party in the Commons. He was also a South African, a Spaniard and a German.

On 6 October, an article appeared in the *Telegraph* about a Malay cook with the unusual name of Alaska. The same story, with suitable American embellishments, appeared in the *New York Times*. A sailor named Dodge had met the Malay who claimed he had been robbed by Whitechapel whores and promised to mutilate and murder as many as he could. He carried a large knife to prove his point. As with the Portuguese cattlemen fingered by

Edward Larkins, there seems to be little more than xenophobia attached to this tale. John Binney, who wrote to the City Police, believed the whole thing to be a red herring. 'Alaska' was almost certainly a corruption of 'a lascar', the lowest Indian caste.

P.C. of Queen's Park had a cunning scheme to trace the killer by finding out who was reading Ripper-related articles in the newspapers! William Gow of Argyll, Perthshire believed that the body parts removed from some victims were being used as amulets by the Hill tribes of India. L.C. Ingham from West Vale near Halifax wanted a lock of a victim's hair or item of clothing 'worn close to the skin'. Mrs Painter of the Strand, Ryde, Isle of Wight had no doubt been reading too much Edgar Allen Poe; the murderer, she contended, could be an ape – 'There are wild animals in London. The animal would be swift,' Mrs Painter was sure, 'Cunning, noiseless and strong ... disappearing in a moment, hiding its weapon perhaps high up in a tree [in Whitechapel?] and returning home to shut itself up in its cage.'

There is no doubt as to the oddity of one of the City writers, the Swedish traveller Nikaner Benelius. He wrote from Goswell Road, London on 18 October asking to meet the Lord Mayor. He also wanted to meet two young ladies 'at the same cathedral' (St Paul's?). He preached in the streets and was interviewed by both Constable Walter Dew and Inspector Edmund Reid, especially over Liz Stride's murder. He was harmless, if paranoid, and was arrested in November for illegally entering a lady's house and grinning at her!

One name that is missing from any of the letters relating to the Ripper case is one that will not go away, that of the artist Walter Richard Sickert. Born in Germany of German-Danish and English parents, Sickert's family moved to England in 1868 to avoid the conscription which was the norm in the states that would become a united Germany three years later. He attended King's College School in Wimbledon and the Slade School of Art. Intriguingly, in the context of the Ripper letters, he spent four years as 'Mr Nemo' ('Nobody') in Henry Irving's theatrical troupe. He worked as assistant to James McNeill Whistler and Edgar Degas and in 1885 married Ellen, the daughter of the radical Richard Cobden MP, champion of free trade in the 1850s and '60s. He became notorious for his womanizing on both sides of the Channel, having a house in Dieppe where, importantly, he was living during most of the period covered by the Whitechapel murders.

Outside art circles, Sickert was virtually unknown before being put in the frame by journalist Stephen Knight in his 1976 nonsense *Jack the Ripper: The Final Solution*. To simplify an impossibly tortuous story, Knight met artist and portrait-painter Joseph Gorman, who claimed to be Sickert's grandson. Since Sickert is not known to have fathered a child this seems unlikely, but the journalist in Knight knew a good story when he found one and his subsequent research (sloppy and assumptive to say the least) 'uncovered' the scandal of the 'highest in the land'. Unwilling to accept far more humdrum – and likely – explanations as to why the police did not catch Jack, Knight concluded that there was a cover-up of huge proportions.

Sickert, said Knight, was engaged by the royal family to teach fine arts to Prince Albert Victor, the Duke of Clarence, heir to the throne and grandson of Queen Victoria. The artist had a studio in the East End and on one of his visits there, 'Eddie' as Clarence was known in the family, met and fell in love with a street girl, Annie Crook, who worked in a local florist's shop. The pair had a child, Alice, who, had history travelled down the other trouser-leg of time, might one day have become queen of England. The existing queen was horrified. Unlike today, the prospect of a commoner as part of the royal family simply could not be allowed to happen. In desperation, Victoria turned to her trusted advisor, the Physician-in-Ordinary, Sir William Gull, and his solution was to silence Annie Crook forever. Using a coachman, John Netley, to drive him to Whitechapel and with Sickert as a guide, Gull, a secret Mason and maniac, found Annie, had her incarcerated in his private asylum and then proceeded to butcher a number of street women, either to cover up the fact that Mary Kelly was a friend and accomplice of Annie or that all the women were. John Netley then spent years trying to find – and kill – little Alice; without success, hence the later existence of Joseph Gorman, Alice's son.

Gripping fiction though this is – it has been the plot of several Ripper movies – nothing about it makes sense and there is no hard evidence for any of it. But Sickert became lodged in the canon of Ripperology and the story was taken up in various formats by Melvyn Fairclough in *The Ripper and the Royals* (1991) and allegedly corroborated by Florence Pash who was a sponsor and possible lover of Sickert. There is actually nothing in the way of a Ripper connection in the manuscript of the unpublished book on Sickert's letters which Florence was working on with Violet Overton Fuller.

Enter novelist and forensic scientist Patricia Cornwell. She met John Grieve, deputy assistant commissioner at the Met, who believed that Sickert was worthy of further research. Ms Cornwell discovered a hatred of women in Sickert's art, not noticed by art experts and certainly not borne out by the artist's colourful love life. She attributed this hatred to a physical problem – a penile fistula – which made intercourse impossible. The problem with this theory is that the surgeon who carried out an operation on Sickert in St Mark's Hospital, Dr Alfred Cooper, worked on the far more common *anal* fistula; and once again, Sickert's supposed problem does not square with his numerous affairs.

Ms Cornwell annoyed the Ripper community with her book *Portrait of a Killer* by having *Case Closed* as a subtitle. In the world of Ripperology, that is a bold statement to make and few people were convinced by it. Although the subsequent edition softened the tone a little, Ms Cornwell still clings to Sickert as a likely Ripper. Is it possible that he at least wrote two of the letters?

The first clue lies in the use of paper. Paper historian Peter Bower, much respected in this particular line of research, found that two of the Ripper letters matched some newly-produced stationery used by Sickert in three of his other letters. This paper came from a batch of twenty-four sheets produced by Leppard and Smith, with a Gurney Ivory Laid watermark. This makes it possible, perhaps even probable, that Sickert was a Ripper letter-writer, but that, of course, does not make him the Whitechapel murderer. In fact, in 1888, from Sickert's other letters, we know that he was using a different type of paper from earlier and later examples.

The other line of research that Ms Cornwell followed was DNA. Checking Sickert's known correspondence with Ripper letters, she discovered similarities on the stamp used on the letter sent to Dr Thomas Openshaw, curator of the Pathology Museum in London referred to in the next chapter. Unfortunately, Ms Cornwell's research relies on the limited data provided by mitochondrial DNA. While these results are shared by only 1 per cent of the population, that still means that 40,000 people in London alone could have licked that stamp. Further research in 2006 by Professor Ian Trilby, using more sophisticated techniques, indicated that the sender, along with Maria Coroner et al, was probably female.

So, *Portrait of a Killer: Jack the Ripper: Case Still Wide Open*!

Chapter Fourteen

The Signs of the Zodiac

W ere any of the Ripper letters actually written by the Whitechapel murderer? As we have seen, Patricia Cornwell believes that at least two of them were written by Walter Sickert, who also, she contends, killed women in the East End. Frank Spiering in *Prince Jack* believes that the 'Dear Boss' letter and the 'Saucy Jacky' postcard that followed it were penned by the misogynist J.K. Stephen, tutor and mentor to Prince Albert Victor, the central character in the now discredited 'highest in the land' theory.

To attempt to answer the question above, can we learn anything from other times and other crimes? One of Jack's contemporaries was Thomas Neill Cream, born in Glasgow in May 1850. In common with many families in impoverished Scotland, the Creams moved to Canada when the boy was 5. At first joining his father in the lumber business, he enrolled in McGill College, Montreal, and quickly gained a reputation as a flash student, dressing expensively and driving a carriage and pair. He qualified as a doctor in 1876, having delivered a lecture on 'the Evils of Malpractice in the Medical Profession'. He soon practised this for real. His first victim may have been his first wife, Flora, who was dead by August 1877. Her death certificate read 'consumption' and Cream pocketed $200 of insurance money with which he went to London.

As a post-graduate medical student, he joined St Thomas's Hospital but failed his exams the first term, qualifying only on the re-take. He was back in Canada a month later and a girl who worked at a local hotel was found dead in a privy with a bottle of chloroform by her side. Cream was carrying out abortions by this time and the girl was one of his clients. He left Canada in a hurry and went to Chicago. Up to his old ways again, Cream murdered two more women and sent his first blackmailing letter to Frank Pyatt, the pharmacist who had made up the prescription for Miss Stack, his second Chicago victim. He next murdered Daniel Stott, using the man's epilepsy as a cover and took the widow, Julia Stott, as his mistress. Once again, Cream took to letter-writing, this time pointing the finger to the district attorney at the pharmacist who made up Stott's medicine. Caught on the run in Canada, he was found guilty of murder in the second degree and was sentenced to life in Joliet Prison. Astonishingly for someone guilty of such a premeditated crime, Cream's sentence was reduced to seventeen years and then still less for good behaviour. He was free by July 1891 and sailed for Liverpool on board the *Teutonic*. For those who cling to the nonsense that Cream was Jack the Ripper, a prison stretch in Joliet makes a pretty watertight alibi!

In October of 1891, Cream embarked on a series of murders of prostitutes, all younger and prettier than the Whitechapel victims. Ellen Donworth died on the 13th; Matilda Clover a week later. In April 1892, after a few weeks in Canada, he killed Alice Marsh and Emma Shrivell. Strychnine was used in all cases and Cream stood trial for murder at the Old Bailey on Monday, 17 October 1892.

The letters that Cream wrote were not of the 'Ripper' type, with their boastfulness and threats. He wrote them for a specific purpose, either to lure his victims to a rendezvous or to smear somebody else and lead the police in the wrong direction. The first one he wrote to Eliza Masters, asking her to meet him, and he specifically told her to keep the letter because he wanted it back later. Eliza tore it up anyway. Instead of keeping his date with Eliza, Cream targeted Matilda Clover. He wrote her a letter too.

At the end of November 1891, Cream wrote to Dr Broadbent, an eminent physician, under the name of M. Malone. It was effectively a blackmail threat: 'Malone's' detectives had uncovered the fact that Broadbent had caused Matilda's death and £2,500 would make the problem go away. Correspondence was to take place by the *Daily Chronicle*'s first page. 'I am not humbugging you,' he wrote. 'I have evidence to ruin you for ever.' In fact, the evidence damned Cream – he mentioned strychnine as the cause of death and only Matilda's murderer could have known that. He persistently made the same mistake with references to his other victims.

Typical of serial killers who cannot stay out of cases they themselves have created, Cream, posing as a private detective, A. O'Brien, wrote to G.P. Wyatt, East Surrey's deputy coroner, on 19 October offering his services in the murder of Ellen Donworth. For that, he expected the government to pay £300,000!

Not content with pointing a finger at Broadbent over Matilda's murder, he tried the same letter tactic with Frederick Smith of the Strand. This time, he called himself H. Bayne and had found two letters from Smith in Matilda's lodgings soon after her death – 'I can save you if you retain me in time, but not otherwise.' On 25 April, Cream wrote to Dr Harper of Basingstoke with the tragic news that his son, a medical student at St Thomas's, was responsible for the murders of Alice Marsh and Emma Shrivell – 'If you do not answer me at once, I am going to give evidence to the Coroner.' This time it was signed W.H. Murray. At the time, the defence did not contest the fact that the handwriting was Cream's and they also acknowledged the watermark on the paper – Farfield Superfine Quality – which was an American brand not on sale in Britain. The graphologist employed by the prosecution was Walter de Grey Birch who had worked in the Manuscripts Department of the British Museum for twenty-seven years. He attested that Cream had written them all, although he denied it at first, and the various letters were shown to the jury. The only exceptions were a series of blackmail notes written at Cream's dictation to Laura Sabbatini, a secretary who testified in court.

In summing up, defence counsel pointed to Cream's habitual drug addiction, implying that the content and tone of the letters were the result of this and had no links with reality at all. The Crown made relatively little of the letters, other than to remind the jury that they constituted powerful evidence of guilt.

Judge Henry Hawkins, known, unfortunately for Cream, as 'hanging Hawkins' pointed up the letters and even read the one to Dr Broadbent to the jury during his own summing-up. The jury took just ten minutes to find Cream guilty. He had nothing to say before the black cap was placed on Hawkins' head, as the judge intoned the usual grim words 'And may the Lord have mercy on your soul'.

The *Chicago Tribune* was on to Cream years before he met the executioner. On 19 June 1881, the paper accused Cream of sending 'the vilest sort of postal cards through the mails'. Such an offence carried a fine of up to $500 or ten years in prison. The letters' recipient was a fur trader, Joseph Martin, who Cream insisted owed him $20. Martin denied this and was horrified to receive the postcards claiming that Martin's family were all suffering from a disease that had come from him. 'I will learn that damned vixen of a low wife of yours,' Cream ranted, 'to speak ill of me.' He also accused Martin of abandoning a bastard child in England.

'This thing,' said the *Tribune*, 'of sending scurrilous postal cards though the mails and thereby attempting to blacken the reputation of people, has gone far enough.' Judging by the tiny number of such court cases in Britain over the Ripper letters, it is clear that the authorities here were less perturbed than their American counterparts.

***

But the world had changed considerably by August 1969, especially in California. This was an extraordinary time in American culture; a brave new world of the young, personified by the West Coast and hippies who opposed the Vietnam War and wore flowers in their hair. Under the surface, however, there was a darker side.

On 8 August, the 'family' of Charles Manson attacked the occupants of 10050 Cielo Drive, killing the caretaker, Steven Parent, then torturing and murdering the others: 'Voytek' Frykowski, 'Gibby' (Abigail) Folger, Jay Sebring, and the actress Sharon Tate and her unborn baby. Manson's supporters were there, they said, 'to do the devil's business'.

But if the case brought about a media frenzy in America (which it did), a killer of an altogether different kind was already operating in the San Francisco Bay area around Vallejo and Napa Valley. On 20 December 1968, 17-year-old David Faraday and his 16-year-old girlfriend Betty Lou Jensen were sitting in Faraday's mother's Rambler station wagon off the Lake Herman Road, Vallejo, arms around each other, on their first date. A solitary figure emerged from the darkness and fired a .22 pistol into the boy's head. Betty Lou screamed and ran from the car but fell as five bullets hit her in the back, killing her outright.

Investigating policemen interviewed the couple's families and friends, focusing on jealousy among teens as the most likely motive. As weeks and months went by, interest in the case waned and enquiries got nowhere.

On 4 July 1969, while America was enjoying a national holiday for its Independence Day celebrations, Michael Mageau, 19, and his 22-year-old girlfriend, waitress Darlene Ferrin, were sitting in their car in the Blue Rock Springs Golf Course car park in Vallejo. They were suddenly blinded by a flashing torchlight and a lone gunman fired two shots into the car with a 9mm pistol. Darlene died instantly, but Mageau survived, despite four bullet wounds. All he could remember of the assailant was that he was heavy-set and wore glasses.

At 12.40 am the Vallejo Police Department took an anonymous phone call. A gruff, probably disguised voice said: 'I just shot the two kids at the public park. With a 9 millimetre automatic. I also killed those kids last Christmas [Faraday and Jensen].'

On 1 August, just a week before the Manson family's spree, letters were sent to both San Francisco's daily papers, the *Chronicle* and the *Examiner*, and to the *Vallejo Times-Herald*. They were nearly identical, in clear, unjoined letters, coherent but with occasional spelling errors. One third of each was in the form of a cryptogram. Since the writer described the gun, the position of the bodies and the clothing worn by Darlene Ferrin, the cryptic letters had to come from the killer. The letters insisted that the papers publish them or there would be a killing spree of the type Vallejo had never seen. The symbol on the letters was a circle divided by a cross: the sign of the zodiac.

Unlike Neill Cream, whose letters were cunning, self-serving and limited in terms of publicity, the Vallejo murderer craved the limelight. Not only did all these papers publish his letters, they gave him a *nom de mort* nearly as reverberating as Jack the Ripper: the Zodiac Killer. More letters followed, especially via the *Examiner*. In what would become his last letter for the moment, Zodiac wrote that solving the cryptogram would solve the case. Experts were called in and failed.

> 'This is the Zodiac speaking,' the killer wrote, 'Up to the end of Oct I have killed 7 people. I have grown rather angry with the police for their telling lies about me. So I shall change the way the collecting of slaves [victims]. I shall no longer announce to anyone, when I commit my murders, they shall look like routine robberies, killings of anger and a few fake accidents, etc. the police shall never catch me because I am too clever for them.
> 1. I look like the description passed out only when I do my thing, [killing] the rest of the time I look entirely different. I shall not tell you what my descise [*sic*] consists of when I kill.
> 2. As of yet I have left no fingerprints behind me contrary to what the police say.
> I thought you would need a good laugh before you hear the bad news you won't get the news for a while yet.
> PS Could you print this cipher on your front page? I get awfully lonely when I am ignored, so lonely I could do my Thing!!!!!!'

Despite its similarity to several of the Ripper letters from 1888–91, there is a lot that is different about the Zodiac. The fact that the syntax is generally sound makes his spelling mistakes ('descise' for disguise, for example) all the more obvious as a weak ploy to evade detection. Unlike Jack or any of 'his' letter-writers, the Zodiac had to be aware of fingerprint analysis, both at crime scenes and on the letters. His threat to disguise future murders is genuinely terrifying. Jack himself was a *lustmorderer*. He *always* killed one social class by means of strangulation, throat-cutting and mutilation. The

Zodiac was about to undergo a transformation very unusual in serial killers and his targets would change too.

In the meantime, a Salinas high school teacher and his wife (both amateurs) beat the code of the cryptogram. It read:

> I like killing people because it is more fun than killing wild game in the forest because man is the most dangerous animal of all to kill something gives me the most thrilling experience.
>
> The best part of it [is] when I die I will be reborn in paradice and all the I have killed will become my slaves. I will not give you my name because you will trs to sloi down or stop my collecting of slaves for my afterlife.

In terms of motivation, at least one expert read into this signs of sexual inadequacy, perhaps impotence. After all, the victims were courting couples. The notion of slaves and paradise, however, went far beyond that; and why, even in a cryptogram, maintain the peculiar spelling mistakes?

True to his word, the Zodiac struck again, this time on 27 September at a picnic spot at Lake Berryessa in Napa County. Gone was the furtive night attack: this time the killer hit his targets in broad daylight. He wore a square-cut hood with a zodiac logo and forced the couple – Bryan Hartnell, 20 and Cecelia Shepard, 22 – out of their white sports car before tying them up. Although he was brandishing a gun, the Zodiac now used a knife, stabbing Hartnell six times. He saved his greatest ferocity, however, for Cecelia, driving his blade twenty-three times into her body in the rough shape of a cross. Then he went back to the car and wrote on the door: 'Vallejo 12 – 20-68/ Sept 27 – 69 6.30 by knife'.

Thirteen days later, he struck again. This was a high-risk killing and the first to involve a single victim. Paul Stine, 29, was a part-time cab driver working on a PhD and he picked up the wrong passenger. In Cherry Street, Presidio Heights in San Francisco, the Zodiac ordered the car to stop and he shot Stine dead. He tore the driver's bloody shirt off and took it with him, the first trophy he had removed from a victim. He got away on foot but was seen by three teenagers who called the police. The killer was aged between 20 and 25, with an auburn crew-cut and thick glasses. Police enquiries got nowhere on this, although they could now attribute another killing – presumably one of the seven that he boasted about – to the Zodiac.

Night attacks, day attacks, couples, a singleton, guns and knives. Panic spread throughout the Bay area; nobody was safe. The next day, the *Chronicle* received another Zodiac letter, accompanied by a piece of Paul Stine's bloody shirt. 'Schoolchildren make nice targets,' the letter read. 'I think I shall wipe out a school bus some morning. Just shoot out the tyres, then pick off the kiddies as they come bouncing out.' This scenario became part of the script of Clint Eastwood's noir thriller *Dirty Harry*, in which Andy Robinson gave an unforgettable performance as a lunatic serial killer calling himself Scorpio and writing warning letters to the mayor.

Ten days later, the Zodiac made another phone call, this time to Oakland Police Station, saying that he would give himself up if he could be represented by celebrity lawyers F. Lee Bailey and Melvin Belli. He also wanted air-time on an early-morning talk show. Astonishingly, no doubt in the hope of catching him, this was agreed to, but talk-show host Jim Dunbar waited in vain for his arrival. During the show, a phone call came through from a soft, boyish voice who said he was the Zodiac. He called back fifteen times, each time too briefly for the call to be traced, and talked to Melvin Belli about the headaches he suffered from. No one who had survived the Zodiac's attacks recognized the voice at all. Belli received a letter in the Zodiac's writing two months later, claiming eight victims with a ninth to follow soon.

In March 1971, the Los Angeles *Times* heard from him again:

> If the blue meanises are ever going to catch me, they had better get off their fat asses and so something … The reason I am writing to the *Times* is this, they dont bury me on the back pages like some of the others.

Several books on the Zodiac interpret 'blue meanises' to mean menaces, i.e. the police force hunting him. Equally, however, it could be a reference to the Blue Meanies, the music-hating monsters of the Beatles' psychedelic animation feature, *Yellow Submarine*. By 1974, the Zodiac had written again to the police, now claiming thirty-seven victims. This could have been bravado, but bearing in mind his promise to disguise his work as robberies gone wrong or even accidents, we have to wonder if the body count, over a three-year period, might not be accurate. Nothing more was heard from the Zodiac killer.

Over the Zodiac's ten-month reign of terror, more than 2,500 suspects were interviewed by the police. The most likely, Arthur Leigh Allen, died in August 1992. His DNA was taken and bore no match to the cryptic letters that were the killer's hallmark.

***

While the Zodiac earned widespread notoriety, John Linley Frazier has vanished without trace. In 1970, he murdered Dr Victor Ohta and the four members of his family for a cause. Those who see a 'noble' motive in Jack's crimes, for example, highlighting the economic and social misery of the East End in 1888, use Frazier as an example. An early advocate of 'green', he left a typed note promising death to all who ruined the environment.

Firemen found Ohta's house blazing and the five members of the family all dead in the swimming pool. The youngest was Taggart, aged 11. Ohta's secretary, Dorothy Cadwallader, was there too. All of them had been hit, execution-style, with a bullet to the back of the head. A note left under the windscreen-wipers of Ohta's Rolls Royce read:

Halloe'en 1970 [the murders took place on 19 October] Today World War III will begin, as brought to you by the people of the Free Universe. From this day forward, anyone and/or company of persons who misuses the natural environment or destroys same will suffer the penalty of death by the people of the Free Universe. I and my comrades from this day forth will fight until death or freedom against anyone who does not support natural life on this planet. Materialism must die or mankind will stop.

The letter was signed, with more than a hint to the Tarot pack, 'Knight of Wards – Knight of Pentacles – Knight of Cups – Knight of Swords'.

Mrs Ohta's station wagon had been abandoned on a railway track in a tunnel near the San Lorenzo River. A goods train hit it, but there was no derailment or injury to the train's passengers.

This was northern California and the area was still reeling from the Manson murders and the Zodiac. The summer of love had long ago turned to bitterness and hippies were given a rough time by the police. The 'people of the Free Universe' boiled down to one 24-year-old drop-out, separated from his wife and working as a car mechanic. High on mescaline, he joined a hippy community in Felton and developed a hatred of materialism before targeting the Ohtas as a successful middle-class family – all the things John Frazier hated. Although he denied everything when the police arrested him, an eyewitness saw him driving Mrs Ohta's station wagon after the murder and his fingerprints were all over the Rolls Royce and inside the partially burned-out house.

The irony was that Ohta himself was hardly an uncaring member of the bourgeoisie. The son of poor Japanese immigrants who were interned as a matter of routine by the American government in 1941, he enlisted in the US army where an older brother was killed. He worked as a track-layer after the war while studying medicine, specializing in eye surgery. He not only sponsored the hospital where he worked, but often treated poor patients for nothing.

Although Frazier's letter-writing was confined to one brief note, it spoke volumes as to his mindset and his own particular need to kill:

> Because Craig is Craig so must the streets be filled with Craig (Death) and huge drops of lead poured down upon her head until she was dead.
> Yet, the cats still come out at night to mate
> And the sparrows still sing in the morning.

***

The '.44 Caliber Killer' was first known to the media because of the weapon he used for murder, but when David Berkowitz began to add taunting letters to his career, the media changed their minds and followed his lead – 'I am deeply hurt by your calling me a wemon [*sic*] hater. I am not. I am the "Son of Sam".'

In the world of American youth culture, the drug-fuelled late sixties had all but vanished by the middle of the next decade, especially in grimy old New York, a world away from the flower people of the West Coast. Disco fever was all the rage, glitterballs twirled overhead and everyone wore big hair and platform shoes.

Donna Lauria, 18, and Jody Valenti, a year older, were sitting in Jody's Oldsmobile in Buhre Avenue, the Bronx, on 29 July 1976. America was in a bubbly mood, celebrating that month 200 years of freedom from the British Empire. The girls were out late; it was one in the morning and Donna's parents, on their way back from a wake, spoke to them briefly before retiring for the night in their apartment not far from where the car was parked. They had not long been inside when shots rang out in the street below. Their daughter was dead and Jody was wounded and screaming hysterically, thumping the car's horn to attract attention. They were the third and fourth victims – although Donna was the first to die – of a pudgy postal worker who was born in June 1953. The future Son of Sam was the child of Betty Broder and Joseph Klineman and within days of his birth, he was given out for adoption by Pearl and Nathan Berkowitz of the Bronx. Richard became

David Berkowitz. A moody, difficult child, he was fascinated with fire, one of the classic 'triad' psychoses of many serial killers, the other two being late bed-wetting and animal cruelty. He served in the US army between 1971 and '74 and he tracked down his birth mother, which psychiatrists would later claim contributed to his problems. He saw himself as discarded and worthless.

His first attack took place on Christmas Eve 1975 when he stabbed Michelle Forman and a friend. He was never in the frame for this and moved to Yonkers soon afterwards. The attack seven months later that led to Donna Lauria's death proved that Berkowitz had now gravitated to a gun rather than a knife (this 'learning curve' is common to serial killers but it rarely manifests itself in a change of weapon). Jody Valenti described the shooter as white, male, about 5ft 9in tall and weighing about 160lb. He drove a distinctive yellow car.

While police enquiries were under way by New York's finest, Berkowitz struck again. Donna DeMasi, 16, was chatting to 18-year-old Joanne Lomino on the stoop outside the girls' apartment in Bellerose, Queens. A man in military camos asked them directions in a high squeaky voice but had not finished his sentence before he opened fire, his .44 wounding them both. Joanne would be crippled for the rest of her life.

Berkowitz was back to vehicle targets by 30 January 1977 when he opened fire on Christine Freund, 26, and her fiancé, 30-year-old John Diel, in Forest Hills, Queens. They had just been to see Sylvester Stallone's hit movie *Rocky* and were on their way to a dance. The girl died in hospital hours later, having been shot twice, while the wounded Diel drove away in a panic. By this time, the shootings were being linked. Young couples, two of them in cars, and all female victims had long, dark wavy hair. All the bullets came from a .44. At this stage, however, police believed they were looking for more than one killer, possibly a copycat. For example, the victimology was suspiciously similar to the Zodiac three years earlier.

Virginia Voskerichian was 19 and lived a block away from Christine Freund. On the evening of 8 March 1977, she was walking home from the library of Columbia University and was shot in the head. Eyewitnesses saw a 'chubby teenager' running away from the scene. The press was having a field day, with daily bulletins that saw the *New York Post* and *Daily News* circulation figures rocket. Even the foreign press used these stories, from the USSR's *Izvestia* to the Vatican's *L'Osservatore Romano*. None of this, or the frantic police work behind the scenes, saved the lives of Alexander Esau, 20, and Valentina Suriani, 18, who were killed in Valentina's car in the

Bronx. Now the 'chubby teenager' was regarded as a witness and an older, dark-haired man was the suspect. Since the killings had all happened in a relatively tight area, it stood to reason that the murderer was a local man, but 'murder-mapping' was at best an infant science in 1977 and no conclusions were reached.

But there was a new twist in the Esau-Suriani murders; a note, written in block capitals and left at the scene for Captain Joseph Borrelli of the NYPD. Once this was released to the press, the signature 'Son of Sam' became nearly as infamous as Jack the Ripper.

'I am the "Son of Sam",' the letter went. 'I am a little "brat".' The writer blamed his violence on a drunken father who abused him and ordered him to kill. He had buried his victims' bodies in their back garden and he himself watched the world go by from his locked attic room. It read like a B feature horror movie script, except that there were some lines that rang grimly true:

> I feel like an outsider. I am on a different wave length than everybody else – programmed too kill …
> I am the 'Monster' – 'Beelzebub' – the 'Chubby Behemoth'. I love to hunt. Prowling the streets looking for fair game – tasty meat.

And he had a word of warning for the police:

> Let me haunt you with these words; I'll be back! I'll be back! To be interpreted as – bang, bang, bang, bang – ugh!! Yours in murder, Mr Monster.

There was one phrase in the letter that took Borelli's detectives in the wrong direction: 'me hoot [heart] it hurts sonny boy', which they assumed was Scots dialect. Two of the victims were medical trainees, proving how easy it is to read too much into letters like Sam's. The point was that the letter was all about control: the victims, the police, the inhabitants of Queens, even the media, were all now dancing to the Son of Sam's tune and he loved it. It was exactly the same motivation that could be attributed to the Ripper letter-writers. The psychological profile the police drew up in May 1977 talked of neurosis, paranoid schizophrenia and even demonic possession; Sam was not actually the killer's father at all, but the devil.

At the end of May, another letter appeared, this time addressed to Jimmy Breslin, a journalist with the *Daily News*. By the 1970s, arguably television was a more powerful media outlet than newspapers but the bulletins and chat shows could be relied upon to give ample coverage to events like this. The Son of Sam sent his greeting to Breslin from the gutters, sewers and sidewalk cracks of New York. He thanked the journalist for taking such an interest (rather as Maria Coroner had written her letters, she claimed, to boost newspaper sales) and he was clearly lying when he said, 'I don't care for publicity.' In a line taken directly from innumerable 'Dear Boss' letters, he wrote 'I love my work' and urged people not to forget what a dear, sweet girl Donna Lauria was. He then gave himself four different aliases, either to confuse or as a mirror of his schizoid mind. He also claimed to be a rapist and suffocater of young girls, which was totally untrue.

The letter was articulate and there were well-executed graphics with it, prompting the police to check the DC Comics studio to see if anyone recognized the handwriting or art style. NYPD detectives even watched Robin Hardy's *The Wicker Man*, starring Christopher Lee, since one of the letter's aliases was the 'Wicked King Wicker'. When the *Daily News* published portions of the letter on its front page, sales rocketed to 1.1 million copies and, as with the 'helpful' letters sent to the City Force in 1888, NYPD was inundated with theories and suspects that led precisely nowhere.

On 26 June the Son of Sam struck again, shooting but failing to kill Sal Lupo, 20, and Judy Placido, 17, as they sat in their car in Bayside, Queens. They had been talking about the murders only moments earlier. Witnesses identified two possible shooters, one blond, the other dark, and a partial licence plate number.

The last shooting took place on 31 July and followed the by now territorial pattern. Stacy Moskowitz and Robert Violante, both 20, were shot in their car in Bath Beach, Brooklyn. Queens was in lock-down, but Berkowitz was wise to that and struck elsewhere. Moskowitz was killed, but Violante survived, albeit virtually blind as a result of the gunshot to the head. Umpteen witnesses described the killer, wearing a wig and driving a yellow Volkswagen and several rang NYPD's Son of Sam hotline. Berkowitz was operating in an alien part of the city and his sang-froid probably deserted him as a result. Road-blocks were quickly set up and hundreds of motorists questioned.

On 10 August, police finally closed in on Berkowitz. He drove a yellow Ford Galaxy and there was a rifle in the back, together with maps showing various crime scenes and a letter in Son of Sam style addressed to Inspector Timothy Dowd of the Task Force. Detective John Falotico held his gun to Berkowitz's head and said:

'Now that I've got you, who have I got?'
'I'm Sam,' Berkowitz said.
'You're Sam? Sam who?'
'Sam. David Berkowitz.'

The mayor later announced: 'The people of the City of New York can rest easy because of the fact that the police have captured a man whom they believe to be the Son of Sam.'

Berkowitz confessed in less than half an hour during a police interview. 'Sam' was Sam Carr, a neighbour, and his black Labrador was the demon who demanded blood. Interestingly, this was the year in which David Seltzer's *The Omen* stunned cinema-goers with its demonic Rottweilers. Astonishingly, the killer was allowed to write to the press and warned of other 'Sams' 'God help the world'. Serial killers are usually loners and derive a bizarre comfort from the belief that they are part of a community.

David Berkowitz, for all his murders and the warped sentiments expressed in his writings, was declared fit to stand trial and on 12 June 1978 was sentenced to twenty-five years to life for each murder, to be served consecutively. In June 2005, one of his lawyers, Hugo Hamatz, was sued by the killer when he tried to write a biography based on the Son of Sam letters. There was a settlement out of court and all the money went to the victims' families.

***

Mugshots never bring out the best in people. Theodore John Kaczynski is no exception. His hair is long and wild, his beard straggly and greying. Only his eyes are chilling and dead. For seventeen years, he was the Unabomber and he held a doctorate in mathematics from the University of Michigan. In the photograph taken soon after his arrest, he could easily pass for any of the 'lunatics wandering at large' in Whitechapel in 1888.

Kaczynski was born in Chicago and graduated from Harvard in 1962. In 1967, he became assistant professor of mathematics at Berkley but two years later suddenly left to live as a recluse in a log cabin in Lincoln, Montana. A friend described him as a loner, 'an old man before his time' who was set apart from his peers by his IQ of 167 and passion for figures. He remained aloof and isolated throughout his time at Harvard but was perfectly friendly on a one-to-one basis. In Montana, he tried to live a self-sufficient lifestyle in a decade when survivalism and the 'good life' were deemed important to that particular generation. It was while he was there, brooding and introverted, that he developed a hatred for the property-developers who were, in his eyes, ruining the wilderness.

'From that point on,' he said later in an interview, '... I would work on getting back at the system. Revenge.' The only way to stop increasing technology was to destroy it and ironically he used technology itself to do so. 'Ted' posted his first bomb to a professor of materials engineering at Northwestern University in May 1978. It was a pipe bomb and damaged the hand of the university's security officer who opened the package. Minor cuts and bruises were the result a year later when a graduate student at the same university fell for the same sub-standard gadgetry. In November 1979, Kaczynski turned his attention to airlines, targeting American Airlines Flight 444 from Chicago to Washington DC. The twelve passengers on board were terrified by an explosion in mid-flight, but smoke inhalation was the only result. Between 1980 and 1995, individuals at various universities and the Boeing Company were sent bombs through the post. The first death was that of Hugh Scrutton, a computer store owner, in Sacramento, California in December 1985. The second was that of Thomas J. Mosser, an advertising executive in North Caddwell, New Jersey. The third and last was a timber industry lobbyist, Gilbert Brent Murray, again in Sacramento.

Kaczynski, now labelled the 'Unabomber' because he targeted universities and airlines, began writing to the media in April 1995. The FBI was on his case and there was a $1 million reward for information leading to a conviction. He demanded that the *New York Times* publish his 35,000-word thesis *Industrial Society and its Future*. He promised to end his reign of terror if this was done. The *New York Times* and the *Washington Post* published the work; the titillation magazine *Penthouse* was rejected by Kaczynski as not being reputable enough. As with Berkowitz and Frazier, the letters to the press spoke of 'we', as though the Unabomber was merely part of a larger, and therefore more deadly, force. Idiosyncrasies of spelling made it clear that the letters were the work of Ted alone. Experts generally agreed that they were the work of 'neither a genius nor a maniac' and that the anti-technology views were held quite commonly in society. If the writer were a madman, said Professor James Q. Wilson of Harvard MIT, so were Jean-Jacques Rousseau, Tom Paine and Karl Marx. Perhaps not the wisest of comparisons! Others could not fault the writer's logic, but universally condemned his use of violence to make his point.

In fact, Kaczynski had been writing diatribes to newspapers since the 1970s and his own family became suspicious of him as a result. By now, the

FBI was fully aware of the links with 'murder-mapping' and believed that the bomber came from Chicago (his birthplace, as it turned out) and had links with both Salt Lake City and San Francisco. They were right on all counts.

Copycat letters appeared almost at once after publication and the FBI and local law enforcement were kept frantically busy sifting through hoaxes without number. But it was the linguistics comparisons between the thesis and the letters that led to the Unabomber's arrest, by the FBI, on 3 April 1996. In the Lincoln cabin, they found bomb parts, 40,000 pages of handwritten journals and one live bomb, ready for the post.

Bizarrely, after the arrest, the media linked Kaczynski with the Zodiac killings, although there was no similarity either in handwriting or content. Declared fit to stand trial, the former maths professor pleaded guilty to all charges and was given a life sentence without the chance of parole. In 2012, when routinely approached by the Harvard Alumni Association for the fiftieth reunion of the class of 1962, he listed his occupation as 'prisoner'.

***

We have already discussed the case of Peter Sutcliffe, dubbed the 'Yorkshire Ripper' by the press. In 1981, the lorry driver was convicted of murdering thirteen women and the attempted murder of seven others. Unlike the Unabomber and Frazier, Sutcliffe's motivation involved sex. In that sense, he is closer to Jack than any other killer in this chapter. But Sutcliffe wrote nothing to the police or the media. What interests us is the tape recording sent by 'Wearside Jack' to the West Yorkshire police investigating the case.

The Yorkshire Ripper's handiwork attracted *huge* media publicity and the local police were criticized, not unreasonably, for mishandling the situation. To be fair to them, neither DNA nor computer technology was available to them. Files were still maintained on paper and cross-referencing took weeks to finalize. In that sense, Assistant Chief Constable George Oldfield was not much further forward than Charles Warren, James Monro or Robert Anderson and their shoe-box filing system of 1888.

On 8 March 1978, Oldfield received a letter:

> Dear Sir
> I am sorry I cannot give my name for obvious reasons. I am the Ripper. I've been dubbed a maniac by the Press but not by you, you call me clever and I am. You and your mates have a clue that photo

in the paper gives me fits [shades of 'Dear Boss' again] and that bit about killing myself, no chance. I've got things to do. My purpose to rid the streets of them sluts. My one regret is that young lassie McDonald [a 16-year-old shop assistant, unlike the other victims, not a prostitute] did not know cause changed routine that night. Up to number 8 now you say 7 but remember Preston '75 get about you know. You were right I travel a bit. You probably look for me in Sunderland, don't bother, I am not daft, just posted letter there one of my trips. Not a bad place compared with Chapeltown and Manningham [the murder sites] and other places. Warn whores to keep off streets cause I feel it coming on again.
  Sorry about young lassie
  Yours respectfully,
  Jack the Ripper
  Might write again later I not sure last one really deserved it. Whores getting younger each time. Old slut next time I hope. Huddersfield never again, too small close call last one.

The police took this letter seriously, although everything in it could have been gleaned from the extensive media coverage. 'Preston '75' came as a surprise and in 2011, thanks to DNA technology, the murder of Joan Harrison there was attributed to Christopher Smith. In one respect, however, the writer had made a salient point. Unlike the original Jack, who killed on foot yards from his home and 'lair', the Yorkshire Ripper could travel far and wide. As a long-distance lorry driver, Peter Sutcliffe knew the roads, major and minor, like the back of his hand. He got to all his murder sites by car.

  Fifteen months later, after two more letters, both postmarked Sunderland, and with no breakthrough in the case, George Oldfield received a tape cassette. A dull, matter-of-fact voice said, in a Wearside accent:

  I'm Jack. I see you are still having no luck catching me. I have the greatest respect for you, George, but Lord! You are no nearer catching me now than four years ago when I started. I reckon your boys are letting you down, George. They can't be much good, can they?

The technology had changed, but the same taunts had been delivered to the police in London ninety-one years earlier in the original Jack's time. At the end of the tape, a piece of Andrew Gold's *Thank You for Being a*

Friend was played. The FBI, consulted because of their obvious expertise, assured Oldfield that this was a hoax, but the Sunderland postmarks on the letters and the accent convinced the West Yorkshire force that it was genuine.

Voice analysts, using the rather arcane science of dialectology, decided that the sender of the tape came from the Castletown area of Sunderland. A Dial-the-Ripper hotline was set up, similar to the one for the Unabomber and not unlike the 1888 newspapers printing the 'Dear Boss' letter. If, then, the handwriting could have been identified, the voice recognized, perhaps some headway would be made. The publicity campaign cost £1 million, apart from the police overtime involved in interviewing 40,000 innocent men in the Sunderland area. The satirical magazine *Private Eye* could not help joining in the national ridicule of the West Yorkshire police. Its stop press read 'Ripper – I am a woman' and claimed that another tape had been received in which '[the Ripper] claims, in a strong Irish accent, to be leader of the Liberal Party'.

Sutcliffe, from Bradford, across the Pennines and 78 miles from Sunderland, killed three more women after the tape was received. He was eventually arrested in his car with a prostitute (one of the luckiest women in the country at the time) and charged accordingly. George Oldfield himself became a victim of Sutcliffe in a way. Worn out and ill, he took early retirement and died in 1985.

The case of the hoaxer was closed in 2003 but two years later, a technological breakthrough was made on a small piece of gummed seal from the tape's envelope. DNA analysis linked to a routine drunk and disorderly conviction put John Samuel Humble in the frame. He admitted to both the letters and the tape, facing trial in January 2006 for perverting the course of justice. It was clear that Humble was an alcoholic but that defence did not work and 'Wearside Jack' was sentenced to eight years in gaol in March of that year. He was released three years later, but even with that latitude, Humble's experience makes us realize just how lightly Maria Coroner and co. had got off 118 years earlier.

Chapter Fifteen

The Lusk Letter

Neill Cream, the Zodiac, John Frazier, David Berkowitz, Ted Kaczynski and John Humble all wrote letters to the press and/or police. All but Humble were serial killers whose motives varied. All wanted publicity, either to boast or to frighten or to highlight a cause. Some of them used phrases very similar to the Ripper letters, perhaps because all of them had access to at least some of them by way of newspapers, books and libraries. Ripperology did not exist in Cream's time but by the 1970s, it had become an industry.

Earlier writers on the Whitechapel murders assumed, as did sections of the press and police at the time, that most if not all the Ripper letters were penned by the killer himself. Some modern 'experts' still cling to this. Patricia Cornwell, in her 2002 *Portrait of a Killer*, wrote, 'It is obvious that the actual Ripper wrote far more of the Ripper letters than he has ever been credited with. In fact, I believe he wrote most of them.' Determined to lay the murders at Walter Sickert's door, Ms Cornwell attributes various examples of possible art in the letters as the painter disguising his skill, just as he disguised his handwriting. Sickert's Ts, Ss and Ws, she contends, are written differently in various correspondence, so making her point. Could the writer have disguised his writing by tilting the paper or using the 'other' hand? Of course, but it brings us no closer to Jack.

Sue Iremonger, document-researcher, believes that several letters in the Scotland Yard files were written in the same hand as the 'Dear Boss' original. If this is so, all it tells us is that journalists Best or Bulling were working harder than was thought, not that the writer was Jack.

But the Lusk letter is different. We know that George Akin Lusk was president and chairman of the Whitechapel Vigilance Committee set up at the Crown pub, Mile End Road, on 10 September 1888. As such, he received a considerable amount of publicity, partly because it raised awareness of the Ripper's existence and partly, I suspect, because Lusk enjoyed the limelight. He styled himself 'builder and decorator', specializing in restoration of music halls, and no doubt the attention he received would help in that respect.

What he did not welcome, I also suspect, was the letter and parcel that arrived on 16 October 1888. It read:

> From hell
> Mr Lusk
> Sor
> I send you half the Kidne I took from one woman presarved it for you tother piece I fried and ate it was very nise I may send you the bloody knif that took it out if you only wate a whil longer
> signed Catch me when
> you can
> Mishter Lusk

This letter no longer exists. It was passed to Scotland Yard from whose archive it vanished. A photograph of the original has also been lost. Chief Inspector Swanson transcribed it in a report on 6 November which he sent to the Home Office. The 'from hell' address has been hijacked by Alan Moore in his graphic novel of 1999 and by Albert Hughes in his film of the same name which starred Johnny Depp and was released in 2001. 'Sor' and 'Mishter' may be attempts at cod Irish, echoing the primal fears of the Fenians we have discussed elsewhere. Interestingly, there is no mention of Jack or the Ripper and the chilling contents hint at that most taboo of human aberrations: cannibalism. In the Weimar Republic of 1920s Germany, Fritz Haarmann ate portions of the fifty boys he killed and sold the rest as beef in a street market. Georg Grossmann killed young girls and made them into sausages. In America, the sadomasochistic Albert Fish raped, murdered and stewed 12-year-old Grace Budd, writing one of the most sick 'confession' letters ever written to the girl's mother. Jeffrey Dahmer undoubtedly ate body parts of his victims, keeping them in his fridge and freezer for the purpose. Andrei Chikatilo, the 'Mad Beast' of Russia, killed an estimated fifty-two child victims in the 1980s, eating their genitals.

Against revolting examples such as these, Jack almost appears normal! It is only the Lusk letter that mentions cannibalism and the kidney referred to was believed to belong to Kate Eddowes. All of this could be dismissed as macabre lunacy or a sick joke gone too far, were it not for one thing. With the letter, in a 3in-square cardboard box wrapped in brown paper was a human kidney. Suddenly, contemporaries who had already written off the Ripper letters as hoaxes had to sit up and take notice.

October was a quiet month for the Whitechapel murderer but it was a busy one for the writers of hoax letters. As early as 17 September, the first ever letter said 'Lusk can look forever he'll never find me but I am rite under his nose all the time.' This was signed 'Catch Me If You Can' and had a similar chaotic handwriting style to the 'From hell' correspondence. Lusk had only been part of the Vigilance Committee for a week by this time and his press appearances were still minimal. It is likely therefore that the writer knew him personally and was indeed 'rite under his nose'.

On 12 October, Lusk received his first letter. It carried a Kilburn postmark and read:

> I write you a letter in black ink, as I have no more of the right stuff, I think you are all asleep in Scotland Yard with your bloodhounds, as I will show you tomorrow night (Saturday) I am going to do a double event, but not in Whitechapel. Got rather too warm there. Had to shift. No more till you hear me again. Jack the Ripper.

This was followed by a postcard:

> Say Boss –
> You seem rare frightened, guess I'd like to give you fits, but can't stop time enough to let you box of toys play copper games with me, but hope to see you when I don't need to hurry too much.
>   Goodbye, Boss.

'Box of toys' is defined by the slang expert Eric Partridge as Cockney rhyming slang for noise, but the sense here is of boys. Various contemporary accounts claim that Lusk regarded all this as the work of pranksters, especially after 27 September when he petitioned the queen to grant rewards for information leading to the killer's arrest. Inevitably, the press ran with this, even printing the man's address in Alderney Road.

On 15 October, it looked as though the writer was indeed going to meet the builder face-to-face. Miss Emily Marsh was working in her father's leatherware shop in 218 Jubilee Street, Mile End when a tall, scruffy-looking clergyman came in, pointed to one of Lusk's reward posters in the window and asked Emily whether she knew Lusk's address. Suspicious, but probably mollified by the dog-collar, she referred the visitor to Joseph Aarons, landlord of the Crown at Number 74 and fellow member of the Vigilance Committee. The clergyman seemed less than happy with that, so

Miss Marsh found a recent newspaper that gave Lusk's address, but no house number. The visitor wrote it down in a notebook and left. Emily sent John Cormack, the shop boy, to follow him, but the clergyman merely walked past the Crown and did not try to find Lusk's house either. She described the man later to the police as 6ft tall with a dark beard and moustache and an Irish accent. We have already noted the alarm that Fenian terrorism caused in the capital and the 'Irishisms' of the Lusk letter rang bells when all this scattered information was put together.

Lusk himself had seen a similar-looking man hanging around his house. He told an inspector from Bethnal Green that the man was 5ft 9in tall, with an unkempt beard and moustache, a dent on the bridge of his nose, a florid complexion, wide nostrils, sunken eyes and a deerstalker hat. He also had a broken left boot, a rusty-coloured frock coat and a round-ended cane. Either Lusk was a *very* good observer of passing people or he was describing someone he actually knew, rather like George Hutchinson's over-detailed account of the man he saw talking to Mary Kelly on the night she died.

Henry Labouchère's newspaper *Truth* wrote days before this, on 11 October, re the letters generally, 'The handwriting is remarkably like that of the forgeries which *The Times* published and which they ascribed to Mr Parnell …' Charles Stewart Parnell was the colourful MP who led the Irish bloc in the Commons. The letters referred to were forged by a journalist, Henry Pigott, in an attempt to discredit him. Continuing with the anti-Irish theme, the *Daily Telegraph* referred to Lusk's demands for rewards 'which would convince the poor and humble residents of the East End that the government authorities are as much anxious to avenge the blood of these unfortunate victims as they were the assassination of Lord Cavendish and Mr Burke.' These two had been ambushed and murdered by Fenian terrorists in Phoenix Park, Dublin in May 1882, causing outrage across the country.

The details of the Lusk package are notoriously difficult to pin down. Various papers at the time give slightly different reports and later memoirs cloud the issue still further. The most likely sequence of events is as follows. Lusk received the cardboard box, kidney and letter on 16 October, meaning that it was probably posted on the 15th. The postmark was barely legible but it implied the East End and had two 1d stamps on it. It had not been sent by the usual parcel post and was too big to fit into a conventional post box. The only two Post Offices with larger boxes were at Lombard Street and Gracechurch Street, so it may have been posted in either of those. Alternatively, it could have been handed to a postman direct.

Lusk's first reaction was that the kidney belonged to a sheep – Smithfield meat market was not far away – and he regarded it as a joke. That night, however, in consultation with Aarons, Lewis and Reeves of the Vigilance Committee, it was decided to take it to Dr Frederick Wiles of 56 Mile End Road for an expert opinion. He was not in, but his assistant, F.S. Reed, did the honours. He concluded that the kidney was human and had been preserved in spirits of wine. However, he needed a second opinion and the expertise of Dr Thomas Openshaw, curator of the Pathological Museum at the London Hospital.

Aarons returned to the Vigilance Committee to say that Openshaw believed the kidney to be human, female, specifically the left kidney and that it had been removed from a body within the last three weeks. He also said that it was 'ginny', in other words belonging to a woman who was an alcoholic. Everything except the time scale pointed to Kate Eddowes as its original 'owner'. The 'double event' during which Kate died had taken place six weeks before Openshaw examined the kidney.

Lusk then took the letter and kidney to Leman Street police station, where Inspector Abberline took charge. He forwarded the kidney to Inspector James McWilliam of the City Force (since technically, the Mitre Square murder fell within their jurisdiction) and the letter to Scotland Yard. Here it was photographed and sent by Chief Inspector Swanson to the City Force where it was again photographed and the original sent back to the Yard. This distribution of evidence belies a view that was once common among Ripperologists, that the two police forces did not co-operate. On the contrary, Swanson and McWilliam now met daily to discuss developments. To add a third medical opinion, the kidney was examined by Dr Frederick Brown, the highly-capable City Police surgeon who had made such a thorough job of the murder scene and post mortem of Kate Eddowes. He, too, believed that the kidney was human.

On the surface, it looks as though there was agreement on the medical front, especially when two other doctors were consulted, most notably Dr Henry Sutton, a colleague of Sir William Gull, who was senior surgeon and lecturer in physical anatomy at the London Hospital. He stated that the kidney had been placed in spirits within hours of its removal so could not have come, as some people thought, from a student helping himself to the organ from a dissecting room. If the kidney came from Eddowes, the logic ran, then the letter was written by her killer.

So far, so good, but all was not what it seemed. On 29 October, Openshaw, now of course prominent in the news, received a letter in handwriting very similar to that sent to Lusk. It read:

Old Boss you was rite it was the left kidney I was going to hopperate again close to your ospitle just as I was goin to dror mi nife along of er bloomin throte them cusses of coppers spoilt the game but I guess i wil be on the job soon and will send you another bit of innerds, Jack the Ripper.

And there was a curious PS:

O have you seen the devle
with his mikerscope and scalpel
a lookin at a kidney
with a slide cocked up.

There were a number of anomalies about this letter. It was full of inconsistent spellings, with very unsubtle 'Cockneyisms' of the type that Charles Dickens used when trying to create working-class characters. Why, for example, was 'ospitle' spelled that way when the address on the envelope (in the same handwriting) spelled it correctly? 'Pathological' and 'curator' are accurate too. Clearly, the writer was determined that the letter should arrive at the right place and the missive itself was designed to confuse.

Interviewed by the *Star*, Openshaw denied that he had made such bold claims about the kidney to Aarons and Lusk. He could not say that it was specifically the left kidney or that it was female, and there was nothing about it to suggest alcoholism. There was much discussion about Bright's disease (nephritis) in which William Gull and Henry Sutton were experts, and although the kidney was pale, alcohol does not affect the kidneys in this way, only the liver.

Doctors still differ over this. Richard Whittington Egan, one of the doyens of Ripperology and perhaps the only one with dissection experience, believed that Kate Eddowes' kidney was removed by accident and the murderer had no anatomical knowledge. Nick Warren, on the other hand, as a practising surgeon, believes the reverse; the kidney is difficult to locate from the front and Brown's detailed inquest report says that it had been 'carefully' extracted. There was argument too over a portion of the renal artery still attached to the kidney. Major Henry Smith of the City Force wrote in his 1910 memoirs *From Constable to Commissioner* that two inches of the artery still remained in Kate Eddowes' body and that one inch was attached to the Lusk kidney. Dr Brown maintained at the time that there was no renal artery attached, so the likelihood is that Smith got his facts wrong more than twenty years later.

Both Patricia Cornwell and Professor Ian Findlay of the Gribbles Molecular Science forensic lab in Brisbane tested the Openshaw letter. Findlay, using a DNA technique 100 times more reliable than the team working for Ms Cornwell, believed the stamp to have been licked by a woman, muddying the waters still further.

So what are we left with? Graphologist Patricia Marne finds both the Lusk and Openshaw letters to be

> completely chaotic in form and erratic in rhythm. The long downstrokes to his small g and y are a sign of aggression, the periodic pressure reveals anger with emotional instability, leading to violent mood variation. The pointed t bars with their symbols of knives or daggers in the cross bar and their sharpening points indicate, and are symbolic of, the murder weapons used to mutilate victims.

We have already noted that graphology is an imprecise science. In fact, looking at the Lusk and Openshaw letters side by side – as they are in Patricia Marne's book – it is not at all clear that they were written by the same person.

Given the medical variance over the authenticity of the kidney, there seems to be only one conclusion, at least as far as the Openshaw letter is concerned. The PS gives the game away. Evans and Skinner, in their work on the letters *From Hell*, give a possible source for this: a Cornish folktale published in 1871:

> Here's to the devil
> With his wooden pick and shovel
> Digging tin by the bushel
> With his tail cock'd up!

But the important thing about the Openshaw version is the mention of microscope (however badly spelled), scalpel and, above all, slide. Only a scientist would know that slides (glass plates) were used with a microscope in 1888, so the Openshaw letter at least was probably the work of a medical student, infamous at the time, as they are still, for juvenile behaviour.

As to the Lusk letter and the accompanying kidney, the jury is, infuriatingly, still out.

Chapter Sixteen

'Lewis Carroll was Jack the Ripper' and 'The Matrix is real – we're living in it.'

T he last document in the bulky files on the Whitechapel murders, currently held in the Public Record Office, concerns a letter written on 14 October 1896. Even for those who believed (wrongly) that Frances Coles, known as 'Carrotty Nell', was a Ripper victim, the killings had stopped five years before this letter was sent. It was written, unsurprisingly, in red ink:

Dear Boss
You will be surprised to
find that this comes from yours
as old old Jack-the-Ripper. Ha. Ha.
If my old friend Mr Warren is dead
you can read it. you might
remember me if you try and
think a little Ha Ha. The last job
was a bad one and no mistake
nearly buckled, and meant it to
be the best of the lot & what curse it,
Ha Ha Im alive yet and you'll
soon find out. I mean to go
on again when I get the chance
wont it be nice dear old Boss to
have the good times once
again, you never caught me
and you never will. Ha Ha
You police are a smart lot, the lot
of you could not catch one man
Where have I been Dear Boss
you d like to know, abroad, if

you would like to know, and
just come back, ready to go on
with my work and stop when
you catch me. Well good bye
Boss wish me luck. Winters coming
'The Jewes are people that are
blamed for nothing' Ha Ha
have you heard this before
                    Yours truly
                    Jack the Ripper

There is nothing original in this letter. On the contrary, the red ink, the use of phrases – 'buckled', 'I mean to go on', 'my old friend' and the reference to the Goulston Street graffito – were all intended to revive the sense of panic engendered by the original letters. Since it had been some time since the last letter arrived (the previous dated correspondence was 27 April 1891), the authorities spent some time investigating it.

Chief Inspector Swanson, who had presided over the original case, thought that disseminating copies to police stations was not a good idea. Along with others, he compared this letter with the original 'Dear Boss'. Detective Inspector Payne of H Division wrote a report on it. The consensus was that there was no cause for alarm but at the same time a watchful eye should be kept. Acting Superintendent L. Cross wrote: 'Writer is sending letter no doubt considers it a great joke at the expense of the police.'

A second report was prepared by Henry Moore, now chief inspector. He had replaced Abberline when the Dorsetman was seconded to the Cleveland Street brothel case and ran the Ripper enquiries on the ground. By 18 October, Moore had re-read all the Ripper correspondence (how many of them there were, at that date, is anybody's guess) and made comparisons. He was particularly interested in the original 'Dear Boss' letter and the 'Saucy Jacky' postcard that followed it, still clearly believing that both these were written by the murderer. The 'y', 't' and 'w' letters were similar, as was the vocabulary. Tantalizingly, Moore says 'Besides there are the finger smears'. Both Herschel and Galton had taken the science of fingerprinting further than ever before, but Galton's classification system of the previous year was still too complicated to use. In 1893, the Troop Committee had recommended that prints be added to anthropomorphic records in Scotland Yard's files. Without a positive means to establish a match, however, this process failed to do the job. Ironically, in the year that Moore was reporting on the last Ripper letter, Edward Henry, Inspector General of the Bengal Police, was in London on leave, meeting Galton to discuss ways forward on the fingerprint front. It was all too late to catch Jack or even the senders of the anonymous letters.

When Moore reported on the Goulston Street words, a marginal note from Swanson reminded the world that those were not the exact words used. Moore's conclusion was that the recent letter was not written by 'Dear Boss', if only because it was addressed to Commercial Street Police Station and not to the Central News Agency. So, the whole business of the Ripper letters, such an important part of the case itself, ended with an inconclusive whimper.

As the 'science' of Ripperology developed, theories about the authorship of the letters abounded. Perhaps the first journalist to write extensively on the case was Leonard Matters, an Australian who served in the Boer War prior to becoming editor of the Buenos Aires *Herald* and briefly (1929–31) MP for Kennington. The authors of the definitive *Jack the Ripper A–Z* speak highly of him – 'Neither his character nor his book warrant ... condemnation; failure to trace his main source does not justify concluding that he invented it.'

Perhaps not, but journalists from T.J. Bulling, via Frederick Best and Harry Dam, right up to Stephen Knight, have all, in various ways, muddied the waters of genuine research and Matters' *Jack the Ripper* is at least guilty of ludicrous leaps of logic. His villain is the shadowy Dr Stanley who, as we have seen, was bent on revenge for the death from syphilis of his son. In his chapter 'Who Wrote the Letters?', Matters cites Dr Forbes Winslow as being convinced that Jack would be discovered in the 'upper classes of society'. This of course flies in the face of all recent research into serial killer behaviour and victimology. Matters then carps that he has not been allowed into Scotland Yard's 'black museum' to see the surviving correspondence for himself. He also, unhelpfully, refuses to print the 'Dear Boss' letter 'in full because it is repulsive in tone'. This is the same letter, forgery as it is now universally held to be, that was printed in various newspapers at the time and reproduced in handbill form. And this was 1888, at a time of far more genteel sensibilities than the 'roaring 'twenties' in which Matters wrote.

The Australian falls for the obvious – the phraseology in 'Dear Boss' marks the writer out as an American – 'probably a self-educated sailor, whose penmanship was first class but whose mind was not well tutored'. Apart from Edward Larkins' Portuguese sailors and the Malay Cook, 'Alaska', there were others who were watched by the police, which probably explains Matters' leap of logic that a sailor must be responsible. No one who was not a local could get away with what Jack did; a passing sailor would have run straight into a police patrol. All this is even more surprising in that Matters' final conclusion is that 'Dear Boss' was a hoax anyway!

Fast forward to 1965 and Tom Cullen's *Autumn of Terror*. It was a milestone publication at the time and Cullen is still highly-regarded today. He claims that Scotland Yard received 1,400 letters in a single month and the most recent he had come across was sent to *Reynolds's News* in February 1959! He expresses his indebtedness to Donald McCormick's *The Identity of Jack the Ripper*, published in that year. Perhaps Cullen had to tread warily because of libel issues. In *Jack the Ripper: Letters from Hell*, authors Stewart Evans and Keith Skinner cannot make up their minds about McCormick!

I must come clean and admit that I met Donald McCormick, who also wrote as Richard Deacon, on an unrelated project; he and his wife were utterly charming and great company. The fact is, however, that he was not above inventing evidence and twisting facts to fit a theory. As someone on the fringes of Cold War espionage, this is hardly surprising.

McCormick referred to research on the Ripper letters carried out by Dr Thomas Dutton of Bayswater, who was a friend of Inspector Abberline. Dutton died in 1935 at the age of 79 and left three handwritten volumes *Chronicles of Crime*, which were his random jottings on all things criminal over a period of sixty years. The doctor was an expert in microphotography and used this science to examine 128 letters and postcards in the Ripper archive. He concluded that thirty-four were in the same handwriting, and that the writer was not a skilled forger in that he formed his Cs, Hs, Rs and Ts in too many ways; he was trying too hard to confuse. Dutton also claimed to have photographed the Goulston Street graffito at the request of the police and that he had attended the post mortem of at least one victim.

Dutton subscribed to the 'murderer on the move' theory in that he believed two letters from Liverpool and one from Glasgow were written by Jack himself. Again, this runs counter to modern profiling beliefs, in which a serial killer acts in an area in which he is most comfortable, i.e. Whitechapel.

'Subconsciously,' McCormick wrote, 'the Victorian psychological viewpoint manifests itself: that is to say, [the police] could not imagine a madman making a joke about his crimes. A maniac, they argued falsely, must be a person without a sense of humour.'

As if to redress that imbalance, McCormick produced a poem, which appears nowhere in any original record, along the lines of *Ten Little Indians* (to use the rather more politically correct title):

Two little whores, shivering with fright,
Seek a cosy doorway, in the middle of the night.
Jack's knife flashes, then there's just one,
And the last one's the ripest for Jack's idea of fun.

Dr Dutton was real enough, unlike Matters' Dr Stanley, who has never been identified. He was educated at Guy's Hospital, Edinburgh and Durham universities, served in a medical capacity with the Royal Navy and wrote a number of popular medical books. At the time of the Ripper murders, he was living at 130 Aldgate High Street. On his death from heart disease in Bayswater in 1935, the *Sunday Chronicle* carried the story that the three volumes referred to above were left to a patient, Hermione Dudley. In the *Chronicle of Crime*, Dutton subscribed to the Dr Stanley thesis. To date, no one has tracked down either Miss Dudley or Dutton's jottings and we are left, as so often in the Ripper case, with half-truths and rumours.

None of the early writers on the Whitechapel murders could have envisaged the future, which, at the time of writing, belongs to social media, 'fake news' and the superhighway of technology which is actually taking us backwards. When I began to write this book, I looked up, online, the '52 Biggest Celebrity Conspiracy Theories' on the MSN entertainment newsfeed.

Prominent among these was a belief in certain quarters that *The Matrix* is real and we are living in such a world today, which no doubt explains why the weather is all over the place and Donald Trump is not only president of the United States but in line for a Nobel Peace Prize! *The Matrix*, for the uninitiated, was a blockbuster science-fiction film of 1999 starring Keanu Reeves. It grossed more than $460 million worldwide and in its day used mind-boggling slow-motion camera techniques that influenced a generation of film-makers. The Matrix itself is a simulated reality run by robots who are trying to control mankind. Because the themes and even the dialogue made references to Descartes, Kant and Plato, the story seemed to have a depth and resonance which, in fact, it did not. It is simply an ingenious sci-fi movie, but the followers of social media, who often cannot tell a video game from reality, give it far more credence. This is part of the fake world of cyberspace, a technological extension of that inhabited by Ripper letter-writers in the nineteenth century.

The conspiracy theory concerning Jack, which seems to have been plucked at random from dozens of celebrities as murderer stories, focuses on Lewis Carroll. Just for the record, let us give it the attention it most certainly does not deserve.

Lewis Carroll was actually the Reverend Charles Lutwidge Dodgson and immediately, to the ill-informed who frequent social media sites, that is suspect. Why does the man have an alias? And wasn't a man called Charles Ludwig briefly believed to be the Whitechapel murderer in that he attacked prostitute Liz Burns in the Minories in September 1888? To scotch these at once, Dodgson has no links at all with the 'lunatic at large' in the Minories and he used Lewis Carroll as a pen-name when he wrote his two *Alice* books. The links to Jack were highlighted by Richard Wallace, a psychotherapist and social worker who wrote *Jack the Ripper: 'Light-hearted Friend'*, itself a quotation from one of the fraudulent letters. Wallace's theory is that Carroll and a colleague, Thomas Vere Bayne, carried out the murders between them. Much of the evidence Wallace attributed to the anagrams of which Carroll was fond. The book received harsh reviews, one commentator referring to 'Wallace in Wonderland'. The mathematical vicar may well have been a repressed paedophile – his photographs of Alice Liddell went far beyond the cute family snaps we expect of the Victorians – but he was not the Whitechapel murderer. His only known link with Jack is a conversation he once had with his friend Dr George Dabbs in 1891 while Carroll was holidaying on the Isle of Wight; Dabbs had a medical practice there. Neither man left to posterity what Dabbs' ingenious theory was.

The 'Lewis Carroll was Jack the Ripper' nonsense is no more ludicrous than many other theories that have been bandied about in the last 130 years. The difference with today's social media is that everything is about soundbites, ill-informed tosh that requires no evidence, no proof and no truth. At least writers on books on Jack have to provide an argument. It may be spurious, it may be far-fetched, but there will be approximately 200 pages of debate and factual content. Writers of blogs today are under no obligation to produce works like this. The web giants such as Twitter, Facebook, Snapchat and Instagram claim not to be journalists and are not, therefore, bound by the rules of the game. They are instead 'platforms', allowing any idiot, however warped or misled, to say their piece, in perfect anonymity, online.

We have so much technology surrounding us now that it is difficult to step back and see our true selves. One of the latest books on Jack – *Ripper Confidential: New Research on the Ripper Murders* – reminds us on the first page that they had electricity, typewriters and telephones in 1888. It also reminds us that the denizens of London's East End, from which Jack and his victims came, had none of these things. The people of the Abyss were the people that time forgot. But the technology of 1888 is as nothing to that of today. In the most recent available statistics, more than 80 per cent of adults in Britain have a smart phone. Such gadgetry is not remotely necessary for actual communication; it is merely a means to join the insane bandwagon of social media.

There are still a few old-school journalists who rail against this. Richard Littlejohn in the *Daily Mail*, for instance, recently referred to Twitter as a drug more invasive and destructive than tobacco or alcohol. With the astonishing campaign against smoking which has seen the rise of fume-laden vapes and the identification of old-fashioned smokers as social pariahs, huddled outside pubs, the great British public has turned to another addiction. And Littlejohn has his tongue only partially in his cheek when he writes, '[social media] can reduce users to gibbering wrecks and is responsible for broken marriages, ruined careers and a spate of suicides. Side-effects include sleep deprivation, delusions of grandeur and paranoia.'

When even heads of state like Donald Trump and Vladimir Putin make pronouncements by it, what chance has Joe Public got?

What this book shows is that the social disease is not new, any more than 'fake news' is new. The shock of the Whitechapel murders caused the great majority of the British public at the time to shudder. It caused journalists to rush to their pens or typewriters. It caused a minority to write letters and postcards, some offering 'helpful' advice to the authorities, most mocking a tragic and appalling series of crimes. These were the 'trolls' of their day, hiding behind the anonymity of the name 'Jack' in all its variations and threatening individuals and society at large with murder. Because so few writers were prosecuted – only four of the many hundreds who put pen to paper – we cannot know if any of the writers actually committed the atrocities they promised in their letters. The likelihood is that they did not, but the *intent* was there and that is the central thesis of this book.

Many people today believe that we live in a more violent, volatile and disturbed society than at any time in the past. Historians disagree. Much is written today about knife crime, especially in the capital, as though it is a new phase of criminality. On the Isle of Wight in the fourteenth century, although we do not have accurate population figures, murders by knife were commonplace. In fact, statistically, a man was 200 times more likely to die on the island then than in London today.

We do not live in more violent times, and the content and tone of the Ripper letters proves it. Of course, Maria Coroner and Miriam Howells, two women who were caught writing letters, dismissed it all as 'a lark'; they were trying to belittle their guilt and get lesser sentences as a result. Today, threats, especially for religious or racial 'hate crime', are taken far more seriously, yet the internet, like the letters of 1888, is notoriously easy to hide in. It encourages the same kind of cowardice shown in the original letters themselves.

The Whitechapel murderer might have been the first of his kind: a disturbed sociopath driven to kill on the murky streets of the East End. But following him, as surely as thousands follow Twitter today, was a small army of Jack wannabes. Historians should revise their views of the Victorians as a result.

Bibliography

Altick, Richard, *Victorian Studies in Scarlet* (J.M. Dent, 1970)

Begg, Paul and Bennett, John, *Jack the Ripper: CSI Whitechapel* (Andre Deutsch, 2012)

Begg, Paul, Fido, Martin and Skinner, Keith, *The Complete Jack the Ripper A-Z* (John Blake, 2010)

Clack, Robert and Hutchinson, Philip, *The London of Jack the Ripper: Then and Now* (Breedon Books, 2007)

Cornwell, Patricia, *Portrait of a Killer: Jack the Ripper – Case Closed* (Time Warner, 2002)

Cullen, Tom, *Autumn of Terror* (Fontana Books, 1966)

Eddleston, John, *Jack the Ripper: An Encyclopaedia* (Metro Publishing, 2002)

Evans, Stewart and Rumbelow, Donald, *Jack the Ripper: Scotland Yard Investigates* (Sutton, 2006)

Evans, Stewart and Skinner, Keith, *Jack the Ripper: Letters from Hell* (Sutton, 2001)

Evans, Stewart and Skinner, Keith, *The Ultimate Jack the Ripper Sourcebook* (Robinson, 2001)

Fairclough, Melvyn, *The Ripper and the Royals* (Duckworth, 1992)

Fido, Martin and Skinner, Keith, *The Official Encyclopaedia of Scotland Yard* (Virgin, 1999)

Fielding, Steve, *The Hangman's Record*, Vol. 1 (Chancery House Press, 1994)

Gibson, Dirk C., *Jack the Writer: A Verbal Analysis of the Ripper Correspondence* (Bentham Books, 2017)

Glyn Jones, Richard (ed.), *True Crime Through History* (Paragon, 1989)

Guy, William, Ferrier, David and Smith, William, *Victorian CSI* (History Press, 2009) (reprint of 1844)

Haining, Peter, *Sweeney Todd* (Robson Books, 2002)

Knight, Stephen, *Jack the Ripper: The Final Solution* (Grafton Books, 1977)

Krafft-Ebing, Richard, *Psychopathia Sexualis* (Creation Books, 1997) (first published 1886)

Marne, Patricia, *The Criminal Hand* (Sphere Books, 1991)

Marriner, Brian, *A Century of Sex Killers* (True Crime Library, 1992)

Matters, Leonard, *Jack the Ripper* (W.H. Allen, 1929)

Morton, James, *Sex, Crimes and Misdemeanours* (Warner Books, 2000)

Partridge, Eric, *A Dictionary of Slang* (Bibliophile Books, 1982)

Perry Curtis, L., *Jack the Ripper and the London Press* (Yale University Press, 2001)

Schechter, Harold and Everitt, David, *The A–Z Encyclopedia of Serial Killers* (Pocket Books, 1996)

Science Against Crime (Marshall Cavendish, 1982)

Sindall, Rob, *Street Violence in the Nineteenth Century* (Leicester University Press, 1990)

Spiering, Frank, *Prince Jack* (Jove Books, 1980)

Sugden, Philip, *The Complete History of Jack the Ripper* (Robinson Publishing, 1994)

Trow, M.J., *The Thames Torso Murders* (Pen & Sword, 2011)

Trow, M.J., *Jack the Ripper: Quest for a Killer* (Pen & Sword, 2009)

'Walter', *My Secret Life* (Granada, 1972)

Wescott, Tom, *Ripper Confidential*, Vol. 2 (Crime Confidential Press, 2017)

Wilson, Colin and Seaman, Donald, *Encyclopaedia of Modern Murder* (Pan, 1989)

Zangwill, Israel, *Children of the Ghetto* (William Heinemann, 1893)

Index